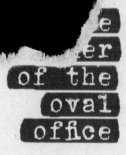
e
er
of the
oval
office

www.penguin.co.uk

from the corner of the oval office

one woman's
true story
of her
accidental
career
in the
Obama
white
house

Beck Dorey-Stein

BLACK SWAN

TRANSWORLD PUBLISHERS
61–63 Uxbridge Road, London W5 5SA
www.penguin.co.uk

Transworld is part of the Penguin Random House group of companies
whose addresses can be found at global.penguinrandomhouse.com

Penguin
Random House
UK

First published in Great Britain in 2018 by Bantam Press
an imprint of Transworld Publishers
Black Swan edition published 2019

This edition published by arrangement with Spiegel & Grau, an imprint of
Random House, a division of Penguin Random House LLC, New York.

A CIP catalogue record for this book
is available from the British Library.

ISBN
9781784164126

Designed by Debbie Glasserman.

P   S.p.A.

for   ature
                                                           de from

Certain names and identifying characteristics have been changed to protect the privacy of individuals. I've used pseudonyms, composites, and other forms of disguise. In some instances, I have rearranged and/or compressed events and time periods in service of the narrative. I have re-created dialogue to the best of my ability, with the help of texts, brutal-to-revisit journal entries, notes on my phone, and emails to my mother. Readers who believe they recognize themselves should refer to the third track of Carly Simon's *No Secrets*, or perhaps make themselves a stiff drink and retire to "that notoriously uncomfortable bed" as described by the ineffable Joan Didion.

BECK DOREY-STEIN

For the scrappy ones

TURN THE GOD DAMN MUSIC UP!
MY HEART FEELS LIKE AN ALLIGATOR!

—HUNTER S. THOMPSON

CONTENTS

GUIDELINES FOR ASPIRING STENOGRAPHERS

Abide by the rules, grammatical and otherwise.

Show up early and say nothing.

Be discreet and neat—like a librarian or a well-paid prostitute.

Neutral tones set the tone.

Breathe quietly or not at all.

Apply semicolons sparingly; do not question convention.

Live to type, don't type to live.

Exude femininity in a strictly nonsexual way.

No hanky-panky in the workplace—or anywhere, ever.

Do not aim for perfection. *Be* perfection.

And above all else, keep the secrets to yourself.

I SHOULD NOT BE A STENOGRAPHER.

PROLOGUE

This Place

Any minute now, President Obama will deliver remarks in the East Room of the White House. Across one parking lot, down three hallways, and up five flights of stairs in the Eisenhower Executive Office Building, I lie on the couch in my little office as the setting sun drenches the room in flammable orange. The Voice of God is the anonymous person who announces the president. I wait to hear him.

Any minute now.

I've become so good at waiting.

Remember when you were small, those rare nights when you would return to your elementary school after dinner to perform in the holiday concert or the spring play? You'd run ahead of your parents and past your sleeping classroom, toward the sound of kids laughing, teachers shushing. Each step pulsing with kinetic mischief, your heart racing to be in this sacred space at such a magical hour. Round the corner to the big kid hallway and there they are, all your friends, already lined up in their matching black pants and white button-downs, beckoning for you to join them because tonight, anything can happen. You're in the right place.

Finally, I hear the Voice of God and walk over to the closed-circuit television to turn up the volume. A minute later, the president appears on the screen, cracks jokes, and takes his characteristic pauses before addressing the topic of the evening. He speaks eloquently, evenly, sincerely. Applause drowns him out when the president blesses the audience and the United States of America. I type the transcript, proofread it, and send it to the press office before zipping up my jacket, putting on my backpack, and closing the wooden office door behind me.

It's past nine as I walk through the empty hallways at the end of the night. The black-and-white marble floor echoes with secrets and electric possibility.

For the past five years, this house was my home. For so long, this was the only place I wanted to be. Not anymore. Ever since November, each day here feels like a funeral. I have the hallway to myself—even the janitors in their blue aprons pushing their heavy cleaning carts are somewhere else. Doors left ajar reveal bare desks, naked walls, empty black frames, piles of paper next to overflowing wastebaskets. Each room diagrams a different stage of an inevitable divorce.

I walk through the slow automated glass doors of the EEOB and into the chilly darkness of another January night. From the top of the Navy steps, I see clusters of people loitering under the streetlamp after their West Wing tour. The only sound is the hollow clank of halyard against flagpole. This place already feels more like a memorial, less like the well-oiled machine I've known it to be. A full moon hovers just above the White House like a flag at half-mast.

This is my school. This is my house of worship. This is my everything—and it is disappearing with each passing day.

I walk by his car and drag my finger across the bumper, knowing agents are watching from their idling SUVs. After waving goodbye to the new guard stuck on night duty, I scan my badge, hear the buzz, the click, the groan of the gate, and walk out onto an empty Pennsylvania Avenue.

This place.

This place.

This place could break your heart.

Everyone keeps talking about the end, but I keep going back to the beginning.

Act I
2011– 2012

We can do this. I know we can,
because we've done it before.

PRESIDENT BARACK OBAMA,
STATE OF THE UNION ADDRESS, 2012

CONNECTING THE DOTS

2011–January 2012

"SO WHAT DO YOU DO?" IS THE FIRST QUESTION D.C. PEOPLE ASK, AND the last question you want to answer if you're unemployed, which I am. It's October 2011, and since the summer, I've spent nine to five at my kitchen table writing cover letters no one will ever read. I keep setting the bar lower and lower, and I'm no longer hoping for actual interviews, but just generic acknowledgments that my applications have been received so I know that I haven't actually disappeared from the universe even if my savings and confidence have. I've grown to appreciate employers considerate enough to reject me properly with a courtesy email. The halfhearted Google spreadsheet I keep on my desktop shows zero job prospects but tons of student loans, and rent due in four days. And now it's time to go blow more money I don't have at a bar full of douchebags.

Dante failed to mention the tenth circle of hell, which is for people pretending to be happy at a happy hour full of young politicos at a lousy bar with sticky floors two blocks from the White House. These are soulless TGI Fridays–type places, except that the cocktails are $17, and every time I walk into one, the soundtrack from *Jaws* plays in the back of my head.

I know the question is coming; it's lurking just below the surface like a patient predator: *What do you do? What do you do? What do you do?*

Happy hours in D.C. are thinly veiled opportunities to network, hook up, or both. I'm not trying to do either, but here I am at Gold Fin because I promised my boyfriend I'd talk to his coworker's girlfriend about doing research at her think tank. However, now that I'm here, talking to Think-Tank Tracy seems like a waste of everyone's time. I'm not a good fit for a think tank, or a PR firm, or a nonprofit; I haven't even received a generic rejection in weeks. I'm slowly figuring out that I'm not a good fit for this city in general, where everyone acts as if they know something you don't and dresses as if they're going to a mob boss's funeral in 1985. Black on black on black. And not cool New York black. Boring, uninspired, ill-fitting Men's Wearhouse–meets–Ann Taylor Loft black.

So instead of looking for Think-Tank Tracy, I look for the bartender. I try to get drunk right away so I can stop worrying about my bank account and how I'm going to answer the inevitable "What do you do?" question. As the edges of the room begin to blur, the floor feels less sticky, and life seems beautiful and ironic and funny.

As I wait at the bar for another drink, I watch the pantomime of ladder-climbing bobbleheads who eagerly anticipate the moment they can offer up their freshly minted business cards. These twentysomething Thursday night kickballers and Saturday night kegstanders are as interesting as the bleached walls of this bar, and yet they're so arrogant, I must be the one missing something. After all, they are real people with real jobs earning real paychecks. They are young professionals who don't go grocery shopping in sweat pants in the middle of a Wednesday afternoon. Staring into the bottom of my drink, I wonder, *When did I fall so far behind? When did I become some loser twenty-six-year-old without a job or a life plan, who isn't even financially responsible enough to do her drinking at home?*

I'm two Cape Codders deep and waiting for a third when a guy with a severe side part and a visible desperation to be his father sidles up next to me, introduces himself, and then casually asks, "So what do you do?"

I know that other people in my predicament say, "I'm between things," or "I'm weighing my options," but everyone knows what that means and I hate bullshitting. So instead I look this baby-faced Reaganite in the eye and tell him I don't have a job.

He keeps an urbane smile pasted on his lips, but I can see him recalculating, the wheels turning. He tilts his head, as though he might be able to assess my condition better from a different angle. *This is how three-legged dogs must feel*, I think.

The funny thing is, nobody cares what you do. They don't ask because they're curious about how you spend your day or what you're interested in. What D.C. creatures really care about is whether you're important or connected or powerful or wealthy. Those things can help advance a career. But a jobless girl getting buzzed at the bar can't do anything for anyone.

The Reaganite backpedals away once he gets another beer, doesn't even bother to offer me a business card, and so I quickly knock back my third drink and leave the bar before Think-Tank Tracy shows up. On my walk home, I text my boyfriend to say I'm done with happy hours. They make me too depressed.

I'D MOVED TO D.C. IN THE SPRING OF 2011, BY MYSELF, FOR A SEMESTER-long tutoring job at Sidwell Friends School. I would live in the nation's capital for three months, and not a moment longer, because who wants to live in D.C.? I had enough friends to make a three-month stint exciting, but enough self-respect to know that D.C. and I would never really be into each other. D.C. is the girl who never swears and always wears a full face of makeup; the guy who makes a weekend "brunch rezzie" for him and his ten closest bros and thinks tipping 15 percent is totally solid. I moved to the city with two suitcases and my eyes wide open—I'd use D.C. to build my résumé, and D.C. would take all my money for rent and bland $11 sandwiches.

An exclusive Quaker school, Sidwell Friends flaunts quite a roster of notable alumni, from Teddy Roosevelt's son to Bill Nye the Science Guy to Chelsea Clinton. In such a pressure cooker, where the Friday speaker series includes parents who also happen to be members of Congress, I was not surprised to learn that Sidwell students were unbelievably worried about not being smart enough or good enough at oboe/squash/debate/all of the above to get into college. So in addition to essay structure and thesis statements, I spent a solid portion of my tutoring sessions reassuring sixteen-year-olds that they were plenty smart, definitely going to college, and absolutely prom-date-worthy. In other words, my job in the spring of 2011 was to help those hormonally charged stressballs chill the fuck out.

Sidwell's grounds were beautiful, and so were the smoking-hot, super-fit male teachers I saw in the hallways. I assumed the school boasted some top-tier experimental outdoor physical education program to have drawn all this masculine brawn. As a single woman with limited time on campus, I didn't waste a precious moment playing coy. But every time I looked over to say hi to one of these human Ken dolls in a short-sleeved button-down, he'd look back at me with a quick, close-lipped smile, completely uninterested.

Sitting across from one of the square-jawed teachers in the cafeteria one day, I went for it and introduced myself. He gave me a sheepish smile and explained that he was working. "Working on what?" I asked. He didn't have a stack of papers, a pile of tests, or even a pen in his hand. He sat there with nothing in front of him, but he was working? He said it again and threw his head in the direction of a group of girls sitting at a table diagonally across from us. I was confused, until one of the girls shrieked "Malia!" and the whole table cracked up laughing.

Oh, right. The Obama girls were at Sidwell, as were Joe Biden's granddaughters. These guys weren't male models moonlighting as gym teachers; they were Secret Service agents.

I gave up on the agents around the same time I gave up on D.C. in general. The city was too buttoned-up for me, too obsessed with politics. When my job at Sidwell ended in June, I'd pack up and go wherever the next job took me, abandoning my large group of college friends that had migrated to D.C. after graduation.

Not that D.C. was all bad—I'd miss spending time with Sarah, Erin, Charlotte, Emma, and Jade—five of my former lacrosse teammates whose apartments in Foggy Bottom were as close to one another as college dorms. Living in the District with a deep bench of friends had been like being a senior on a small campus all over again. I was dizzy-busy. There was always a rooftop happy hour or birthday party to attend, or jazz in the National Gallery Sculpture Garden on Friday nights, or boozy brunches on Saturdays that started at noon and ended after dark. We would meet up for runs in Rock Creek Park and make our way down to the National Mall, winding our way among the monuments and lamenting how slow we were compared to our mile times during preseason.

"It's kind of funny," Sarah said one Saturday in May as we walked arm in arm to a party on Seventeenth Street. JD and Elle, also Wesleyan alums, were throwing the first barbecue of the season. "It's kind of like D.C. is the new Wes."

"Only without the papers or stress or freezing lacrosse games in Maine," Jade said, shuddering at the memory.

"Or boy drama," Charlotte said. "Or *is* there boy drama?"

I feel her elbow in my ribs as they all stop to look at me.

"Nope!"

"Really?" Emma asked. "Any luck with the Secret Service agents?"

"Definitely not. But it's fine, because I'm not dating guys while I'm in D.C."

"Does that mean you're dating girls?" Jade asked.

I shake my head. "I'm only here for one more month. I'm not going to waste my time dating Napoleon wannabes."

Washington is great for a long weekend to see the monuments and the cherry blossoms, but I find the ethos of this one-trick-political-pony town as seductive as Patrick Bateman in *American Psycho*. Even the cashier at Trader Joe's asked me what I did for a living as he bagged my groceries with the spatial reasoning of a Tetris champion.

For once, my social life seemed straightforward. I'd friend-zoned the entire District and felt great about it, because the last thing I wanted in the spring of 2011 was to get tied down to a guy in this ego swamp of a city.

Which is why, of course, I did not fall so much as face-plant in love that night at the backyard barbecue.

It was a hot, humid evening, and I was draining my second Cape Codder when the upstairs neighbor walked out onto the porch with a beer and a bowl of chips. He was tall, with sandy brown hair and the casual friendliness of a displaced Californian. "Hey, I'm Sam," he said, extending his bear paw of a hand.

Between the sportsman's scruff and the moss-green eyes, I was sure he had the cutest face I'd ever seen, even if it was still caked with mud from an all-day rugby tournament. Every time he looked at me, my heart flailed in my chest like one of those car dealership inflatables. When Sam laughed at one of my jokes, I nearly passed out. After an hour or so, I saw him saying goodbye to his friends when my song came on—Dr. Dog's cover of "Heart It Races." Before he ducked out, he whispered in my ear that Dr. Dog was one of his favorite bands, too.

"It was like lightning!" Sarah squealed on our walk home that night.

"Hasta la vista, boy hiatus!" Jade laughed.

"JD says Sam just asked for your number," Charlotte said, smiling down at a text.

"Give it to him!" Emma yelled.

SAM WASN'T LIKE OTHER YOUNG WASHINGTONIANS. I MEAN, SURE, HE worked at a PR firm and was more political minded than I was, but so was everyone. And yes, he had volunteered on the Obama campaign in 2008, but everybody my age in D.C. had been involved in Obama for America—it was part of the standard D.C. pedigree: high school, four-year college, OFA. When I told people I'd been teaching in the fall of 2008, they squinted, confused. Why would I have spent 2008 teaching when I could have been volunteering for the greatest president we've ever had? The idea that I needed to start paying back my student loans after graduation—that even if I'd known about volunteering, I wouldn't have been able to afford it—never crossed their minds.

But Sam got it, and got me. He loved that I was a teacher, that I didn't care about business cards or job titles. We started to text all day and see each other every night, aware but unafraid of our break-neck romantic clip.

Two weeks after the backyard barbecue, Sam and I were in the checkout line at Whole Foods. As we unloaded our cart, I asked, "You're my boyfriend, right?" and just like that, we were official. Two weeks after that, he was at my brother's wedding, meeting my entire family in the middle of a stress torpedo. My mom liked Sam's can-do attitude. (He fixed a bench in the front yard.) My dad liked his handshake. (Firm but not a death grip.) My little sister liked his Converses. My big brother, the groom, thought I was "fucking crazy" for dragging a brand-new boyfriend to a family wedding, "and Elizabeth agrees with me," he said of his future wife over the phone.

But that night, while everyone danced under a big white tent in the backyard, Sam told me he loved me. We were about a hundred feet from my childhood bus stop. My brother was right: I was totally fucking crazy. Luckily, Sam was, too.

GOOD PARTNERS HELP YOU GROW, AND THEY FORCE YOU OUT OF YOUR comfort zone, and Sam did both in short order. His default mode was optimism. Between his kisses and his laid-back SoCal vibe, I felt so much more relaxed, as if a kitten were sleeping on my chest at all times.

Most nights that summer were drunken, musical dream walks. Sam spent his days at the PR firm, and his nights jamming in a band called Fear of Virginia. He knew all the underrated bars in D.C. and had so many friends I began to call him the mayor. We couldn't walk down Eighteenth Street without his stopping to say hello to the dish-washers on break outside Lauriol Plaza or a crowd of former cowork-ers eating mussels at L'Enfant Cafe.

In many ways we were opposites: Sam was a night owl, whereas I liked to beat the sunrise on my morning runs. Sam had a million friends, whereas I had a solid core team. He saw the gray in every situation when I just wanted neat boxes of black and white, wrong and right. I spoke with my parents, big brother, and little sister most days, our group text thread always active, while Sam was more independent of his L.A.-based family. He knew how to julienne vegetables, and I didn't know what "julienne" meant. Sam could recognize any congressperson who passed us, and he had an opinion about every legislative bill. I knew exactly none of them.

But deep down, we shared values and wanted the same things. We left large tips at restaurants, since we'd both waited tables. We loved dancing at concerts and playing team sports on Saturdays— rugby for him, soccer for me. We lived for the thrill of a new song and led the aggressive applause for an encore. We loved reading and drunk eating at midnight. He despised the name-dropping, aspiring-politician jackasses downtown as much as I did. "I call them D.C. creatures," he told me one night as we clinked glasses at a crowded, ego-packed happy hour. Sam and I would spend Sunday afternoons at the dog park on S Street, pointing out the mutts that were our favorites. We both wanted fulfilling, kick-ass careers—we didn't know how we'd get there, but we knew it would happen. We knew we would get everything we wanted now that we'd found each other.

With Sam around, I became less anxious about my future. I stayed in D.C. after Sidwell let out for the summer, and I decided that my next adventure would be here, in the District, with Sam. "Love and happiness," Al Green crooned as we cooked dinner, "will make you do right."

I moved in to a row house on Swann Street, just north of Dupont Circle, with Emma and Charlotte. Our Swann house had a porch perfect for midsummer stooping and a backyard designed for all-day brunches, which we'd already mastered in college. But the best part about the Swann house was that it was just around the corner from Sam's place. It took less than five minutes to walk to his group house, and the dog park was on the way.

By the end of the summer, the only holdup was that I still didn't have a job. Emma was working on Capitol Hill for Senator Leahy, but Charlotte and I were navigating unemployment together. We were young, bright, hardworking women; we'd figure it out.

. . .

OR WOULD WE? AS THE DAYS GROW DARKER, I'M BLOWING THROUGH MY savings and I'm not getting called for interviews. Maybe I should have listened to my dad when he'd warned me about the Great Recession making it nearly impossible to find a job. In the fall of 2011, I can't even get an unpaid internship because all the slots are already filled—not that I could afford an unpaid internship anyway. Each morning, Charlotte and I grudgingly open our laptops at our kitchen table, less and less convinced with every passing day that we will ever find work in this town.

Intimately aware of my deflating confidence, Sam sends me a quote from Steve Jobs: "You can't connect the dots looking forward; you can only connect them looking backward. So you have to trust that the dots will somehow connect in your future." I love the quote so much I write it with blue crayon on white computer paper and tape it to the Swann Street refrigerator.

It's a gray Tuesday in October when I finally get a call. It's my former boss at Sidwell, who says they'd like to rehire me while the full-time tutor eases back into the workforce after six months of maternity leave. "She's feeling overwhelmed," she explains, and I make sympathetic clucks in an effort to contain my excitement. I'm ecstatic to be asked back—not just because I need the money desperately, or because it means they liked me, but also this means I might be able to get my foot in the door for a full-time teaching gig.

I return to campus like a seasoned athlete with home field advantage, friendly with the lunch ladies and Secret Service agents who recognize me from last spring. I catch up with my students in my little office overlooking the turf field and revel in how much I love spending time with teenagers, even when they're near tears over SAT prep—maybe even *especially* when they're near tears over SAT prep.

I'm happier, but I'm still stressed about making rent. Sidwell is just a part-time job, so I cram all of my tutees into Wednesdays. This way, I can patch together a few more jobs to make ends meet.

By January 2012, I have five: substitute teaching at Washington International School, waitressing at Kramerbooks & Afterwords café, my Sidwell gig on Wednesdays, and tutoring some kids at their houses. I'm also working twenty hours a week at Lululemon, which is a culture shock ($100 for yoga pants?!). I run around the city with three different uniforms in my backpack, I'm covering expenses, but I'm exhausted and so busy I hardly ever see Sam. On my various commutes, I start thinking more about the white whale: a single full-time job, with benefits and a cool title. A bunch of fellow English majors are in law school, and it's easy enough to picture myself carrying a briefcase, making a solid salary, and wearing my hair in a bun. Since I don't know much about lawyers other than what I've learned from *To Kill a Mockingbird*, *A Few Good Men*, and *Legally Blonde*, I start to do to some basic online research.

When I see a posting on Craigslist for a stenographer at a law firm, I apply but laugh when I get to the section that asks me to attach a cover letter. A cover letter about how excited I am to type? I've written four dozen cover letters, and I doubt a single one has ever been read. I'm certainly not going to waste my time writing one for a job posted on Craigslist for a stenographer gig, which I would take only on the condition that I could move up to be a paralegal.

And so when "Bernice" responds to my application with "Thanks for applying—I see your résumé but you failed to attach a cover letter," I respond, "I believe my résumé speaks for itself," as though I'm Robert De Niro and not some twenty-six-year-old who buys a tub of tomato soup at Safeway for a week's worth of lunches. I don't imagine I'll hear back from "Bernice," but she invites me to come in to take a test, which I assume will be a typing test. No sweat.

It's a Friday when I arrive at an office building on Sixteenth Street. I ask the man at the front desk to hide my slush-soaked Uggs so I can change into the heels I've carried in my bag. I ride up to the fifth floor, where a woman leads me to an empty office and says I'll have an hour to complete the exam.

But it isn't a typing test. The questions are multiple choice, and there's even an analogy section, like the one on the verbal GRE practice exams I took when I first considered graduate school. Fun! I actually enjoy taking the test and am eager for feedback, especially if it confirms that I'm secretly a genius and have just been super unlucky in my job search. A job offer—any job offer—would give me a much-needed boost of confidence in my own competence.

The following Monday, Bernice emails to say I did well on the test and could I come back for a sit-down interview?

I know three things when I say yes to an interview with Quantitative Employment: One, I don't want to work there; two, I need to practice my interviewing skills; and three, cover letters are, just as I thought, total bullshit.

The day I'm supposed to interview with Bernice, my training session at Lululemon runs long. I don't want to tell the manager I need to get going to a job interview because she's one of those terrifying double-zero mean girls from Long Island who announces she needs to lose five pounds and then stares at you and waits for you to tell her how pretty and perfect and skinny she is. I'd chew off my own arm before having to tell her anything other than that I've folded a couple of extra stacks of Power Y tank tops before my break. So I blow off the interview with Bernice.

When I finally namaste my colleagues and leave the store, my phone is dead. So it's not until two hours after my scheduled interview that I email Bernice and apologize for not showing up, ignoring the tight fist of anxiety in my chest. Who blows off an interview? Only a dumb twenty-six-year-old nobody going nowhere.

As I head to the post office to mail my big brother a birthday package, I feel like a grade-A asshole. I tell myself I don't really need a sixth part-time job. Maybe I can become a manager at Lululemon—a nice one, who doesn't count other people's calories out loud during lunch.

In line at the post office, I see I have a new message from Bernice. She's going to tell me I'm a horrible, thoughtless person who's never going to get hired in this town—or anywhere—if I can't even show up for an interview. I contemplate deleting it without reading it but decide I deserve to hear whatever she has to say, however unpleasant.

Hi Rebecca,
I understand you're busy. For transparency's sake, I wanted to let you know this is a job at the White House, and you'd be trav-

eling with the President on his domestic and international trips. Let me know if this changes things.
Bernice

I drop my phone. Or maybe I fling it. Either way, it lands with a crash on the tile floor. But when I pick it up, the screen isn't cracked, and that insane message is still there.

"This is D.C., it might not be a prank," Charlotte says when I show her the email in our living room. Her job search has been as fruitful as mine, which is to say, fruitless. But Charlotte's eyes twinkle as she skims the email, the corners of her mouth curling up into a smile. At least one of us isn't convinced this is a mean joke. I haven't trusted the Internet since the sixth grade, when I was talking to Brian Littrell of the Backstreet Boys on AOL Instant Messenger and then found out it was some nine-year-old girl who only confessed her true identity after her mom threatened to cancel her birthday party.

I INTERVIEW WITH BERNICE THE FOLLOWING WEEK. YOU CAN SEE THE White House from Bernice's corner office. "There's an opening to be the president's stenographer," she says, which apparently is still a real thing in the twenty-first century. While I'm picturing myself in cat's-eye glasses and a beehive hairdo clicking away on a tiny typewriter, Bernice explains that I'd be responsible for recording interviews, briefings, conference calls, and speeches, and then typing them up afterward in the stenographers' office.

No, I won't be expected to type in real time.

No, I don't need to learn shorthand.

Discretion and accuracy are more important than speed.

I'd learn to release official White House transcripts to the press office and presidential archive. I'd go wherever President Obama went. It would be full-time with benefits. In fact, it would be more full-time than most full-time jobs, because there would be work on weekends.

"I taught at a boarding school for two years," I tell Bernice. "I'm used to weekend duty."

Bernice raises her eyebrows and looks down at her apple red fingernails. "Right," she says. "Only this is the White House."

I apologize to Bernice for ditching the first interview before telling her how excited I am to have this opportunity to meet with her, to possibly be a front-row witness to history. I'm near tears and my hands are shaking. If she doesn't hire me, I'll have only myself to blame after my no-show, but it would suck to get so close to something so cool and not get the part. I ask why she posted a job like this on Craigslist.

"I'd run out of people from the State Department," she says, tossing her pen onto her desk and reclining in her leather chair. "Since that had never happened before, I wasn't sure how else to find candidates. You stood out because of your Sidwell experience. If you got clearance to be around the Obama girls, you can probably be around the president." She goes on to explain that there's another interview with the woman who would be my immediate supervisor over at the White House, Peggy, as well as a comprehensive background check by the FBI. "We can't have you flying on Air Force One if you have any criminal history," she says, ending the interview.

I don't want to jinx it, but I'm pretty confident I'll ace that background check—I only got high in college once, and that was by accident.

I'm so nervous and excited when I meet with Peggy that within minutes of shaking her hand, I blurt out that I love Barack Obama, that he was my college commencement speaker, and that I nearly fainted when I got to shake his hand after receiving my diploma. I tell her that I went into teaching and not advertising because in his speech he told us to give back. When I finish my fast-talking gush, I realize she may hate the president; hers is a contract position, after all, not a political appointment.

But Peggy smiles and leans forward. "I love him, too," she says. "I've had my job at the White House for nearly thirty years. I started with Reagan, and this is my favorite president by far."

The next day, I'm at Sidwell, in the cafeteria, when I realize I should grab my phone in case Bernice calls. I get up in such a hurry that I bump into a tall middle schooler who's busy looking at a marked-up paper. I'm halfway up the stairs to my office before I realize that the tall middle schooler was Malia Obama. Within minutes I'll know whether our encounter was auspicious or ominous.

Turns out it was the best hip-check I've ever received. I get the job.

I RETURN TO THE AGENCY OFFICE TO FILL OUT PAPERWORK THE FOLLOW-ing week. As I sign my name on the final page and slide the stack of papers back across the desk to Bernice, I ask if she has any advice for me. She doesn't say anything, just smiles, then leans back in her leather chair to think.

"Do you have a boyfriend?" Bernice asks.

"Yes . . ." I say slowly, unsure how this is relevant.

"Good," Bernice says. "Keep him."

I laugh uncomfortably.

"I've seen lots of people fall in love with the wrong people around here," she says, her eyes dark, her voice a razor blade cloaked in a whisper. "Stay with your boyfriend," Bernice says. "And stay away from the Secret Service agents."

I laugh, genuinely this time. The agents? Seriously? I'd already tried that ride at Sidwell.

As I leave Bernice's office, I find myself skipping down the side-walk, making all kinds of promises to myself as I pass people who look at me as if I'm nuts. "I have a job!" I want to tell them. I swear to myself that I'll keep up with the news, I'll get to the office early, I'll buy a new pair of heels, I'll work extra hard so everyone will like me. I start to laugh as I think about Bernice's advice. *And I'll stay with my boyfriend.* That part is easy. I love Sam.

The next day, snow falls in an all-day celebration of white con-fetti. I decide to walk to Georgetown sporting a hot-pink workout jacket and new black yoga pants from Lululemon (thank you, em-ployee discount). Even though I haven't started yet, the promise of a steady paycheck allows me to act on things I've been thinking about for months: a haircut, new running shoes, a brand-new belt for Sam, White House–appropriate clothes for myself.

My dad calls as I continue walking toward M Street. He wants to know if I'm excited about my new job, because he certainly is—just the fact that he's calling reflects his enthusiasm. My dad is soft-spoken and shy—not the kind of dad to yell from the soccer side-lines, grab a beer with the guys (he doesn't have guys), or call up his daughter just to chat. Except tonight, that's exactly what he does.

"I'm a little nervous," I tell him, which I didn't realize until I'm say-ing so. My dad is a psychologist and has this magical power of getting me to realize things and say them out loud. He's the best listener I know, unless he's watching an Eagles game—then he's useless.

"What are you nervous about?" He doesn't mind the long si-lences. I guess that's part of being a good listener.

"I mean, Dad, at the end of the day, I just signed a contract to type for a living." He knows the power in a pause, letting me untangle the knot myself. "I get that it's for the president and it's at the White House and I'll see historic stuff and, if nothing else, now I'll have benefits and an income, but it's just typing, you know? It's not hard. No one's going to think I'm smart."

Again, silence.

"Do you realize I'm getting paid not to talk?" This makes my dad laugh.

"Yeah," he finally says, "that might be a problem."

Before we hang up, my dad reminds me that nothing is perma-nent and that this is a pretty cool opportunity not only to see history but also to take notes, to write about it.

"Since you can't talk, listen. And really, what's the worst that could happen?"

That's my dad's go-to question whenever I'm anxious. He has a point. We say goodbye and I put my phone in my pocket. I feel better. I take a deep breath and walk into Banana Republic.

As I make my way through the stores of M Street, I try on blazers and blouses, and also attempt to mount several pairs of high heels. Before I disembark from the institutionalized torture devices better known as women's professional footwear, I catch a glimpse of my-self in the mirror: black skirt suit, white button-down, black heels. I look as if I belong. It's like the rom-com makeover montage, only in reverse: free spirit converts to workaholic.

I can do anything if I can pass for a D.C. creature, I think as I put my hair into the tight bun of a corporate cutthroat, smile, and hand the cashier my credit card. In a six-month period, I've gone from alone and lost in the world to in love and employed at the White House. In the immortal words of LL Cool J, "Don't call it a comeback."

That weekend, Sam and I binge-watch *The West Wing,* which Sam insists is required viewing before joining Obamaworld. We eat too much Mexican food and drink too many margaritas. "Hey," Sam says, jabbing me in the ribs. "You'll probably fly on Air Force One pretty soon." I laugh and blink back tears of joy as I curl up in his lap.

On Sunday night, I can't sleep, I'm so excited for my first day. While Sam snores next to me, my mind races. I look over at my black skirt suit hanging on the back of the door. I feel so lucky. As I lie awake, I figure that maybe I needed the table of drunk guys at Kramerbooks to stiff me a tip on a $300 bill, and maybe I needed the manager at Lululemon to ask me if I'd ever thought about cutting my carbs. Maybe I needed the depressing happy hours, the lonely nights berating myself for lackluster ambition. Maybe this would be my big break. Maybe Steve Jobs was right: *You have to trust that the dots will somehow connect in your future.*

WELCOME
TO THE
NEIGHBORHOOD

February

PEGGY SENDS ME AN EMAIL FIRST THING MONDAY MORNING, MY FIRST day of work. "Our office is on the fifth floor of the EEOB—that big building to the right of the White House," she explains. "Since you don't have an official badge yet, you'll need to go through the visitors' entrance—just make sure to bring ID. I've already set up an appointment for you." I'm so excited to get to 1600 Pennsylvania Avenue, I almost miss the final line of Peggy's email: "Welcome to the neighborhood." I get goosebumps.

Peggy meets me inside the visitors' entrance at Seventeenth and State Place and gives me a hug like I'm her niece and not her newest employee. She's noticeably tall—close to six feet—with gentle blue eyes and very straight auburn hair down to her shoulders. I'm not great at guessing ages but I think she's close to my parents'—late fifties, early sixties.

"Today will probably be a little overwhelming," she says with a smile, "but you'll have the hang of things in no time."

After I pass through security, she takes me on a tour of the Eisenhower Executive Office Building.

The building is named after President Eisenhower, Peggy tells me, because he saved it from being torn down. And I'm glad he did, because it's beautiful, inside and out. It's also huge—five stories high and a whole city block long. "The stenographers are on the fifth floor, in the bird's nest," she says as we walk up a set of impressive marble steps. At the top, two heavy wooden doors slowly open for us, and it feels like that moment in *The Devil Wears Prada* when Stanley Tucci yells, "All right, everyone, gird your loins!"

Once inside, Peggy explains that the grand spiral staircase connects each floor, and if you stand at the center on the ground floor, you can see all the way to the top, where there are stained-glass skylights.

It's hard to believe that this is where I will come to work every day.

As we walk along the ground floor, Peggy points out Ike's, the EEOB staff cafeteria. "Over there is the post office and down this hall is the medical unit."

"Medical unit?"

Peggy nods. "It's very convenient, because we'll need to get you updated on your immunizations before you travel overseas. They'll dispense the malaria pills and all that kind of stuff. The doctors and nurses travel for the president, but they're very nice and take care of all of us." This is unreal.

"Down there are some Secret Service offices, the gift shop, the travel office," Peggy says with a wave. "Oh, and downstairs is the bowling alley. You can reserve it at night and bring your friends. WHCA is also downstairs."

"WHCA?"

"White House Communications Agency," Peggy explains. "They're our heroes. They help us with audio. And like the medical unit, everyone in WHCA is active duty military." I look at her with saucer eyes. "Most of them have already completed several tours in Iraq and Afghanistan," she says as we climb the stairs to the first floor.

The floors themselves are incredible: black-and-white-checked marble, as though you're on a gigantic chessboard. The hallways are long, and the sound of high heels clicking against the marble echoes with such portent I feel as if I'm in a Hitchcock film.

I look around trying to catch someone's eye. I like to say hello to everyone, which is why my friends in Manhattan are embarrassed whenever I visit them. But everyone's too busy to smile. The suited staffers are staring down at their phones or straight ahead. No one says hello.

At an elevator bank, Peggy presses the up arrow. "These things are notoriously slow," she says, shaking her head. "Even though we're up on the fifth floor, sometimes I think it might be faster to take the stairs." The elevator doors open with the resentful groan of an arthritic grandfather. Peggy and I pile in with a bunch of other people in suits.

When we get out on the fifth floor, Peggy tells me to look up.

"Wow. It's like we're in church," I whisper as we stare at the stained-glass ceiling.

"Are you religious?" Peggy asks.

"I am now," I say.

THE FIRST THING I THINK WHEN I WALK INTO THE STENOGRAPHERS' office is: small. Very small. There are five desks lined up against the walls. Three people at the desks are staring at me. Peggy introduces me to a guy my age named Lucas who helps cover the vice president. He shakes my hand, puts on earphones, and resumes typing.

Then Peggy says, "This is Lisa, and this is Margie." The two girls are my age and look alike, with long brown hair, brown eyes, bold red lipstick, and perfectly shaped eyebrows. They're both dressed all in black: Margie in a black dress, Lisa in black pants and a black sweater. I wonder if they're sisters, or if you just start to resemble your colleagues if you stay in a tiny office long enough.

It's Valentine's Day, and I'd desperately wanted to bake heart-shaped cookies for my new officemates, but Sam had advised against it. "Just get a feel for the place before you start doing all your teach-ery things," he'd said.

That night I tell Sam that I think the girls in my office don't like me. He laughs and shrugs between mouthfuls of spaghetti he's made for us. "It was your first day—you won't know how they feel about you for at least a month."

Before I fall asleep, I convince myself I'll get those girls to like me. Happiness is contagious, and I've never been happier. I have a kick-ass boyfriend, a kick-ass house with kick-ass roommates, and now I have a brand-new kick-ass job.

THE NEXT DAY, I MEET THE WOMAN I'M REPLACING. CONNIE HAS BEEN a White House stenographer for nine years but wants to try something new, and this job has opened doors. Yet another selling point. Maybe my time in the White House will help me realize I want to be a reporter, or shape policy, or pursue law school after all.

Peggy asks Connie to bring me to a press briefing that's beginning in T minus five minutes. Our speedwalk turns to a jog as we cross the parking lot that separates the EEOB from the West Wing. "This is West Exec," Connie calls over her shoulder, yelling over the hum of a dozen big black idling SUVs.

From the fifth-floor bird's nest in the EEOB to the briefing room in the West Wing is an easy seven-minute stroll but a tough two-minute sprint. We run and powerwalk through corridors, push through three sets of doors, race up one stairwell, smile at two guards, press one large square button, and descend two steps into the lower press office. It's here that Connie catches her breath and I assume we've arrived.

Two women in their twenties sit behind large computer screens. Connie introduces me and everyone pauses. Later I'll be able to identify this pause as the shuffling of hierarchical introductions, of finding order in the snaking ribbons of rank.

A blond man in glasses steps toward me from behind a wall of faces. With an extended hand he says, "Hi, Rebecca. I'm Jay Carney." As I lean across Connie to shake Jay's hand, I wonder why his name sounds so familiar. The press corps is on the other side of two thick wooden doors painted royal blue. "They've been waiting," Connie explains, "so just make your way to the back. If there are open seats, feel free to grab one, but it's supposed to be packed today."

I hear tons of people talking on the other side of the doors, but when Connie pushes open the door, it's suddenly silent. I'm walking onto a stage after the curtain's gone up. Everyone is staring at us. Dozens of faces and countless camera lenses are frozen in anticipation. Connie strides confidently across the room and the silence gives way to the chatter as the reporters realize it's not the press secretary arriving for the daily briefing, just the stenographer and some girl trailing her.

I follow Connie's lead and cross in front of the first row of well-dressed and professionally coiffed reporters. Later I'll learn that they're from the television networks, that only the Associated Press and Reuters are both print and first row. *The New York Times*, *The Washington Post*, and *The Wall Street Journal* are in the second row. BuzzFeed is somewhere near the back.

For now, I feel their eyes on me. It's not particularly warm attention, and I focus on smiling the way a fish might focus on swimming out of the peripheral vision of a shark. Connie sits in front of the first row holding out a microphone and inserting her earbuds, and I continue to the back, my chest beating out of my dry-cleaned shirt, now damp with sweat.

Not even a minute later, a parade of four people emerges through the blue doors. There it is again—the sudden silence—as Jay Carney mounts the small stage and rests his binder on the lectern.

"Good afternoon and welcome to the White House for your daily briefing. I have one announcement to make before I take your questions." The room is packed, questions fly, Jay fields them all with the calm resolve of a major league shortstop. He's patient but responsive. He does not rush. Soon I'll grow used to the back-and-forth of the briefing room, but today I'm rapt with the heady thrill of watching the opening pitch for the first time, awed by the sight from beyond the nosebleed seats.

I text Sam as soon as I get out, and he makes fun of me for not knowing who Jay Carney is. He had watched the whole briefing on C-SPAN and had spotted me in a couple of the cutaway shots. He's so proud.

POOL DAYS

March

THIS NEW JOB IS LIKE BEING BACK AT BOARDING SCHOOL, WITH EARLY
mornings, late nights, and weekend duty. When I crawl into bed
each night, Sam teases me that I'm even busier than he is.

"Will we ever see you again?" my mom asks over the phone one
Saturday morning. I'm rushing to work to cover an in-towner, which
means an event in the D.C./Maryland/Northern Virginia region,
where we can just motorcade and be back in a few hours. Today,
POTUS is visiting a school.

"Mom, come on, I'm coming home for Easter. Did you get my
email?" I ask.

"I'm saving it for tonight as a special treat."

I've been emailing my mom long letters detailing my White
House adventures. I'd just sent her ten pages describing my first
background briefing in the Roosevelt Room—which journalists

were there, who spoke to me, where everyone sat, what David Remnick, the editor of *The New Yorker*, looks like in person.

"Okay, I've got to go," I tell my mom as I stand outside the White House gate, the Secret Service agents waiting to buzz me in. "I need to find the pool. I'll call you after."

I hold up my badge outside the first metal gate and wait. When the officer on duty buzzes me in, I push open the gate and then pull open a heavy metal door that leads to the security hut. I say good morning to the officers, scan my badge over the keypad, type in my password, drop my bag through the X-ray machine, and walk through the metal detector, which inevitably goes off because of my gold alligator necklace. The guard with the wand knows this, knows me, smiles, and says, "That dang gator."

As much as swamp monsters scare me, I love my alligator necklace. The best way to manage a fear is to adopt its ferocity as your own. When I get lost in the EEOB or forget a senior staffer's name in the West Wing, I touch my gold gator not only to ground me, but also to remember my strength, my teeth.

I grab my gear and find Marie the press wrangler and the camera-clad pool lined up outside the lower press office. The "pool" is the group of thirteen reporters and photographers from the White House press corps who are responsible for traveling with the president and tracking his every move. On a slow day when the president stays at the White House and has private meetings, there will be only a handful of pool reports. On a busy day on the road, the poolers will send out more than twenty, ranging from "The motorcade is rolling to an unknown location" to highlights from Jay's gaggle to "Here is the menu for tonight's state dinner." Just as I start to say good morning to everyone, my phone rings. "Uh-oh, we've got a rookie," Jeff the cameraman announces. "Best to keep that thing on silent as long as you work here," he says to me with a smile.

THE NEXT COUPLE OF MONTHS FLY BY DISASTER FREE AS I TRY TO FOL-low protocol, find my way through the windowless tunnels that are the West Wing halls, and make friends. The first time I enter the

Oval Office, I'm so focused on recording the audio, holding my own in the stampede of reporters, and standing exactly where Lisa told me to—behind the big lamp on the side table, between the president's chair and the tan sofa—that it's several minutes before I look up from my recorder.

My hands start to shake uncontrollably. President Obama is sitting not even four feet away and gives me a quick nod and tight-lipped smile before beginning his remarks to reporters. Lisa had told me to stand between the press and the president, because part of our job is to act as a neutral buffer, but I feel anything but neutral. The Oval Office is smaller than I expected, and more inviting, lived-in. The two long sofas look comfortable, and there's a bowl full of perfect apples in the center of the coffee table begging to be eaten. Behind the Resolute Desk is a table covered with framed photographs of the Obama family.

I'm still absorbing the details of the room when the press wrangler announces we're leaving, the photo op is over. As I linger, trying to remember every detail to tell my mom, I realize Vice President Biden is standing by the glass door to the Colonnade, thanking and joking with various reporters as they exit. When I pass him, the vice president eyes my newly minted blue badge, smiles, and says, "Welcome."

THERE'S A BIT OF A LEARNING CURVE AS I PICK UP THE WEST WING JAR-gon and try it out with the same broken stutter I have when I try to speak Spanish. Lisa tells me that on the road, "RON" means Remain Over Night, and "hold" means waiting room or wait (depending on whether it's being used as a noun or a verb), and "the Beast" is the heavily armored black Cadillac limo the president rides in. The "CAT" guys are the Counter Assault Team, which rides ahead of the Press 1 vans, the back window open with these black-clad, Van Damme–built men gripping huge guns, ready to defend the president. When reporters refer to the president as "Obama," I cringe with the rest of the staffers; to us, he's "POTUS" or "the president," never just his last name. I nod when Steve Holland from Reuters says, "Just another day of hurry up and wait" as we huddle outside the Roosevelt Room for a "pool spray," which is the term for a photo opportunity for the press.

Before the daily press briefing, I turn on my microphone when Jay and two deputy press secretaries walk through the blue wooden doors. The room falls into a silent hush. Jay mounts the stage, opens his binder, looks up. But before he opens his mouth, I say Jay's opener in my head: "Good afternoon, ladies and gentlemen, and thank you for coming to the White House for your daily briefing." I can't help but grin—I've got this job down.

SOON ENOUGH, PEGGY SAYS IT'S TIME TO SPREAD MY WINGS: IT'S TIME for me to fly on Air Force One by myself. The night before my first overnight trip to Oklahoma, I don't sleep—not because I'm nervous, which I am, but because I have no idea what to wear. I need outfits for the workday but also pajamas and workout clothes, and what about something more comfortable for the flights? Can I wear a sweatshirt on the plane, or will people think that's unprofessional or, worse yet, unpatriotic? My closet is less prepared for this trip than I am. Charlotte and Emma try to help me, but it's a lost cause. I throw half my bureau into an old red duffel bag from my club soccer days and hope that when I open it, it will reveal someone else's more stylish wardrobe.

The next morning, in a blind panic, I pack several more outfits and two pairs of boots, just in case there's a hurricane or a flood or a forest fire. I zip up a month's worth of clothes for one night away and feel like an idiot. But it's too late to change course. I'm late. Everyone else traveling with the president has already dropped their suitcases off in the luggage room, on the ground floor of the EEOB.

As I drag my overstuffed duffel down the EEOB corridor, I hear Lisa call my name. "Wait up!" she says. She takes a look at my bag. "You're bringing *that*?"

Lisa wears only brand-new black clothes from fancy labels, so I know she hates my bag even more than she hates my green dress, which at least is from this decade. She falls into step next to me, trying to cram as much information as she can into my head before

I ride off and potentially tarnish the stenographers' reputation with my bright dress, my brandless bag, and my tendency to say hi to people. As we walk down the Navy steps toward the idling white eighteen-passenger vans parked on West Exec, it's clear that she's even more nervous about my first solo trip than I am. I've already shadowed her on day trips to Albany, New York, and to Columbus, Ohio, but she still thinks my independent debut is premature. Peggy had confided in me that she usually has new stenographers wait six months to travel, but because this is President Obama's reelection year, she expects we'll be traveling a ton and wants me to be a seasoned pro when the campaign schedule heats up over the summer.

After I pound my overnight bag into submission in the back of a white van, Lisa introduces me to Skye, who is part of the traveling team. Skye works with a big group of people that ranges from the advance office to the military aides to the valets to ensure President Obama and his traveling staff get where they're going on time and without any sort of logistical holdup (visas, passports, bad weather, political coups, et cetera). Skye smiles at me and says, "Nice to meet you, Rebecca."

"Oh, actually, I just go by Beck," I tell her. She looks confused and refers to her clipboard, which holds the manifest of names for the vans and Air Force One.

"It says Rebecca here," Skye says, showing me my name on the manifest.

"Right, that's my full name, but I've gone by Beck for forever."

"Not Rebecca?"

"Nope, just Beck."

"I've never heard that as a nickname before," Skye says, using a black Sharpie to cross out my name on the manifest. She cocks her head to the side, writing in my nickname. "That's different."

It's only when Skye looks back up at me from her clipboard that I notice: She's really pretty and very thin, with long jet-black hair and glacier-blue eyes. She's wearing a tight pencil skirt and steep Tory Burch high heels. I can't help but eye her, and then I realize she's eyeing me, too. I'm about to tell her how much I love her cream-colored blouse when something in the glint of those ginormous blue eyes tells me not to.

"You have everything?" Lisa asks. We stand on the sidewalk, just a few feet from Skye as she checks in the other staffers. Lisa's concern is actually kind of cute, like a worried mom at the bus stop on the first day of school. "Microphone, XLR, recorders, converters, batteries, laptop, foot pedal, chargers?"

"Roger, dodger," I tell her, shaking the contents of my heavy black backpack.

"What about your hard pin?" Lisa asks, eyes wide.

"Right here!" I show her the shiny red metal octagon, no bigger than a quarter, pinned to my dress. The hard pin is priceless; it's proof to the Secret Service that you're part of the bubble, and it allows me to go wherever the president goes, except "secondary hold," which is code for the bathroom.

"Just text me if anything comes up," she says, straightening the collar of my blazer.

"So is Skye our boss on trips?" I ask Lisa. I can't get a grip on the hierarchy. When I was the new teacher, everyone jumped in to help me get up to speed. At the White House, there's no hand holding. I'm not sure whom to go to if I need help.

"Not really," Lisa says. "We don't have, like, a supervisor on trips. I guess technically Jay is our boss, since we work for the press office."

"So should I go to him if I have any problems?"

"No!" Lisa shrieks. Skye and a young man in glasses look over. "Just call me," Lisa hisses, "and don't bother anyone else."

In the carpet van, no one looks up as I climb in and ungracefully make my way to the back row. It's an unspoken rule that senior staff get the first few rows, which, luckily, Lisa had explained to me in the elevator. I take note of the senior staffers as they click-clack away on their BlackBerrys. A woman with curly red hair is in the first row, tapping away on her phone. She has gold bangles up to her elbow, and they jangle along with her typing. Just as I pass her, she whispers something to Pete Souza, the chief official White House photographer, who's playing Words with Friends on his phone. Pete's cameras sit next to him like well-traveled lapdogs as he and the red-headed woman burst out laughing, her bangles clanking along with her body. I smile, but then I feel like an idiot because I don't know what they're laughing about, and maybe I've tucked my dress into my underwear again.

On the ride to Joint Base Andrews, I try to breathe as quietly as possible and look at my phone with the same serious consternation as everyone else does. No one speaks, except some of the senior staff in the front rows, but it's more like talking to each other in one-word codes as they're responding to various emails. It's not a conversation so much as a "Jesus," or "Can you loop me in on that?" or "He said yes about tomorrow, right?"

We arrive on the tarmac, and the suited professionals board Air Force One with sporty bags and light-looking briefcases. Every piece of luggage I see is black; my overnight duffel is a big bull's-eye. The redheaded woman carries a black Tumi carry-on, and she shoots me a look as we stand in line at the bottom of the airstairs that says she already knows I'll never be able to afford a bag like hers.

The Air Force Ravens check each person's name off the manifest before we're allowed to board the plane. When it's my turn to say my name, I apologize for my hyphenation.

"Sorry, my parents were hippies," I tell the Raven. He smiles as he scans his paper looking for my name and, eyeing my duffel, asks if I'm a soccer player.

"Used to be," I tell him, shifting the weight of the bag as the strap digs into my shoulder.

"Great sport," he says. "My daughter plays."

I nod, ask him how old, which position, before realizing this Raven is the first person who has engaged me since Lisa back on West Exec. Behind me, a senior staffer clears his throat. I've held up the line. The Raven also hears the throat clearer and stands up straighter, smiles, and tells me to go on up.

Entering Air Force One, I don't board so much as lumber, trying not to knock anyone over as I navigate the cabins with my wide load. As I unintentionally pin a flight attendant against the wall, I'm almost too overwhelmed with anxiety to form words.

After I apologize to the flight attendant, I look up and see Jim Carrey near the front of the plane. I'm about to ask someone why Jim Carrey is traveling with us when someone yells, "Jason," and the man turns around. Not Jim Carrey—his D.C.-dressed doppelgänger.

I head to the staff cabin—Lisa had shown me where to sit on my training trips—and find the seat with my place card in the cup holder. "Welcome aboard Air Force One, Ms. Dorey-Stein," it says, printed in blue. I cannot believe this is my life. I love this seat. It's next to a window, with only one seat next to it that Lisa says is usually left empty. Every chair can recline nearly all the way. I have power outlets at my feet.

In front of me is a table that displays a variety of the day's newspapers and a candy tray, complete with Snickers, Reese's, Kit Kats, two types of gum, mints, and, best of all, boxes of Air Force One M&M's. To my left is the staff office, where I can email the audio from the gaggle, the main reason I'm here. A stenographer travels on every trip the president takes because on at least one leg, the White House press secretary will "gaggle"—hold an informal off-camera daily briefing with the thirteen reporters and photographers in the pool. It's my job to stand right next to Jay, record the gaggle, and send it back from the AF1 staff office. During my training trips, Lisa let me cover two gaggles. It was nerve-racking both times—what if the microphone battery died? Or the recorder turned itself off? Or I deleted the file halfway through? Or I sneezed? The two sessions had gone smoothly enough, except at the end of the second gaggle when I'd accidentally socked Jay in the mouth with my microphone. To be fair, there'd been a sudden jolt of turbulence, but that was my last gaggle performance, so I'm nervous about today. I want to make my office proud or, if nothing else, prove to Lisa she can trust me to behave on the road.

I try to ignore the big flatscreen TV on the far wall, as well as the Air Force One Bose noise-canceling headphones, and pillows and blankets. I can't imagine I'll ever be able to sit back and relax. Instead, I decide to take inventory of all my steno gear.

As I heave my backpack onto the seat next to me, Todd, one of the flight attendants, asks if I'd like anything to drink. We still have forty minutes before the president's helicopter, Marine One, will arrive, so the Air Force One crew comes through to offer refreshments. I ask for coffee, trying to wrap my brain around my good fortune.

"Sounds good, and please let me know if you need anything. I'm here to help you," Todd says with a warm smile. Like the medical unit and WHCA, the Air Force One crew is all active duty military. They're also some of the most grounded, kindhearted humans I've met so far.

On my training trip with Lisa, I'd learned that we get "per diems," or, monetary reimbursements, for every day we're on the road. The per diem for expensive cities like San Francisco is significantly more than the per diem in, say, Kansas City, to account for the cost of living. All of this had seemed ridiculous to me—I get paid extra for traveling with the president?—until Lisa said we paid for all our food and drinks on Air Force One and that we rarely had time to eat sit-down meals on trips. Room service, she had explained, was less a luxury and more an imperative, because by the time you arrive at the hotel after a long day full of stress and motorcades and no sustenance, your stomach is grumbling but restaurants are closed, and your eyes won't stay open.

The smell of pancakes wafting through the staff cabin is so delicious I don't care how much they cost or what my per diem is as I settle into my seat. Air Force One is pristine, but I'm quickly ruining that as I unpack my black backpack in search of steno gear. In my rush to get out the door, I'd filled my computer bag with several outfit options and a bunch of my personal stuff—makeup, hair straightener, running shoes, library book.

Only after I've dumped my pajamas onto the seat next to me do I see his shoes, black and shiny. It's Jay Carney, smiling while examining the mess I've made with all my stuff. He takes a sip of his coffee in an Air Force One to-go cup before asking, "You ready for this?" and giving the air a punch. Uh-oh. Jay is clearly well caffeinated and wants to get the gaggle over with so he can play cards in the front with the president. Peggy had told me that President Obama likes to play Spades during flights. Rule number one in my job—don't make senior staff wait for you. Ever.

"Take your time there," he jokes, as I search to find the microphone within the black hole of my backpack. I look up to say something witty, but Jay is suddenly bright red and says quickly, "I'll come back."

What have I done? I didn't say a word. I look down at my mess to try to figure it out. There're the bag of cables, the recorder, the microphone. My running shoes are on the floor, makeup bag is on the seat. I'm holding my hair straightener. . . . Holy shit, my straightener! Oh, dear God, my travel-sized straightener in its little travel-sized hot-pink silk bag looks like a vibrator! Jay Carney thought I was talking to him, on Air Force One, with a vibrator in my hand.

He returns a couple of minutes later and we head back to the press cabin. I consider saying "That wasn't a vibrator" as we walk through the Secret Service cabin, but that would probably make things worse. Instead, I join the reporters and turn on my microphone and recorder.

"Good morning, everyone, and thank you for joining us on Air Force One," Jay begins. A reporter asks Jay if he thinks the antigovernment demonstrations in Russia over President Putin's reelection could turn violent. "As you well know," Jay says, "I won't comment on hypothetical situations."

THE REST OF THE DAY GOES SMOOTHLY, AND SOON ENOUGH, WE ARRIVE at the hotel in Oklahoma City. I've successfully recorded the audio for the gaggle, two sets of public remarks, and one NBC interview. "Great job today," Peggy texts me as I sit in the passenger seat of the Press 1 van. While I'd run around with the pool, Peggy, Lisa, Lucas, and Margie had typed up the transcripts using the audio I'd sent them. Even though I'm exhausted from the day, I already know I love the road—meeting reporters and photographers, navigating the corridors of convention centers, introducing myself to staffers, watching President Obama from backstage, trying not to stare at him when he walks right by me after his speech.

When we pull into the hotel and unload our bags from the back of the Press 1 van, a reporter says, "Way to keep up, new steno." With half of my belongings crammed into my soccer duffel, I waddle toward the elevator bank. A bunch of staffers, including the red-headed woman with the gold bracelets, are already waiting for the elevator and eye me wearily. Their black Tumi bags have already been delivered to their rooms, thanks to the carpet van and Air Force One guys who'd transported it from the EEOB luggage room this morning.

The elevator doors open, and the staffers file in. There's room for me but not for my bag. I ignore how hot my face is and tell them I'll wait for the next one. They smile politely as if to say, yes, you will wait for the next one.

I'm staring at the closed metal doors when Jay Carney appears in normal-people clothes. It's the first time I haven't seen him in a suit. He looks like a cool dad in jeans and a black V-neck T-shirt. "Coming to the bar?" he asks. I shake my head and shrug.

"Yeah, it was a long day," he says through a yawn. "Have a good night." He walks away smiling broadly, more to himself than at me. I fight the urge to yell out, "It wasn't a vibrator!"

VAGIANTS

April

WORK IS QUICKLY TAKING OVER MY LIFE, AND SAM AND I ARE LIKE SHIPS passing in the night. He likes hearing my stories, and I promise him I'll write everything down.

On my next flight on Air Force One, we're traveling to North Carolina, where the president will talk about college affordability, and then to California for fundraisers. Although I have the hang of the job, I still don't get the social breakdown or the protocols.

I do have one friend, finally: Hope. I thought she was kidding when she first introduced herself—President Obama's videographer just happens to be named Hope?

Hope is magnetic. She has big brown eyes like Jeanne Moreau, high cheekbones, and wavy brown hair long enough to betray the Californian in her. Although she's been a professional filmmaker for most of her adult life, she carries herself like the accomplished gymnast she once was, and at five foot two, she's a compact package of strength. You'd never guess she's in her forties. Besides her beauty and bouncy personality, Hope stands out because she says hi to everyone. She's the opposite of a D.C. creature.

Now on the plane, I stand up as Hope comes over to my seat and gives me a hug before fluttering off to greet someone else. She's in the middle of talking to one of the deputy chiefs of staff when she says, "Wow, look at all these women!" I look around and see what Hope sees: The traveling staff are almost all women. It's a rarity, even in the Obama White House, so Hope organizes a photo in the staff cabin "to celebrate badass females getting things done on Air Force One."

I'm not sure if I should get in the picture because I'm new, so I pretend to be too busy reading my book to notice. As I skim the page, Hope calls my name from across the cabin and summons me to join the group. As I tentatively walk over, I feel the woman with curly red hair watching me. Her sleeve of gold bracelets jangles, the rattle of a snake before it attacks. The way she looks at me makes me feel as if I don't even know all the ways I'm screwing up. I've never felt so abashed or intimidated or self-conscious. I pretend not to care, even though I feel my hands growing sweaty. I tell myself that the Rattler doesn't even know me and that I'm probably being too sensitive, reading way too much into things.

While Chuck, one of the five White House photographers, adjusts the settings on his Canon, I shuffle over to the group. No one introduces themselves. As we huddle together for the photo, someone among the female senior staff says something about vaginas, and I figure I must have misheard. I put my arms around Skye and Hope, the only people whose names I know. Afterward, I ask Hope if she'd heard someone say vagina.

"The Vagiants," she says with a half smile. Hope goes on to explain that after President Obama took office in 2009, there was widespread criticism about the lack of female senior staffers in an administration that had championed diversity on the campaign trail. By the time I arrived in 2012, the male-female ratio had dramatically improved—there were two female deputy chiefs of staff, a female photographer, a female National Security Council representative, and a female ambassador to the United Nations. "Some of the most powerful women in the Obama administration," Hope tells me, "call themselves Vagiants."

My stomach immediately starts to cramp. Why does "Vagiant" make me feel bad? Am I being too sensitive? Prudish? I wouldn't especially love it if the men in the West Wing nicknamed themselves the 10-Inch Senior Staffs.

When we get back to D.C., I head out with Lisa, who seems to hate me for being too enthusiastic. I ask her about the Rattler and she snaps, "Why? Did you say something stupid to her?" When I shake my head, Lisa says, "Well, I don't know what you did, but she likes me. We traded *Cosmo* articles on the plane last week." I shrug, embarrassed, and breathe in the fresh air as we exit onto West Exec. Lisa is right, I must have done something wrong.

Halfway down the parking lot, I stop cold.

"Whose car is that?"

Lisa shrugs. How would she know and why would she care?

It's a 1989 Jeep Grand Wagoneer just like the one I grew up in— the same navy blue paint, same dark wood side paneling. For the better part of twenty years, my mom chauffeured my siblings and me every day of the week to our sports practices in that woody. I lost my first front tooth in the backseat of that car. When I was finally tall enough to ride shotgun, my brother and I would take turns sitting up front and fighting over the radio station. I spent half my life in that car, and now here it is, an old friend from the happiest part of my childhood, waiting for me on West Exec.

"It's someone pretty senior," Lisa warns as I peer through the passenger side window. *Same tan pleather interior.* "You know, to be parked on West Exec."

"This person is, like, my soulmate."

I'm only half kidding. This parking lot, with designated parking spaces for senior staff, is full of Priuses and Chevys: sensible, undistinguished cars. Nothing like the wagon, with its rust peeking out under the wood. I press my face against the driver's window, looking for clues about the owner.

"I need this car," I say to myself.

Lisa rolls her eyes. "Can we go?"

THE
CIRCUS

May

I'M IN A HOTEL ELEVATOR WHEN IT HAPPENS THE FIRST TIME. An older woman clutching her pocketbook sees the red pin on my blazer and asks us, "Are you part of that group?"

"Part of the circus?" I ask.

"Yes, we are," I tell her as I instinctively touch it, this cheap metal pin that is, by far, the most valuable piece of jewelry I'll ever own.

In Mariokart, the star makes you invincible. In the circus, the red pin makes you unstoppable. And so here I go, down another long hallway, past the GI Joes in black CAT gear, big guns slung across their chests, past the doctor, the nurse, the military aide holding the nuclear football, the head of Secret Service, the jugglers, the Vagiants, the SEALs, the clowns, and the Rattler to see the ringleader himself—the president of the United States.

Every time I look up, I'm following POTUS through a different state. As I walk across tarmacs and run along blocked-off streets, Johnny Cash's rendition of "I've Been Everywhere" plays in my head. I start leaving my raincoat on the plane, then a spare pair of shoes, a sweatshirt, an entire extra outfit after a tragic coffee spill. It seems I'm on the plane more than not as the campaign revs up along with the D.C. humidity.

Lisa, Peggy, and I rotate trips so that we're each traveling 30 percent of the time. And because POTUS seems to be traveling 24/7, I barely have time to unpack my suitcase before I'm off again. Some days we hit three states, other times two cities on opposite coasts. It's exhausting but exhilarating, walking into a stadium or state fair to cheers of "Yes we can!" and "Fired up! Ready to go!" U2's "City of Blinding Lights" is the cue for POTUS to take the stage, and Bruce Springsteen's "We Take Care of Our Own" signals the end of his speech. He's a one-man band performing multiple times a day, and we're the hundreds of invisible hands backstage. Yesterday we were in Cincinnati; today we're landing in Denver, shortly after midnight.

I refuse to let the beastly travel schedule interfere with my morning runs, so I wake up early and get dressed, remembering to fasten my red hard pin to my black Lululemon tank top, which was marked down after an unfortunate box cutter incident while I still worked in the store. I like the hole. It reminds me of how lucky I am, how far I've come.

It's just after seven in Colorado, and the rising sun filters through the blinds of the tiny hotel gym, painting the back wall neon pink and creating an impossible glare on my treadmill television screen. Not that I care about what's on TV; I've got my running playlist blasting through my skull. David Plouffe, one of the president's senior advisers, is sipping coffee from a to-go cup behind me and eyeing the dusty weight machines incredulously. I watch him in the mirror and wonder what that jackrabbit of a man is thinking. Marvin Nicholson, the president's super-tall, super-goofy trip director, is cracking jokes with the Secret Service guys as they sweep the gym with their bomb-sniffing German shepherds.

After three miles, I up my speed. Four miles in, I increase it again. *I'll stop at five*, I tell myself. Finally, after seven miles, I slow way down and take a look in the mirror. My face is bright red and I'm WWF-level sweaty. My shirt is soaked through, my hair is wet and matted, even my socks are squishy, as if I stepped in a puddle.

I slow to a stop, and out of the corner of my eye, I see someone step onto the treadmill to my right. I hardly take note. "I thought you'd be faster than that," he says. I look over to see who this joker is. It's the president.

"Hey, guys, don't you think she could have run a little faster?" he asks the agents manning the room as I feel my red face turn purple. They laugh, and he laughs, and I should laugh, but I don't. I'm in shock.

"You could have gone a little faster," he says to me with a wink. The president is wearing a black Kangol baseball cap, black pants, black shirt—his standard workout getup. His eyes twinkle under the visor, his jaw working a piece of gum. He's goading me, but I'm speechless and starstruck and want to pass out and can't come up with anything. I suddenly realize that I forgot to pack deodorant, and that I definitely smell terrible right now, right here, with the president, who's given up on having any friendly banter with the smelly mute girl and is flicking through channels on his TV, looking for SportsCenter.

Mortified, I wipe down the machine and sprint out of the gym. Marvin, the trip director, gives me a high five on my way out. I take the elevator up to my room, shaking from the interaction and worried I'm going to miss bag call. When I get to my floor, I jog down the hallway. Every second counts. If I miss the eight o'clock bag call, I'll have to lug my suitcase to all the different sites today.

I pass room after room, and then a door swings open, and there's Jon Favreau, the head speechwriter, putting his suitcase into the hallway for bag call. He's wearing nothing but a towel around his waist, his Favs abs on full display, glistening postshower. We've never spoken, and we don't speak now, because abs like those will render a girl speechless.

"Morning!" he says, grinning but a little self-conscious. I doubt Jon expected the new stenographer to be right outside his door at that exact moment. I'm still sweating, and I really wish I'd put on deodorant, so I keep moving, embarrassed for both of us.

Back in my room, I strip down and pick out my outfit for the day before stuffing my new blue suitcase with the rest of my things, including my sweaty running clothes from this morning. Wrapped in a towel, I put my bag out in the hallway at 8 A.M. on the dot. Phew.

It's only after a quick shower that I realize what I've done. Still in a towel, I swing open my hotel room door, but my suitcase is gone, and it's too late to run to a drugstore. There's no time to fix this. In my rush to make bag call, I'd packed all my underwear. Today, I'll be traveling commando with the commander in chief.

IN THE
NAME OF
FEMINISM

May–June

SAM AND I ARE AT HIS FEAR OF VIRGINIA SHOW AT ROCK & ROLL HOTEL when we get into a huge fight. I am drinking one Cape Codder after another, waiting at the bar for him to finish sound check. When he comes over to say hi, I stand on my tippy-toes and yank him down for some aggressive, drunk kisses. This is not the best idea, since Sam is sober and his coworkers are all right there, waiting for him to introduce us.

The night deteriorates from there: a fight after the show, first backstage, and then as the band packs up their equipment, and then on the sidewalk outside the venue, before I finally take a cab home, alone. I can't tell you what the fight was about; I don't think I knew even as it was happening. But now I wish I knew. I'm waiting in my bed to hear his footsteps on the stairs, the creak of my bedroom door. Half asleep, I imagine I smell that familiar mix of sweat and Old Spice, musical triumph and bourbon.

In the middle of the night, I wake up and Sam still isn't here and hasn't even texted. That's when I know something is off. Something has been off, because why did I ever get that drunk? And when did Sam ever not at least text me good night?

The next morning, I crawl out of bed with the sinking sense that we're over, and I don't even know why. As I zombie-walk to the coffee shop, I review the last month in search of clues, like an unshowered and possibly still drunk Sherlock Holmes. In the last several weeks, there'd been evidence of something amiss, like the time I stopped to pet a dog on Church Street and Sam scolded me, genuinely annoyed, even though I *always* stop to pet dogs. And there was that time at the bar he ordered a beer for himself and didn't get anything for me when I was standing right next to him. And, perhaps most telling of all, the week before our first anniversary, when I asked him what he wanted to do to celebrate, he shrugged it off and said he didn't think anniversaries warranted anything special. My stomach had sunk to my sneakers. I'd already amassed a collection of presents for him.

By midafternoon I realize I'm an idiot: There had been plenty of warnings and I'd just been tone deaf. I text Sam and tell him we need to talk, can he meet me at Swann Street? If we're going to break up, may as well be right now, before I get any more attached.

"I'm sorry," Sam says before I even open my mouth. We sit down on my front porch. The early spring temperature is perfect—not too warm, not too cold. "I know you're going to break up with me," Sam continues, "and I don't blame you. I've been an asshole, but I love you and I want to be with you."

"I'm sorry I got so drunk at the show," I say, staring into his mossy green eyes. God, I love those eyes.

"It's fine," Sam says, holding my hand. "I mean, it was so unlike you, and I was pissed at the time because those are people I know in a professional context, but it's fine. Just please don't break up with me."

I give Sam a sideways glance. In my head I think, *Halle-fucking-lujah, I don't have to dump the guy I want to marry.*

Sam grabs my hand and kisses me—on the cheek, on the mouth—and then whispers, "I love you, Cookie," which is his nickname for me, since he apparently thought I was one tough cookie the night we met.

"I love you, too," I tell him. "Want to see this funny thing my friend Jen posted on Facebook?"

We go up to my room and I take out my laptop, but when I open my Facebook page, an alert pops up that I have a message from a woman named Wendy—Sam's ex-girlfriend.

"Your boyfriend continues to call me to tell me how much he still loves me, more than he will ever love you" is the opening line of Wendy's message. "In the name of feminism, or some kind of universal sisterhood, I feel like I need to show you this correspondence."

Sam hops off my bed as if it's suddenly on fire, and from somewhere far away I hear him saying, "You have to break up with me, you have to break up with me."

As I click open the attachment, I remember that Wendy had called Sam's cell phone in the middle of the night last week, and the incessant ringing had woken me up. I'd nudged Sam, who seemed surprised and annoyed. "Maybe it's an emergency?" I'd said. They hadn't talked since their ugly breakup. Sam had shaken his head and silenced the phone, spooned me, and said, "Go back to sleep, Cookie."

The attachment is eight single-spaced pages of emails between Wendy and Sam, from April to May. I scroll through them, message after message. And like some sad Greek chorus, a world away, Sam continues to sing his refrain, "You have to break up with me, you have to break up with me." I focus every atom of my being on the emails and calmly register that this is a message in which Sam tells Wendy she's smarter than I am; she's hotter, more open, more sophisticated, better in bed, more creative, more disciplined, more capable of following through and succeeding than I'll ever be . . .

You'd think I would panic; that I wouldn't be able to breathe or think; that I would burst into tears. Instead, adrenaline courses through my veins as I look down at Sam, who is staring at me, tears streaming down his cheeks. I finish reading Wendy's message, my heartbeat in my ears. "Oh, and one last thing," she wrote. "If he's crying, you know he's lying. Don't believe anything he says to you. Now you know the truth."

Remember the mom who lifted the car off her son because of the adrenaline rush? I feel that I could bench-press a stack of Hummers as I watch Sam's tears fall in heavy streams. He apologizes, admits to everything; he has to, it's all there. Sam explains he'd cut things off with Wendy last week, and that's why she'd come for me. He'd stopped responding to her emails, ignored her phone calls, which is why she'd called at night and woken me up.

Sisterhood my ass, Wendy.

I hadn't thought twice about that 2 A.M. call. I'd trusted Sam fully. We were a team. We were the best.

Sam tells me he loves me as he wipes his face with the sleeve of the flannel shirt I got him for Christmas. "You have to break up with me," he garbles through the tears. Sam swears that he didn't mean any of it, that he's messed up. He hates his job, he's unhappy, but he'd never actually cheat—this was just an acting out. My brain is functioning as well as a scrambled egg as I try to dignify emotional cheating over physical cheating—or is it all the same? Does it matter if it's over? From far away, Sam keeps repeating, "You have to break up with me," while looking me in the eye and waiting for the inevitable verdict, waiting for me to scream at him, to throw things and tell him to get out of my house.

But I don't want to break up with him. I love him. This is who I want to marry and have a family with. This is who makes me stay up late to listen to live music, who forces me outside my comfort zone while holding my hand and keeping me safe. This is my best friend. This is who laughs when I roll my eyes, who reminds me to see the best in people, to give everyone the benefit of the doubt.

I look back down at those messages on the screen and it's like trying to negotiate the impossible, trying to fit my Sam into Wendy's Sam, or Wendy's Sam into my Sam. It simply doesn't work.

"You broke us." I say it without a single tear and in a steady, judicial voice I don't recognize as my own.

At some point, Sam leaves. I curl into a ball in my bed and when I hear the front door shut, all that superhuman strength shuts off like a light. This is what it means to be without Sam. After a few hours, I decide this is too much pain. I run to his house faster than I've ever run. In a sprint the length of a blink, I'm at his house, and

I take two steps at a time up to his room. I fit myself inside his arms and for a second, everything feels better.

OF COURSE, IT DOESN'T LAST. IN THE FOLLOWING WEEKS, SAM IS SO sweet, so attentive, that it underlines how absent he'd been. Each night, I dream of him and Wendy. On my walk to and from work, those messages play through my head on a loop. And every time he says that he loves me, or likes my dress, or tells me I'm a good writer, or preemptively stops at the sight of a dog so I can pet it, I'm reminded of Wendy and all the things he secretly believes about me.

In the end, it is Sam's kindness that I find too infuriating to bear. His attempt to be better makes me feel worse, and after a couple of weeks of trying to forgive, I end it. Balancing anger with sorrow and resentment and love is too much. I break up with Sam and burrow into my sadness.

I avoid my friends because I'm too embarrassed to tell them about Wendy, about what Sam said about me. They're used to my being busy with work anyway, so they stop reaching out, and I start going to bed before dark.

BERNICE'S ADVICE RINGS IN MY HEAD, OVER AND OVER—"KEEP YOUR boyfriend, keep your boyfriend, keep your boyfriend." I throw it out my bedroom window, and I throw myself into work.

With a new concentration that borders on obsession, I perfect my routine for off-the-record background briefings. I show up early, hit Record once the meeting is under way, and write down the start time. Then I quickly find a seat against a wall or in a corner, anywhere that's out of the way. When the session wraps, I weave between lingering reporters and staffers to retrieve my metallic minions, hit Stop, and write down the end time. Then I return to my office, where my coworkers and I split the audio, type the transcript, and proofread it before either sending it out to the public—for immediate release—or emailing it only to the press office staff and presidential archive—internal transcript. Then I go to the bathroom to cry.

I return to my desk wiping tears from my eyes and see an email from the press office: "Can we get a steno for this?" It could be anything: a roundtable in the Roosevelt Room, remarks in the Rose Garden, a background briefing in the press secretary's office, an interview in the Library, Diplomatic Reception Room, Map Room, Blue Room, Red Room, Green Room, East Room, State Dining Room, Cabinet Room, or Oval Office.

I scroll down. It's a summons to cover a health care meeting anchored by Attorney General Eric Holder and Secretary of Health and Human Services Kathleen Sebelius. I cross West Exec parking lot ten minutes ahead of time and cut through the West Wing lobby. It's always library-lit in there—dark gold light, oriental rugs, silent. I traverse the lobby on tiptoes and slip into the Roosevelt Room, quiet as a White House dormouse.

The Roosevelt Room wasn't designed with acoustics in mind, so we use six recorders for the long mahogany table, and then a seventh I put directly in front of POTUS's chair, which is slightly higher than the rest. After setting up my recorders, I go around the room and write down who's sitting where. As I scribble down the name of a *Washington Post* reporter, someone puts a hand on my shoulder. I jump, already on edge, and the man behind me laughs.

"You've got to relax," he says with a gentle smile. "I'm Von."

I introduce myself and drink up his kindness as he tells me he's been a butler at the White House for forty years.

"Forty years! Any advice?" I ask.

Von shrugs. "It's just a job."

I nod slowly, in disbelief. I need it to be more than just a job. Without Sam, it's all I've got left. Von excuses himself after he delivers the last cup and saucer. As he exits, he turns back. "Nice to meet you, Beck. And I mean it—relax, it's just a job."

THAT WEEKEND, I AGREE TO SEE SAM. WE MEET AT A COFFEE SHOP, NEUtral territory, and he begs me to forgive him, to come back to him—and I do. I'm still in love with him; I'm still convinced we're going to get married. So I hang on with everything I've got. I refuse to tell my friends or family what's happened between us, because if I name it, I'll make it real.

"My therapist says I displaced all of my career frustrations on you instead of on myself," Sam explains. This makes me feel better, like we'd been driving around in a car with a broken engine and the mechanic has just diagnosed the problem. "I need to work on the Obama campaign, Cookie," Sam says. "In Toledo, Ohio." He looks apologetic, but his eyes sparkle. I can tell he's excited about this, and if he's happy with his work, he won't cheat on me, won't send emails to Wendy.

Even if we have to do long distance, I can tell we're back on track. We're the little engine that could, diagnosed and fixed. Sam will be back from Toledo in November—only five months away—and I'll keep busy at work until then. We will be fine. We will be together once this campaign ends, and maybe the distance is what we need to heal, to prove that we are still the best team.

PARADISE, PARTY OF ONE

June

YOU DON'T EARN POINTS OR SKYMILES ON AIR FORCE ONE, BUT YOU DO when you fly on the Delta press charter. For international trips, all the different media outlets chip in and charter a private plane to streamline travel between countries—no waiting in line to have your visa stamped, no shady pull-aside in Afghanistan or Russia, no real-life scenes from *Taken*, *Taken 2*, or, God forbid, *Taken 3*.

This is my first international trip, and thus my first flight on the charter, which is dubbed the party plane because POTUS and senior White House staff never travel on it. While Lisa is on Air Force One to record the gaggle and travel with the press pool, Peggy and I will stick with the press charter, which will set up at a different hotel than where the president's bubble stays when we arrive in San José del Cabo, Mexico, for the G20 summit.

Lisa, forever fashion-conscious, had given me a heads-up that people dress more casually on the party plane. I'm grateful for the tip; no one is in a suit as we wait together on the tarmac. I see Chuck Todd wearing jeans, loafers, and a blazer. The women wear chunky sweaters over black leggings, and glasses instead of contact lenses. Only NBC's Kristin Welker looks camera-ready, and that's because she just rushed over from doing a live shot at the White House.

Rodney, a cameraman from NBC, greets me with a big hello. Lucas told me that he dresses in destination-related costumes— a leprechaun en route to Ireland, for instance—and when I see him, he's in a sombrero and shaking maracas.

Even though he's not on this trip, Lucas had given me his own heads-up about the party plane, so I'm looking forward to the bar carts in the aisle before takeoff, and the Delta attendants who are specially trained to serve VIPs, which means they don't make you sit down let alone buckle during takeoff. I take my seat and find a little goodie bag from Delta next to my name card. The TV anchors play it cool, but I feel like a movie star.

Peggy sits next to me, and it feels like traveling with an aunt— polite but comfortable. Over the course of the flight, the attendants remember my cocktail of choice and call me honey when they bring me a blanket I didn't know I wanted. There are endless entrées and snacks, and the liquor flows as my Skymiles tick up, up, and away. Then everyone around me starts pulling out their wallets. Peggy's briefed me on this ritual—it's called Seat-O, a charter-themed lottery of sorts. Participants write their seat letter and number on a $20 bill and toss it into the Seat-O sack as Rodney walks the aisles, collecting. The pot is usually between $1,000 and $3,000.

I reluctantly write on the bill (isn't this illegal?) and Rodney booms over the PA system, "Welcome aboard! Who is ready for Seat-O!?" I'm nervous and shy and self-conscious, so I just smile when Rodney comes up to me and says, "Hello, little lady!" The felt yellow balls on his sombrero dance along as he does a little welcome shuffle for me. I drop my $20 after watching Peggy do the same, and Rodney continues down the aisle with his Seat-O sack.

The seat drawing takes place once we reach cruising altitude. Rodney stands where flight attendants normally show you where to find your flotation device. (Adding to the air of infallibility is the fact that there are no safety instructions or videos on the press plane or on Air Force One.) After we reach altitude and Kelly, the White House travel director of press advance, has thanked everyone for traveling with the Obama administration to Cabo, she hands the intercom microphone over to Rodney and the plane erupts in cheers and applause. All eyes are on Rodney as he draws a $20 bill out of the sack. Wriggling his eyebrows and grinning with all his teeth, Rodney announces the name of the winner. It's one of the network producers, and everyone boos because he already makes the most money. When he lands in Cabo, he'll have an extra $1,300 cash. After booing, everyone laughs and claps and congratulates the producer because, hey, we're all getting paid to go to a tropical resort. And for the millionth time in the last four months, I can't believe that this is my life. Or anyone's life. No one deserves to be this lucky.

When we land in Cabo, the air is sweet—a smell I'll come to associate with developing countries, from Costa Rica to Tanzania to Laos. After buses transport us from the airport to the resort, I check in and get a packet with everything I'll need, including an all-you-can-eat, all-you-can-drink white wristband. I see reporters lining up at the pool bar, booze bracelets at the ready, and as Peggy and I go in search of our rooms, I wonder who will be my friend in this press charter world.

Hope, my only White House travel buddy, will stick with POTUS and the travel pool when they arrive tomorrow, and zoom from summit site to elementary school to cultural center to war memorial to black-tie banquet. The president routinely works fourteen-hour days abroad—if anyone deserves booze bracelets during international trips, it's him and the travel pool, but POTUS barely sips his wine at the dinners thrown in his honor, and the poolers gratefully chug lukewarm beers on the press bus back to their hotel at midnight. Only television correspondents and the rest of us traveling on the press charter have the luxury of worrying about how many liquid calories we're consuming as we tan the day away in Cabo.

I get to my room and gasp at the ocean view. How is this my room? Was there a mistake? This is the most beautiful place I've ever been, and the nicest room I've ever had, and I don't even have to share it with anyone—now or ever. Peggy and Lisa had laughed when I'd asked if I'd be sharing a $500-a-night room with a coworker. "No, silly," Lisa had said, patting me on the head as if I were an endearingly dumb dog.

I drop my backpack and unzip my suitcase in search of my bathing suit. The press charter always arrives a day ahead of POTUS and Air Force One so that the TV networks can set up their live shots, usually on a balcony overlooking the ocean, or the mountains, or the city, or the devastated area, depending on the landscape and nature of the trip. I have twenty-four hours to soak in the Mexican sun, read, and sip something pink mixed with Malibu through a swirly straw.

Being the new girl anywhere is always awkward, but now I'm the new girl in a bathing suit walking by myself to a pool full of coworkers who can't seem to remember my name. I have no posse, no one to share sunscreen with, no one I can ask to pinch me because how is this scene my real life?

Several reporters and camera people are already in the water, standing in the shallow end sipping daiquiris from plastic cups, sunburn seeping into their pale skin. The small team from the White House press office are also in the pool—Tim from speechwriting, James from National Security, Marie the press wrangler, Diane and Scott, both deputy press secretaries. I don't want to impose—all these people have worked together for years. They're more than colleagues; they're friends. And so I plop down on a chaise longue at the deep end, far from the quickly developing party.

The scene radiates with good old-fashioned trouble as Tim asks who wants another daiquiri. It's 3 P.M. The last thing I ate was breakfast at nine this morning, back on Swann Street in D.C.

I eye Peggy coming down the stairs and shrink in my chair. If she joins me, the cool kids will never invite me to come hang out. Peggy sees me and waves, and my heart sinks as I wave back. How come I'm the only one with a chaperone? But Peggy keeps walking in the opposite direction, toward the hightop by the pool bar where several cameramen are yelling and laughing at each other. I watch Peggy approach the table and tap Rodney on the shoulder. He turns around, and the whole table erupts. "Peggy!" they yell, enveloping her and asking what she'd like to drink.

I sink even lower into my chair, hoping to disappear. Even my sixty-year-old boss has a group of friends. I mean, of course she does. Tim and James are trash-talking each other as they toss a football while the girls hold a handstand competition with an anchor and producer from CNN.

I try to tune out the boozy party animals and let myself escape into my book. When that doesn't work, I take a deep breath, text Sam, and tell him I wish he were here. Sam texts back: "Just say hi, be you." But I'm shy. Sam senses my reluctance and writes: "Go get a drink. Relax. Enjoy."

I walk over to the pool bar and ask the overworked bartender for a mai tai. "Make it two," James, an attractive spokesman for National Security, says behind me.

"Too cool for school?" he asks, and I turn around.

"Me?" I ask, and not in a flirty, eyelash-batting kind of way. I ask because I need clarification, because too many times in my life I've waved back at someone who was waving to the person standing behind me.

"Yes, you," James says, flashing a devastating grin.

"Um, no, I just—"

"What are you reading?"

I hold up the book—*A Confederacy of Dunces*. My favorite. My literary version of a security blanket. I've already read it three times, but I wanted something familiar for my first work trip abroad.

"I liked it a lot," he says, just as someone yells my name.

James and I both look to where Peggy and her cameramen are waving me over. "You're being summoned," he says, and through his sunglasses I can see his elevator eyes checking me out at every floor. It's flattering and gross and exciting. "Come hang after," he says quietly, and I wonder if he means somewhere not here.

I won't find out, because once I join Peggy and the camera guys, I stick with them until after the sunset. They tell one incredible story after another—about the different administrations, presidents, staffers, international incidents. They were all there for H.W. puking on the prime minister of Japan, Reagan falling asleep before the pope in Rome, Monica, 9/11, Katrina. And I'm their target audience: a bright-eyed tabula rasa, full of questions and forever impressed.

Peggy puts her arm around me and asks if I'd like to join them for dinner. "It's on me!" George jokes, holding up his white wristband. Peggy groans and punches his shoulder. I see myself in her just then: the cool girl with the guy friends, the funny straight shooter, smart enough not to mess around with any of the men who've tried to court her over the years. Although the camera guys are all older than my dad, they treat Peggy with the respect and affection usually reserved for big sisters. We agree to reconvene at seven o'clock after showers.

I skip up the steps back to my room, tipsy and feeling lucky. I text Sam to tell him how the day progressed, but he doesn't respond. For a moment my mind flickers to Wendy, but I push her out of my head as I insert my key card. Before I step inside my room, a door opens at the end of the hall, and there's James, freshly showered, turning the light off before shutting the door behind him. My eyes find the number next to the door before my brain registers what for: 811.

"Hey," he says as he walks by me, a little too close. My stomach flips the same way it did in fifth grade when Nate gave me a nod outside the roller rink. I know what it means, that flip. It's the delicious smell of a double-dog-dare, of an empty bottle spun and now pointing at me in the back of the school yard where the recess aides can't see.

At the end of the hallway, James turns around and gives me a look just as someone calls his name from the stairwell. It's a well-worn and overrehearsed look. And yet . . . in it I see the possibilities, the secrets that swim up at resort pool bars and slither under hotel doors late at night when everyone else is sleeping, the back-corner-of-the-bar acknowledgment that we're all adults here, so let's just have some fun.

When Sam Skypes me before bed, I let out a breath I didn't know I was holding. In the back of my brain I'd let myself worry he was talking to Wendy again. I tell him how the afternoon evolved, about dinner with Peggy and her boys, and about James's look. "Good for you, Cookie," he says, chuckling, the sound of a raucous Toledo bar in the background. "James Lentz is a handsome guy."

A WEEK AFTER CABO, I'M WALKING TO WORK WHEN MY DAD CALLS ME. Either something big happened, or someone is dead. "Beck! He did it! The Supreme Court upheld the ACA!"

"No way!"

"It was five to four! Chief Justice Roberts voted the individual mandate is constitutional!"

By the time I hang up, Sam has already texted me, although his angle is more political: "This is so awesome—Romney is going to have a much harder time now!"

A couple of hours later, POTUS makes a statement in the East Room and the stenographers type up his remarks from our office. "Well, it should be pretty clear by now that I didn't do this because it was good politics," the president says. "I did it because I believed it was good for the country. I did it because I believed it was good for the American people." While the rest of the office complains that their health insurance premium is going to go up, Peggy, Lucas, and I hug. This is the right thing. How many people have I already met on the road who were only alive—or their child was only alive— because of the ACA?

"Fuck yeah, POTUS," I say under my breath as I release the transcript.

DREAM
BIG
DREAMS

July–August

"BECK," PEGGY SAYS ONE MORNING IN EARLY JULY, "I WANT TO TALK TO you about next week." I immediately get nervous—have I done something wrong? I wonder if she's mad because I've been coming in a little late the past few weeks. The only good thing about Sam not being in D.C. is that I go to bed early, wake up at dawn, run, and then spend the morning reading and writing until it's time to leave for work. But once I start writing, I have a hard time stopping. It's as if I slip into some kind of hypnotic state as I recall the week's events to the page, each detail seeming more imperative than the last.

I open my mouth to apologize, but Peggy cuts me off. "The president is going on a two-day bus tour next week—can you go?" I say yes without having to check a calendar. I have no plans these days. This job requires so much time that I've already had to quit my club soccer and lacrosse teams.

"Don't you want to know where he's going?" Peggy asks. I turn around to face her; she's grinning. "Maumee is the first stop," Peggy says. "It's a suburb of Toledo, Ohio."

After shrieking and hugging Peggy, I go out in the hallway to call Sam from under the stained-glass skylights. I can't believe this! I get to see Sam! He doesn't pick up and I'm not surprised: It's ten o'clock on a Tuesday morning. He's probably in a meeting. I text him and use a hundred exclamation points.

The day I get to see Sam, we fly in to the Toledo Express Airport and motorcade to the Wolcott House Museum. While POTUS delivers remarks to a roaring crowd outside, I go into the museum, which is in an old house, to find out where I should set up. After his speech, POTUS will do a handful of five-to-seven-minute interviews with local reporters, which I'll need to record and send back to the office before the next site, where Sam is waiting for me. I find WHCA already camped out in the living room and plug in my audio system with theirs.

POTUS hasn't done local Q&As in a while, and he's rusty during his first interview in the living room. The seven minutes with *Channel 13 Action News* is full of his notorious pauses, the expected talking points, and "but the good news is" transitions. Once the reporter is escorted out of the room, POTUS turns to Jay Carney, who's standing next to me. "I sound like such a politician," he says, grimacing with disgust.

If you're a doctor, you want to sound like a doctor when you're diagnosing a patient. If you're a plumber, you'd better speak like a plumber when you're explaining an estimate. If you're a hairdresser, a fireman, a lawyer, a zookeeper, a principal, or a porn star, you want to sound as if you work in your line of work when you are, in fact, working. But nobody wants to sound like a politician, especially a politician.

Then we go to our next event, and I see Sam. The very sight of him knocks me sideways. He's so cute, all dressed up in a suit, shaking hands with reporters. I walk over and he scoops me up, and I wish I could stay here with him and not get back on the bus for the rest of the campaign trip. When POTUS begins his speech, Sam lets go of my hand and whispers, "I'll be right back—I need to introduce myself to Jay." I nod, proud of him, and stay where I am. It's only when the president's wrapping up that I realize Sam hasn't returned and I need to get going to the motorcade so I don't get left behind.

The applause crescendos as POTUS yells his closing paragraph, his voice already hoarse: "And if we win Toledo, we will win Ohio! And if we win Ohio, we'll win this election! And if we win this election, we will finish what we started, and we will remind the world why the United States of America is the greatest nation on earth!"

I see Sam jogging toward me through the crowd.

"You disappeared!"

"Sorry, Cookie, I kept seeing folks I needed to say hi to." Sam gives me a hug, a kiss on the cheek, and a quick kiss on the lips, then walks me as close to the motorcade as he can before a Secret Service agent stops him. "I need one of these," Sam says, touching the red hard pin on my lapel. I grab his shirt collar and kiss him one more time.

"Come back soon," Sam says with a grin.

"*You* come back soon," I say, mussing his perfectly coiffed hair. I won't see him for at least a month, but I don't have time to think about it. I turn and run so I don't miss the motorcade.

PEGGY WAS RIGHT: THE CAMPAIGN SEASON SPEEDS UP TIME. IT'S ALready the end of August, and after several months on the campaign trail, they know me—the reporters, the photographers, the advance team, the military personnel manning the plane and protecting it by checking off each person's name from the manifest before they're allowed to board. "Go right up, Ms. Dorey-Stein," they say, smiling, before I've opened my mouth.

Todd, the attendant on Air Force One, promises to call me Beck after months of "ma'am." "It's a very hard habit to break, Beck, but I'll try." The press office staffers no longer refer to me as the steno. Jen Psaki knows my name, and Jay Carney is comfortable using it on the bus before the gaggle. Rob Nabors shares his Ziploc bag of cheddar Goldfish with me, and Pete Souza hands me my suitcase without announcement when we arrive back at the White House. I'm slowly getting to be real friends with Hope the videographer, but on most trips I still feel pretty lonely.

And then I meet Shilpa in the Staff 2 van in Florida.

I usually ride in the Press 1 van, but after a private fund-raiser in Coral Gables the motorcade has started rolling, so I run to Staff 2. When I open the door of the van, a pretty girl with straight black hair immediately looks up from her phone, smiles, and says hi: a dead giveaway. She must be new. Most people are too busy putting out fires on their BlackBerrys to acknowledge a van-hopper.

"I'm Shilpa—the newest assistant staff sec," she says, extending her hand. The staff secretary is a senior staffer with a team of five assistant staff secs who are responsible for every piece of paper the president sees every single day. This means they are responsible for not only the president's daily briefing book but also every document from an urgent memo from National Security, to a new bill from Congress, to a thank-you note from, say, Ethel Kennedy.

"Wow, that's such a big job," I tell her, shoving my microphone into my backpack.

"Tell me about it!" Shilpa says, laughing, and gives me the warmest smile.

A WEEK LATER, ON A CAMPAIGN BUS TOUR THROUGH IOWA, I FIND MYself reunited with Shilpa. After a long day of wind turbines and cornfields and farms, we go down to the hotel bar, where we meet Cole, one of the president's traveling aides. Cole is part of the president's inner circle on the road—he's never more than a few feet from POTUS so that he can brief him on each person the president will meet throughout the day and keep him updated on travel plans. Needless to say, you need to be smooth, sociable, and nothing short of brilliant about navigating the politics of politics to be an effective travel aide, and no one is better at working the system than Cole. He immediately asks us a bunch of questions, which I'm not used to from people in this bubble. But Cole, who has bright blue eyes, spiky brown hair, and a whip-smart sense of humor, seems to take a genuine interest in Shilpa and me as the newbies, and I appreciate his friendliness. I don't really get how Cole fits into the social hierarchy—he seems as happy to talk to us as he is to talk to the Rattler, who sits in a corner with other senior staffers, including Jay Carney, Marvin Nicholson, Jen Psaki, Terry Szuplat the speechwriter, and Jason Wolf, the guy I mistook for Jim Carrey.

"Don't you think he's a dead ringer for Jim Carrey?" I ask Cole, nodding at the Rattler's table. As she lifts her glass, the hiss of the gold bangles sends a shiver through my White Russian.

"You mean Jason?" Cole asks.

"Yes!"

"Jason is a character all his own. He's the second-funniest person in this rodeo, after me, of course. Want me to introduce you?"

I shake my head violently. No way do I want to disrupt the Rattler's table of super-important senior staff.

"Then let's stay here and get another round," Cole says cheerfully. "What are you guys drinking?"

As hours disappear at the hotel bar, I'm not so much drunk as giddy about making new friends. I genuinely like Shilpa and Cole, and they seem to like me, too. When the bill arrives in a black book, Cole hands the bartender his credit card without even glancing at the check.

"Wow, Cole, thanks, but here . . ." I say, scrambling for my wallet, feeling panic set in as I realize I don't have cash. Shilpa makes an identical scramble for her purse.

"No way," Cole says, waving us off. "Welcome to the team."

"Cole . . ." Shilpa says, holding out a crisp $20 bill.

But Cole just smiles and shakes his head before lifting his glass. "Dream big dreams," he toasts.

Shilpa laughs, but I don't get it.

"It's what POTUS writes to little kids when he signs things for them," she explains.

"Dream big dreams?" I repeat, trying it out.

Shilpa nods, beaming. We both know that's the perfect thing to tell a little kid. Our president is the coolest.

When I go up to my hotel room, I text Lisa to ask about Cole. She tells me he's very important. As a traveling aide, he decides who the president meets on trips.

"What do you mean?"

"Like, who gets to be in the photoline, who greets him on the tarmac, who gets to say hi to POTUS backstage—that sort of thing."

"That's a lot of responsibility."

"Yeah, he and Noah are really good at their jobs."

"Noah?"

"The other traveling aide."

"I don't think I've met Noah yet."

"He's hard to miss," Lisa texts. "He has very kissable lips."

I tease Lisa for being boy-crazy and thank her for the intel. I'm shocked to learn that Cole is only a year older than I am. He's in his midtwenties and already a power player in the Obama administration. And I'm a . . . stenographer. But maybe that's not the point. Maybe POTUS is right: Dream big dreams.

THE
SCAMPERING
STRATEGIST

September–November

ON SEPTEMBER 30, WE GO TO HENDERSON, NEVADA, JUST OUTSIDE Vegas, for three days of debate prep. On the way there, I text Sam that this is a long trip with lots of downtime, since POTUS is just cramming for the debate in a conference room with John Kerry and senior staff. Sam tells me he won't have much time to talk this week; he'll be busy on the campaign. "Why don't you write? Or go read by the pool?" I track down Hope instead, but she apologizes and says she'll need to work most of the trip—she has eighty hours of footage she needs to whittle down to this week's six-minute episode of West Wing Week. Shilpa, sadly, isn't on this trip.

In the morning, I head out for a run. Vegas is somewhere north-west of here as I jog uphill, away from the hotel and into the heights of empty streets and foreclosed McMansions. These houses have been abandoned ever since the bubble burst. Beyond this ghost town stand the mountains, indifferent to the dry heat, the Great Recession, and the president's reelection campaign.

As my feet hit the pavement, I think of Sam. I can see him and a group of slick political animals going out to the same bar drinking every night, sipping beers and click-clacking on their laptops, spouting out numbers randomly like some campaign version of Tourette's syndrome. I hate it. Sam loves it.

I'm lifted out of my head by a shadow on the cement. Someone is about to pass me! This has never, ever happened with these D.C. creatures. At first I think it must be a Secret Service agent, and I tell myself I can't be upset; they're paid to be in shape. But if it's a staffer, I'll be devastated. The shadow is growing ahead of me as the speedster continues to gain. My God, I hate getting passed. Who is this? Just get it over with already!

As I'm about to turn my head, David Plouffe glides by, giving me a respectful runner's wave as he does so. This is unbelievable! He's twenty years older than I am and infinitely more important. How does he have time to be so fast? My admiration blunts my competitive edge in midstride. I can't be upset that Plouffe is cranking out what must be six-minute splits. Despite the desert heat and the fact that I just got passed, my game face cracks into a grin as I climb the hill. David Plouffe is fast! How cool is that?

At the crest, I see Plouffe about to round the corner, but then he dashes off the street and into the red dirt. He's off-roading, kicking up a cloud of dust as he disappears behind a white stucco McMansion. I wonder what he sees or if he knows of a secret path out there.

When I return to my room, I sit down to write and the day disappears. While the president preps for his first debate against Mitt Romney, I write about my run with David Plouffe. There's no reason to agonize over each word, but I need to, even if no one ever sees it. It's as if my mind has been asleep and I'm jostling it awake, like running through the rust after a lazy winter. By dinnertime, my brain is happily humming as I save my little character sketch to my desktop. I name it "The Scampering Strategist."

The next day we fly to Denver, where POTUS has a horrendous debate. Afterward, all hell breaks loose. Marie the wrangler points out the press van, and I hop in with a few reporters. I sit in my as-signed seat, shotgun, and ask the driver what she thought of the de-bate. "Oh, I think Romney did real good," she says. I look at the presidential seal in the windshield, and it's not there—instead, it's the Romney insignia. Marie had accidentally put us in the Romney press van.

The reporters are busy typing so I say, "Guys, we're in the wrong van," and they start cursing their heads off because the motorcade is about to roll, and it might not look good if *The New York Times* and AP reporters literally switched camps directly after a terrible debate. We get out and start running around, and then Marie finds us. I get a shout-out in the pool report for saving the day, and *The Wall Street Journal* picks it up in its blog: "The White House stenographer put two and two together and said, 'Guys, we are in the Romney van. . . .' Blind panic then ensued."

The following morning I go down to the hotel gym. Just as I step off the treadmill, POTUS steps onto the one next to me. The gym is empty except for us. He gruffly says, "Good morning," and I say good morning back and get the hell out of his way.

ON NOVEMBER 6, 2012, POTUS WINS REELECTION BECAUSE HE'S THE baddest motherfucker in the game. Despite the palpable excitement gripping D.C., my personal celebration night is underwhelming: I watch the returns come in on our tiny television on Swann Street and wait for the president's victory speech because I need to type it. While Lisa and Margie are celebrating in Chicago with the White House bubble, and Sam is in Toledo drinking in his personal Ohio victory as well as the national feat, I am sitting alone in an empty house, sober. Charlotte and Emma and several other friends text me from a party to say they're going to walk to the White House to cel-ebrate, so as soon as I finish typing the transcript I go down to meet them. Pennsylvania Avenue is a sea of happy Obama supporters, cheering and clapping and shaking noisemakers usually reserved for New Year's Eve. Everyone is so joyful, but I'm exhausted after months of nonstop campaign travel.

"What's the matter?" Charlotte asks, shaking my shoulder, her cheeks rosy. She'd been at a watch party where they'd started drinking at five.

"I miss Sam." I'd called him, but he hadn't picked up. I'm guessing he's in a loud bar with his campaign coworkers.

"But we have Obama!" Charlotte shouts, and just then the masses start chanting, "Four more years! Four more years!" and Charlotte and I join in, our voices melting into the euphoric chorus. Charlotte is right. Big picture, everything is pretty amazing. Obama shellacked Romney, and Sam is coming back. As POTUS said in his victory speech that night, "The best is yet to come."

LOOK UP

Later in November

WHILE SAM PACKS UP HIS LIFE IN OHIO TO COME BACK TO D.C., I PRE-
pare to fly with the White House on a big Asia swing before Thanksgiving. We're going to Thailand, Myanmar, and Cambodia. This is
my first overseas trip on Air Force One.

"Good luck, and I can switch in if you get tired," Lisa says before
we take off. I've been assigned to POTUS and the press pool while
Peggy and Lisa travel on the party plane and stay with the press charter. I'm determined to hang with the pool the whole time. I want to
prove to Lisa I can do the job as well as she can.

After the gaggle on the flight to Bangkok, I return to my seat and
settle in for the twenty-hour leg. I take an Ambien, a pretty strong
sleeping aid, because I'm nervous I won't be able to fall asleep when
I'm so close to the Rattler.

A day later, in Myanmar, the humidity is crazy. It feels as if I'm trapped inside someone's mouth and smells like it, too. The crush of bodies makes it nearly impossible to breathe as Hope and I exchange tired glances, scrunched with all the reporters in a narrow hallway in a palace in Naypyidaw, the capital of Myanmar. President Obama and President Thein Sein are wrapping up their bilateral meeting on the other side of the doors at the end of the hall. Sandwiched between two reporters, I watch fat beads of sweat roll down their faces and disappear into their beard stubble. We're waiting to go in for a quick pool spray, but not yet. And so here we stand, squashed together for an unknown amount of time, no one talking, everyone privately coping with jet lag, thirst, and the fact that it's only the first full day of a six-day trip.

Twenty minutes later we're still waiting, one slippery mass of flesh and equipment. The cameramen adjust their heavy gear. Their shirts have been soaked through since Thailand. "It's a throwaway kind of day," Rodney says to me. At my raised eyebrow, he pinches the collar of his shirt and explains, "This thing will not be coming home with me."

We hear one of the big doors creak open, and everyone rustles to attention, groggily returning from daydreams of cold beers and swimming pools. "Okay, guys," Marie the press wrangler whispers. "We're going in—nice and easy." She has attempted to organize us into two single-file lines—one American line, one Burmese—but we're a sweaty knot trying to gain a step on our counterparts. These are always stressful moments as thirty reporters and photographers armed with recorders, cameras, and stepladders throw elbows and bang tripods as we bum-rush the doorway. Bottlenecks are inevitable. Secret Service agents manning the door watch with disdain as we squeeze into the room and feast our eyes on the leaders like eager piglets piling onto a beleaguered sow at lunchtime.

Obama and Thein Sein are seated directly in front of us about twenty feet away in high-backed, oversized wooden chairs with floral upholstery and doilies on the armrests. The room feels like a grandmother's living room, with thick, red wall-to-wall carpet and ornate coffee tables in front of each country's delegates, who sit in much smaller, lower chairs along the margins of the room.

Although we just waited in the hallway for nearly an hour, the leaders' statements are brief, and soon enough we are being escorted out of the room with Marvin saying, "Thank you, pool"—a euphemism for time's up. Dizzy from dehydration, I'm focused on getting back to the motorcade vans where there are bottles of water and barely functioning air-conditioning.

Suddenly we're told to run, which is unusual because we're inside a palace. I jog next to Carolyn Kaster, an Associated Press photographer. We're sprinting down one hall that empties into a bigger hall when suddenly Carolyn yells at me, "Beck! Look at this!" I glance left without slowing down, and there is a gigantic golden Buddha, probably three stories high. "Don't forget about this!" Carolyn yells out as the wranglers continue to shoo us from behind like border collies. "Don't forget to look up!" Carolyn yells as we continue to run. This is the closest I've been to a stampede as I see two photographers— one Burmese, one American—trip over each other and land on the marble floor.

Despite the wranglers nipping at our heels, Carolyn shouts again, her camera aimed at the ornate gold ceiling, "Look up, Beck! This is why we're here!" She is doing drive-by photography with her Nikon, running forward while shooting this overwhelming Buddha, her torso twisted at the hips, her camera shutter clicking so quickly it sounds like a sous-chef chopping maniacally—*ch-ch-ch-ch-ch-ch*. In two years, Carolyn will win the highest award in photojournalism, but for now we are in a grand foyer, laughing at the ridiculousness of it all: this huge, beautiful Buddha so close to that dank hallway where we allowed our interest in this trip to turn tepid.

Other reporters turn around to see what's so funny, and although they have no idea, they start laughing because we're all a little delirious. We keep running, laughter ringing off the walls, and soon we're back in the sun, chasing step after step after step down to the bottom of the world, across the gravel drive, and back into the vans.

In the passenger seat of the Press 1 van, I chug a bottle of water as a Secret Service agent walks over and tells everyone to take off their shoes. Then a wrangler joins the agent and says all the agents will need to take off their shoes as well. The agent balks. She's never had to take off her shoes in all her years of service. A reporter balks, too. She is seven months pregnant and worried she won't be able to get her shoes back on if she takes them off. "These things are watermelons!" she yells at the wrangler, holding up one swollen foot for all to see. I look at her foot in the sideview mirror; it really is the size of a small watermelon.

As the agent continues to argue with the wrangler, the pregnant reporter demands to know why anyone has to take their shoes off. "We're going to a pagoda," the wrangler says over her shoulder as she walks off to the Wire 1 van. She says it offhandedly, as if it's a McDonald's or a stop for gas. But it's not. We're going to Shwedagon Pagoda, the oldest Buddhist stupa in the world.

"It's an actual OTR," the AFP reporter mutters as he unties his shoes.

Usually the president's off-the-record events are not spontaneous at all but planned days and weeks in advance. This stop at the pagoda, however, was added about two hours ago when we were flying into Myanmar. The president, looking out from the plane's conference room window, saw the glint of gold circles and the glare of the 4,531 diamonds that encrust the top of the stupa. He told his staff that he wanted to go to that pagoda, and so now we are going. POTUS remembered to look.

The drive is less than five minutes from Thein Sein's house, and as we jump and run up the steps, the experience is surreal. I hear several agents cursing in their dark suits and sunglasses as they run barefoot beside me to the top of the landing. They are not happy about compromising the president's security to honor the sanctity of tradition, but they're doing it. "You're pretty cute when you're vulnerable," I whisper to one particularly agitated agent when we've reached the top.

"I can still kill you when I'm barefoot," he whispers back.

Shwedagon Pagoda will make you shiver and make you squint. Beams of sunlight strike the gold-sheathed temples in hypnotizing designs that are beautiful but also blinding. The president is getting a tour somewhere inside the pagoda as the pool stand in the middle of it all, not speaking, not believing we would have missed this had it not been for the president's direct order.

And then we leave even faster than we arrived, piling back into the vans en route to Aung San Suu Kyi's house. Standing in her backyard, shoes back on, I watch veteran reporters take photos with their phones and speak in awe of Suu Kyi. No one is complaining about the heat or looking for a bathroom. No one is worrying about the future of the Rohingya. No one forsees the massacres, the barbarism as we wait for Suu Kyi to speak of progress. We are once again standing on fragile history, as intricate and complex as the pagoda.

Suu Kyi emerges from her back porch with the president. She delivers remarks as POTUS stands to her left, all of us hanging on her words as she describes her love for her country, her excitement for what the future holds. She does not linger on the past, but it is so present it seems to stand at her side, between her and President Obama.

Quietly, thoughtfully, we traverse the yard and head to our last stop in Myanmar—the University of Rangoon. Tonight we will sleep in Cambodia, but now we are rolling up to this school that has just reopened. I do not watch the president from my assigned seat by the stage. Instead, I sit in a back room being used as the press file, and I watch as a Burmese man in his late sixties lets his shoulders heave as the president speaks of this country's potential. I see the tears roll down his face, this man sitting by a small black-and-white television, listening to the president of the United States praise Myanmar's progress. I will remember that this is why I'm here. I will remember to look up. I will remember to remember.

I GET LOST MY FIRST DAY IN CAMBODIA. DESPERATE FOR A BATHROOM after five hours at the East Asia summit, I'd left the pool in search of one, and when I'd come back to the press hold (where the pool wait between events), everyone was gone. My hands start to sweat as I realize just how huge the summit site is—it's a gigantic convention center with hallways the width of football fields. Everyone is gone and there's a bilateral meeting between POTUS and Prime Minister Noda with a pool spray at the top in ten minutes. No one is here— except that big guy in the corner with U.S. credentials around his neck.

"No problem, I can show you the bilat space," my savior says. "I'm Teddy, by the way."

An advance associate, Teddy has been in Cambodia for two weeks already and knows the summit site like the back of his hand. The advance team are responsible for ensuring that the president's trips are logistically sound so that the president and his traveling team can focus on furthering their agenda successfully. Advance arranges the hotels, the motorcades, the sites, the meals, and the events—it's basically a posse of wedding planners, because each day on the road with the president is like a wedding, only more expensive, with higher stakes, bigger consequences, and fancier cakes.

Teddy's name is perfect for him. At six foot three and north of 250 pounds, he is built like a big teddy bear. He's babyfaced, and his hands are gigantic, like paws that don't know their own strength.

"Just living the dream?" Teddy teases as I ask him if we can walk faster.

I nod without smiling. My hands are full of laptop, recorders, cables, a microphone, and the mobile wifi, and I'm freaking out that I'll miss the pool spray with POTUS and the Japanese prime minister. When someone mentions "living the dream," it's Obamaworld code for what this life is—amazing, stressful, blurry, tiring, frustrating, but mostly worth it as soon as you remember who you get to work for and what you're working toward. It's also what you say over email when what you mean is *I'm going to kill someone in the very near future if I do not get: some support on this/a five-minute break/coffee/a week's vacation.*

Teddy puts me at ease by laughing. "Just relax, kiddo, we'll get you there in no time."

"Kiddo?" I scoff as I follow Teddy up the escalator. "Aren't we the same age?"

"Maybe. But how long have you been traveling with POTUS?"

"Eight months."

"Yeah? I've got four years on you, kiddo."

Unlike most advance associates, who can be cliquey after spending weeks with a handful of other advance associates preparing for the president's arrival, Teddy is friends with everyone. He's a Labrador retriever in human form—well, a Lab crossed with an offensive lineman.

"You've arrived," Teddy says, patting me on the head when he delivers me to Marie the wrangler and the press pool. They're still lined up outside the bilateral room waiting for the pool spray. "Looks like you missed a lot." Teddy gives me a wink before disappearing back into the sea of ASEAN summit staffers.

"Just in time!" Marie says to me. "We're going in!"

The reporters and photographers and videographers from the United States and Japan are all under pressure to get the best pictures, the best sound, the best angle, the best quotes from what may be only a two-minute photo spray, and so the rush into the room is more aggressive than any Rage Against the Machine mosh pit. A Japanese camera guy accidentally rams his tripod into my ribs, and I see one U.S. photographer throw an elbow into his Japanese counterpart.

Once I'm through the door, I look for the mult box, which will give me a direct plug-in into the president's and prime minister's microphones. The mult doesn't always work, however, so as soon as I plug my XLR and recorder into the mult box, I ninja-roll into the thick of the press pool with my microphone so that I have two options for audio—the mult box and the wild sound from my mic. Bilateral pool sprays are a contact sport. I love them.

After the two leaders deliver their statements, Marvin thanks the pool for coming and points out the exit behind them. I'm halfway down the hallway, chatting with Kathleen from the *L.A. Times,* when I realize I left my XLR and recorder attached to the mult box. Shit! This is not good, especially in a foreign country, where the hosts might think an American intentionally left a recorder running as a spy tactic.

I turn back and run toward the closed doors, brainstorming what I'll tell Mike White, the head Secret Service agent, who is manning the door and will not be happy to open it for me. I'm nearly there when Jason, Jim Carrey's doppelgänger, emerges from the bilat room.

"Hold the door!" I yell-whisper. I'll be less intrusive if the door is already open. Jason definitely hears me but closes the door anyway. When I reach him, he asks what's wrong.

"I left my XLR and recorder in the mult box," I tell him, huffing, too stressed to be embarrassed. "I need to go get it. They're going to think I'm spying on the Japanese."

"That would be really bad," Jason says, sounding not the least bit concerned.

I'm about to bypass him when his face breaks into a gigantic grin and I notice he has very blue eyes. "You don't mean these, do you?" he asks, holding up my XLR and recorder.

"Oh my God! Thank you so much!" Without thinking, I give Jason a big hug. I hear him laugh and realize we've never been introduced.

"Sorry! I'm just so relieved! I'm Beck," I say, taking a step back and sticking my hand out.

"I know. I'm Jason," he says, shaking my hand.

"You're my hero," I say, wiping sweat from my brow. "Thank you so much for this." I start to turn because I need to go find the pool again.

"My pleasure," Jason says. "How's your first overseas trip going?" He's one of the most important staffers on the trip, but he asks as if he has all the time in the world.

"It's been great! Crazy, but fascinating, just, like, a mile a minute," I tell him. "I don't want to hold you up, but thanks again for this, you really saved me!"

"You're not holding me up," he says. "I think they'll be in there for at least another twenty minutes."

"Oh, well, in that case . . ." and then I realize I don't have anything to say. I don't know this guy. I tell myself not to tell him he looks like Jim Carrey. That would be awkward and unprofessional.

"Has anyone ever told you that you look like Jim Carrey?" *What the hell is wrong with me?* Blame it on the jet lag, or just narrowly escaping being accused of espionage.

Jason laughs and looks down at me. He's tall—Sam's height, I think—six foot two, maybe.

"No," he says.

"Really?"

"Really. You think I look like Jim Carrey?" he asks.

"Kind of," I say.

Jason smiles, looks down the vast hallway.

"So does that mean I'm funny, or just funny looking?" Jason wriggles his eyebrows at me, and I can see why everyone loves him, even the Rattler. He's clever, and charming, and I realize I'm more relaxed right now than I've been on this entire trip. He has such a laid-back vibe despite all the chaos that engulfs us.

"It's—It's a good thing!" I stammer.

"Nice to officially meet you, Beck."

"Nice to meet you, too, Jim."

"It's Jason."

"I know!"

I'm already running down the hallway, but I can hear him laughing.

THE LAST NIGHT OF THE TRIP, MARIE THE WRANGLER ASKS IF I'D LIKE to get a drink with her down at the bar. The Raffles hotel in Phnom Penh is straight-up colonial. I can smell the history, almost feel the blood on my hands as I run bathwater before heading down to the bar. Hope and Teddy and Marie are at a table, and I could not be more excited—three of my favorite people! When I order a White Russian, Teddy says, "Oh, wow, I could go for a Caucasian right about now," and orders one, too.

"No one has ever agreed to drink a White Russian with me before," I tell Teddy. "You are now officially the best."

"You're still pretty new," Teddy says, blushing. "There are a bunch of cool people on the road—you'll see." Marie and Hope nod, agreeing with Teddy. I can tell he's like Sam—he looks for the good in people.

"Cheers to a great trip!" Hope says, raising her glass. I need two hands to hold up my ceramic elephant, full of Kahlúa and vodka and milk. We haven't had more than two sips of our drinks, but after a week on the road, we're all pretty loopy and head to bed early.

The next morning, I spot Teddy at the breakfast buffet. As we gorge ourselves on six different types of dumplings, rice noodle soup, fresh mango, and coconut water still in the coconut, we watch Secretary of State Hillary Clinton spend over an hour saying hello and thank you to the kitchen staff.

"She works so hard," I say between mouthfuls.

"Totally," Teddy agrees. "Have you tried the banana rice dumpling yet?"

I shake my head as Teddy gives me a yellow dumpling from his plate.

"They're out of this world," he says. "You're in for a real treat."

It's funny—I just met Teddy, but by the time we heave ourselves up, I feel I've known him my whole life. "That was a good warm-up for Thanksgiving, huh, kiddo?" Teddy says as we lumber toward the motorcade. We're finally flying home.

Forty-eight hours later, I get to my parents' house for Thanksgiving dinner just in time to pass out. Jet lag coming back from Asia is no joke. I curl up under the dining room table as my parents talk and siblings tease one another above my head. Sam is here, too, comfortable with the chaos as he pours my brother and himself too many fingers of bourbon. My mom offers to walk me up to my room as if I'm seven years old again, but I tell her I want to stay and listen, so my dad brings a throw blanket in from the living room. Air Force One might have comfy seats and fancy meals, but lying by my little sister's feet under the dining room table on Thanksgiving is exactly where I want to be.

GUTTED

December

THE PROBLEM WITH CAMPAIGNS IS THAT THEY END, AND EVERYTHING you've poured your heart into is finished, like the day after the championship game. Even though the Obama reelection ended in victory, Sam has to look for a new job, and nothing will measure up. Also, jobs aren't as plentiful as he'd hoped.

Back from Toledo, without an apartment or a paycheck, Sam is living in my tiny Swann Street house, in my room. So now I have a depressed, unemployed boyfriend and two roommates who are understandably getting a little resentful that my bigfoot boyfriend is thumping around our apartment, not paying rent, and not even pleasant company. This is hardly the hero's return I'd envisioned during all those months away. I'd thought the campaign in Toledo would have been enough for Sam. In my head, I thought he'd have had his fill of cheap beer and bad food and no girlfriend. He'd come back ready to settle down with me and work in an office. But this is not the case.

Like the first sip, the first hit, Sam's time in Ohio only makes him want more of campaign life—the competition, the dynamic strategizing, the teamwork, the long hours, the risks, the relationships, the riffs with reporters and late-night epiphanies with colleagues. I know Sam is looking only at campaign jobs—none of which are in D.C., which leaves me in a catch-22. I want Sam to be happy and to have a fulfilling career, but that also means he'll go away again.

My temper grows shorter with the days, but I try to hold on to the light. I'm in my office one Friday morning in mid-December, resetting recorders for the daily briefing and looking out the bird's nest window. It's a beautiful winter day, the temperature climbing to the midfifties, when the news starts to break on the office television. I watch footage of kids being led out of their school, all holding hands, and I think, *Wow, that was a close one.*

Then I start to learn the details, and no, it was not a close one. It was a shooting spree. At an elementary school in Newtown, Connecticut.

More names attached to more tiny faces appear as we learn the details of the massacre. I read that the principal, Dawn Hochsprung, would tell her Sandy Hook Elementary students, "Be kind to each other—it's really all that matters!" Twenty six-year-old children have been gunned down in their own school, along with six of their teachers, heroes, hiding in closets and holding those tiny hands until the end.

Marie the press wrangler gets the call from an assistant in Upper Press, and over the loudspeaker she announces the two-minute warning. We crowd around the television in our office and wait to see POTUS enter the briefing room, our recorders already rolling, waiting.

The front-row television correspondents stop speaking into their networks' cameras when the blue pocket door slides open. The president walks out first, followed by Jay and his senior advisers, who take seats on the sides of the room, which is packed with more than sixty reporters.

The president takes the lectern.

> We've endured too many of these tragedies in the past few
> years. And each time I learn the news I react not as a president,
> but as anybody else would—as a parent.

I look over at Peggy. Her hands are shaking, and I know she's
thinking of her granddaughters. Vice President Biden holds calls
with the press to rally support for gun reform. As I transcribe his
words, I listen to the vice president re-create the massacre in graphic
detail, over and over.

On my walk home, I see wagons full of preschoolers at day care in
Lafayette Park. A little girl with a butterfly painted on her cheek waves
at me as I cross Seventeenth Street, and I fight through this wall of
grief to wave back. I see children as corpses. I see the ashen-faced
Sandy Hook parents who, months from now, will find themselves at
Chinese restaurants, in the frozen-foods section of a supermarket, in
the parking lots of their therapists' office buildings, and inevitably
overhear other families laughing together because the world will
have moved on.

POTUS flies up to Newtown two days later to speak at the prayer
vigil, and Peggy goes with him. When POTUS begins, his voice is
quiet, hoarse. Back in the EEOB, I type the remarks with tears
streaming down my face, and as the president says the name of each
victim, sobs erupt from the crowd. *We've got to do something,* I say to
myself. *Congress has got to act.*

After the president finishes, and I release the transcript of his
remarks, I sit alone in the dark of my office and close my eyes. I
wonder how we let this happen. And for the first time in a long time,
because I have never felt so lost or despondent, I pray. I bow my head
and promise the twenty-six victims we will do better. We will be better, to each other, for them.

Act II
2013

We were never sent here to be perfect.
We were sent here to make what
difference we can.

PRESIDENT BARACK OBAMA,
STATE OF THE UNION ADDRESS, 2013

GET
WHERE
YOU'RE
GOING

January

THE THIRD SUNDAY IN JANUARY, I HOLD UP MY BADGE AT THE NORTH
Gate on Pennsylvania Avenue and wait for the buzz. After nearly a
year at the White House, my morning entry ritual can be reduced to
an assembly line of sounds—the buzz, the clink, the groan, the Secret Service agent making a joke about my alligator necklace after it
sets off the metal detector.

But today, every sound is sacred; even the agents' grumbling
about the possibility of snow assumes gravitas. I volunteered to work
today, because "work" on this sunny winter morning means watching Barack Hussein Obama get sworn in for his second term as
president of the United States.

I walk into the West Wing and bump into Lawrence Jackson, one
of the five White House photographers.

"Where are you going?" he asks.

"To meet up with the pool," I tell him.

Lawrence smirks and shakes his head. "Skip that," he says. "You have a blue badge and a hard pin." He readjusts the camera straps slung over his shoulder as we bypass the press office. "You don't have to wait for the pool," he explains. "Just go wherever you're going."

"Really?" I ask. Peggy and Lisa always say to stick with the pool, but the idea of less hurry-up-and-wait and more just-go-wherever-you're-going is beyond appealing.

Lawrence nods. "You're White House staff, and you have an important job to do." I never thought about it that way. Until Lawrence says it, I've just considered myself the lowliest of staffers with a totally archaic, a-monkey-or-machine-could-do-it job to do.

Lawrence and I walk along the Colonnade toward the East Wing, neither of us saying a word as we take in the Rose Garden. Even in January, it's gorgeous.

The East Wing is fancier than the West. Red carpet stretches out before us as we enter the building, waving to the doctor and nurses in their office, Fred the Secret Service agent at his post. We mosey past the Diplomatic Reception Room, up the grand staircase, and into the Blue Room, where the swearing-in ceremony will take place.

Several minutes later, Marie arrives with the pool and points out the white-taped line that reporters and photographers must stay behind during the ceremony.

Soon POTUS appears with FLOTUS, Sasha, Malia, and their extended family. When Chief Justice Roberts arrives, FLOTUS holds up her family's Bible with both hands so her husband can swear on it. I realize that the ceremony is vaguely similar to a wedding, and by the power vested in Chief Justice Roberts, it's done! POTUS is officially the president, again, and the family rushes together for quick hugs before lots of photos.

And just like a wedding, after those sober vows comes the fun stuff—the inaugural balls. There are more than thirty-five fancy-pants parties: seventeen state society balls and more than twenty unofficial balls. Sam gets invited to the Ohio ball and the campaign staff ball, and I get invited to nothing.

The day of the staff ball, however, Matt from the press office offers the stenographers tickets. The other stenographers don't want to go, so I take their tickets and invite Charlotte and Emma. None of us have ball gowns, but none of us were campaign staffers, either. Might as well dress the part of party crashers.

"I'm excited to meet your work friends!" Emma says as the three of us cram into the bathroom on Swann Street to apply mascara, blow-dry our hair, and complain about having only one bathroom for three girls and one Sam, who is still living in our tiny dollhouse, rent-free, to the chagrin of my roommates.

"Don't hold your breath," I tell Emma. Even though I've been at the White House for nearly a year, my work friends are more like work acquaintances. I don't even have anyone's cell phone numbers; when I contact Hope or Shilpa, Teddy or Cole, it's over government email.

"Cookie! Let's go!" I hear Sam yell from downstairs. He has a bazillion people he wants to say hi to at the ball—friends from Ohio and D.C., but also from the 2008 campaign. It's a big reunion for him, and when we arrive at the convention center, Sam has barely walked through the door when someone calls his name and off he goes like a golden retriever puppy. Everybody loves Sam, which is great, because he's still looking for a job and needs to charm as many people as he can. While I can't stand small talk, Sam is brilliant at it.

"Let's get drinks," Charlotte suggests, and the three of us hunt down the cash bar.

Sam reappears just before POTUS and FLOTUS take the stage to thank the thousands of campaign staffers and volunteers who stand together in thick clumps of locked arms, listening to their commander in chief. When POTUS recognizes Alex Okrent, a twenty-nine-year-old staffer who died while working at OFA headquarters, Sam squeezes my hand. The whole room, already reverent, sinks into a profound, respectful hush. "We don't have a lot of time," POTUS says. "I know when you're young it seems like it goes on forever. It turns out things are fragile. And yet, the thing that outlives each of us is what we do for somebody else, what difference did we make. And we know Alex made a difference."

Sniffles and sobs create a thicket of audible loss below the president's microphone. In a few pivots, POTUS brings back the party spirit, the love and hope and idealism that unified this diverse group, and he ends his remarks by leading the rally in several rounds of "Fired up! Ready to go!" It's impossible not to feel empowered when you join in the Obama battle cry. As we all yell and clap and pump our fists in the air, I get it. I look up at Sam, yelling so hard he'll be hoarse tomorrow, and I get it.

A FEW DAYS LATER, I'M IN THE BIRD'S NEST, RECORDING THE PRESI-dent's personnel announcement in the East Room. When POTUS takes the lectern, he recognizes Chief of Staff Jack Lew for his continued service as he takes his talent to the Treasury Department, and he announces that Denis McDonough will be his new chief of staff. His remarks are standard enough, but then POTUS grins and says, "I thought I'd take the occasion to just embarrass somebody."

Oh, this will be good, I think.

"Some of you may know that today is David Plouffe's last day in the White House," POTUS says.

What?!

"What people don't always realize," POTUS says, "is the reason he does this stuff is because he cares deeply about people."

I've covered Plouffe in a number of background briefings, and it's clear he *is* in public service because he cares about serving the public. He's a good man.

While the other stenographers are downstairs grabbing lunch, I type up the last of the president's remarks, then pull up "The Scampering Strategist" on my monitor to adjust the formatting.

"What's that?" Lisa asks from behind me. I turn around, and she's reading over my shoulder, her eyebrows furrowed. Before I can answer, she reads aloud: " 'With quick, decisive steps, electric and hungry, Plouffe runs the way he thinks.' "

My stomach drops as I close out of the document—Lisa reading my writing feels as glorious as getting a pap smear. Feeling my face flush, I tell her, "It's this thing I wrote about Plouffe during the campaign."

"Why?"

"Why what?"

"Why did you write about him?" she asks, clearly annoyed.

"Because he passed me on a run and I was too impressed to be mad," I tell her.

"So you're just, what? Reading it now?"

"I want to give it to him—it's his last day," I tell her.

Lisa takes a step away from me. "You can't do that," she says.

"Why?"

"Because that's unprofessional," Lisa says. "It's just totally out of line—does he even know you?"

At that, I start to laugh. "Actually, I don't know." He's probably forgotten all about that day. That part doesn't matter. What matters is that I have this thing I think he'll appreciate. And even if he hates it, it's not like I have to see him ever again.

"You can't give that to him," Lisa tells me again, hands on her hips.

"Okay," I tell her as I hit Print.

When Lisa and Margie go out for coffee, I go downstairs, cross West Exec, and enter the West Wing with only one mission: to give this piece of paper to David Plouffe. Forget Lisa—since when has a parting gift been unprofessional? Just because I'm low on the totem pole doesn't mean I'm not allowed to look up. *Be kind to each other— it's really all that matters!* Dawn Hochsprung's words mean more to me than Lisa's as I pass the Navy mess, the National Security Council office. I go up the stairs and am standing outside the Upper Press office when I realize I have no idea where David Plouffe's office is.

"Hey!" I hear someone behind me say. I turn around and it's Jason—he'll know!

I explain the situation to Jason and end by telling him that the only problem is, I don't know where David Plouffe's office is.

Jason laughs. "Well, I can help with that." He leads me into the waiting room outside the Oval Office but then stops, turns around. "Mind if I read it first?"

I shake my head and hand him the piece of paper. I'm standing thirty feet from the Oval Office, showing this senior staffer I barely know a thing I wrote about another important guy I know even less.

Jason takes his time reading, his lips repeating the lines. He looks up at me a few times when he likes a particular turn of phrase. I stand there, trying not to die when he reads aloud, "'*Plouffe, whose spindly legs, laser mind, and pointy elbows inspire a montage of utilitarian edges—book spines, desk drawers, a Wüsthof collection*'—Wait," he says, cutting himself off. "You're a writer?"

"No!" I shake my head. I don't want him thinking I'm some snobby artiste type. "I mean, I like to write, but no. I was an English teacher before this."

Jason shrugs, his blue eyes sparkling. "Based on this, you seem like a writer to me." He turns around and leads me down a hallway on the other side of the Oval Office.

I realize we're in the senior staff hallway; Lisa had pointed it out on my second day at the White House, telling me there would never be a reason for me to come down here.

"Beck," Jason says, our eyes locking for a moment, "this is Jeff, David Plouffe's assistant."

A guy around my age stands up from his desk and extends his hand. As we shake, the insanity of the moment grips my tongue, and instead of saying "Nice to meet you" like a normal person, I burst out with a loud, cheery "'Ello!" like I'm Oliver Twist making the Artful Dodger's acquaintance.

Jeff looks at Jason, who looks at me, and I cup my mouth with my hand. My face is so red it hurts. But I don't have time to say anything, because now Jason says, "Oh! Hi, David!" Leaning past Jeff's tiny office and craning his neck into David's, Jason resembles a giraffe looking for fresh leaves.

David walks into Jeff's office, and the four of us stand there, cramped, as Jason says, "David, I think you know Beck, from the stenographers' office."

Plouffe smiles and says gently, "Yes, of course," and nods at me, as if all of this is completely normal.

"Hi, sir, um, thank you for everything," I bumble, aware that Jason and Jeff are staring at me wondering whether I'm British, American, or just insane. David is looking at me, too, but his is a look of amused curiosity. "I—doubt you remember this," I stammer, "but back in October, in debate prep, you passed me on a run, out in the desert, and—"

"Oh, yeah. I went off the street, into the mountains," Plouffe says, smiling, remembering.

"Right, so, I actually, um, wrote about it, because you were so fast, and here it is," I say, shoving the paper into his hands.

"Wow," Plouffe says. "Thank you. I can't wait to read this."

"No, no, thank *you*. I hope you go on a very fun vacation with your family," I tell him as I walk myself out of Jeff's office. It's all too much for my steno heart to handle, and I speedwalk back to the EEOB and up to my office, flushed with embarrassment.

"Where were you?" Lisa wants to know as she sips her Frappuccino.

"Just stretching my legs."

I'm proud of myself and glad Plouffe has the writing, even if he never gets around to reading it. Then there's a ping—a new email in my inbox. David Plouffe. I couldn't have left his office even five minutes ago.

Thanks so much for the essay—good memories and will be nice in a few years to be reminded I could once move at a decent clip.

You are an excellent writer . . .

I read the lines over and over again. I can't believe it. Can I frame this? And put it on my wall and stare at it for the rest of my life? David Plouffe said I was an excellent writer! I forward the email to Sam. "You ARE an excellent writer, Cookie," he writes back. I'm tempted to show Plouffe's email to Lisa but decide to keep it to myself. This is my secret.

AS THE YEAR TAKES OFF, THE BUBBLE FLIES TO CALIFORNIA. I'M ON A treadmill in a hotel gym in San Francisco. I look to my left, and I see POTUS running alongside me. When I pick up the pace, I realize that, for the first time, I'm not nervous having the leader of the free world less than five feet from me. It's weird how normal it is to say hi to the president in the gym now. The other hotel guests ogle the back of his black Kangol hat and try to take photos discreetly on their phones. At one hotel, a guy ran so fast to impress POTUS that he actually wiped out on his treadmill, which definitely got the president's attention.

As I slow to a stop, music still blasting in my earphones, POTUS gives me a gym rat's nod. Behind him is—well, *him,* on one of the 70-inch flatscreen TVs. The news is showing footage from our Air Force One arrival into San Francisco last night, and in my ears is Young Jeezy singing, "Tell him I'm doin' fine, Obama for mankind / We ready for damn change so y'all let the man shine." As I walk out of the gym, I wave hi to Jason, who's chatting with one of the Secret Service agents by the water fountain.

"Wheels!" he says, putting up a hand for me to high-five.

"Huh?" I pop out an earbud.

"You're so fast!" Jason says. "We were just watching you—very impressive."

"Oh! Thank you!"

"Keep up the good work, Wheels," Jason says.

"I'll try, Jim."

Back in my room, I'm about to text Sam to tell him about how surreal my life has become, but I decide against it. Sam still hasn't found a job; the last thing he needs to hear is how much fun I'm having on the road. Instead, I open my work email to check the departure time, because the motorcade waits for one person, and that person is not me. There are two new messages in my inbox. The first is from Shilpa, asking for my personal phone number because she wants to text me about a party. Holler, new friend alert!

The second message is from Jason:

Good morning! You really are super speedy. Have a good day!

I write him back immediately:

Thank you! Nice to see you!

At breakfast, I sit down next to Hope and ask her about Jason. "He's just a really nice guy," Hope says. "Aside from the president, and maybe Marvin, Jason is the best ambassador we have. He makes everyone feel valued."

Before I can ask anything more, Hope adds that he's in a serious relationship with a woman named Brooke. "I've never met her," Hope tells me between sips of coffee. "Jason never brings her to anything, but her dad is a pretty famous producer in L.A. They apparently have a compound in Beverly Hills that's supposed to be incredible."

"Oh, cool," I say, because I don't know what a compound is. The only time I've heard "compound" used in a real estate context is when reporters described the Osama bin Laden raid. Checking my watch, I gulp down the rest of my coffee, and then Hope and I walk out to the motorcade.

We bump into Jason on our way to the vans—he's standing with a police officer who has silver hair and a matching mustache. "The president appreciates what you're doing here," Jason says to him, shaking the police officer's hand and slipping him a presidential coin.

Hope elbows me in the ribs as we keep walking. "That's why everyone loves Jason." She grins. "He makes sure everyone feels special."

HOPE AND CHANGE

February

SAM FINALLY GETS A JOB. IN NEW JERSEY. THE NEWS KNOCKS THE WIND out of me. This wasn't the plan—but what *was* the plan? Staying in D.C., finding an office job, getting depressed again, and reaching back out to Wendy? I call my mom to tell her about Sam's next move.

"Wow," she says. "I feel like I just got kicked in the stomach."

"How do you think *I* feel?"

"Oh, jeez, Beck," my mom sighs. "Your dad says he feels like he just got kicked in the stomach, too."

"Glad we're all on the same page."

Sam will work on the gubernatorial race for dark horse Barbara Buono against Chris Christie. Part of me is relieved to have my 8x8 bedroom to myself again, but mostly I'm really sad. I miss the days when Sam lived around the corner from me, not hundreds of miles away.

Sam isn't the only one who's abandoning me: Emma wants to live with a coworker on Capitol Hill, and Charlotte is moving to Vermont to attend medical school. Most of my college friends have already left D.C. for graduate degrees or job promotions. I need to find new housemates or give up my perfect stoop on Swann Street.

"Wait—my lease is up at the end of the month!" Shilpa says over lunch. We're sitting at the picnic tables on West Exec, halfway between her office in the West Wing and my office in the EEOB bird's nest.

"Are you thinking what I'm thinking?" I ask, leaning forward, holding my breath.

"Yes!" Shilpa shrieks, and that's how a coworker becomes a housemate.

Quickly, Shilpa and I develop a routine. Before our twenty-five-minute walk to work, we give a thumbs-up or thumbs-down to each other's outfits to make sure my skirt isn't too short or her shirt isn't too tight. We want to be taken seriously, but at the same time, we're in our twenties, and we don't want to wear a nun's habit every day. Well, maybe Shilpa would, because she loves black, but my wardrobe is full of bright colors, from my days as a teacher, which is a problem only because I've been told I'm not senior enough to stray from a neutral scheme. For the kelp of the White House food chain, it's better to blend in than get eaten alive. Only the Vagiants can wear any shade from the J.Crew catalog.

I want to look up to this rainbow of wool pencil skirts and Jackie cardigans. But as soon as I catch myself admiring the women who've climbed the hierarchical mountain, I hear the clatter of bangles.

On a trip to Minnesota in early February, I hear her before I see her. Instinctively, I look down and act busy. But the clank of metal on metal gets louder and louder, and the next thing I know, the Rattler has me. I look up and she's practically on top of me as she pinches my new orange blazer between her two fingers. "Love this," she hisses, not bothering to look at me before continuing to slither down the hall. My heart doesn't start beating again for another minute.

That night on Swann Street, Shilpa rolls her eyes at me and hands me a glass of wine when I tell her about the Rattler's remark, which felt more like intimidation than a compliment. I point out that for someone who publicly prides herself on uplifting her fellow females, her assistant is male, and she has a track record of promoting men over women.

"But hey." I grin. "The Rattler is all about women helping women."

"Especially women with orange blazers and bright pink flats," Shilpa says, an eyebrow raised as we clink our glasses together. "You better watch out, B. She's got your number."

Shilpa gets it. The Rattler was reminding me of the snaking ribbons of rank. Grabbing my orange blazer without looking me in the eye was her way of telling me to stick to neutrals, to the colors of plankton blending into its surroundings. In one quick pinch, she'd let me know where I stand, which is far, far below her. Bright colors are for senior stars, not stenographers.

On Valentine's Day Sam is an hour late picking me up from the New Brunswick train station. He has an early Saturday morning fundraiser for Buono, after which we meet in a diner. Sam shrinks into a booth and confesses he needs to work for the rest of the weekend. "You could go shopping?" he suggests. I look out the window, and there's a defunct pet store and a Joann's Nails.

When Sam drives me back to the train station on Sunday night, he apologizes for such a disappointing Valentine's Day visit. I'll be going back to avoiding James Lentz's crooked smile in the West Wing and eating cereal dinners for one while my boyfriend devotes himself to his underdog candidate. I'm twenty-six years old—isn't this supposed to be the best time of my life?

"I'm sorry about this weekend, Cookie," Sam says as his car idles beside the train tracks. "I just got here and haven't even totally unpacked yet—give me a little time."

I nod, trying to see things from Sam's perspective. He's chasing his dream wholeheartedly while also attempting to sustain a long-distance relationship. It's not easy for him, either.

I leave Jersey with a new resolution: I won't burden Sam with emotional dependence. I'll double down on making friends in D.C. If I have friends around me, I won't miss my boyfriend as much.

That week, I see Teddy in the EEOB with a gym bag over his shoulder and ask him where he's headed. "I have pickup basketball tonight at the Department of the Interior," Teddy says. "Why? Do you play?"

"I did in high school," I tell him. "Is everyone really good?"

"There's definitely a range," Teddy says. "You'll be the only girl, but I think you'll be able to keep up."

That night, Teddy leads the way to Interior's court. The smell of a well-waxed wood floor is in my top ten favorite smells, right up there with dusty library books and freshly mowed soccer fields, and I can't help but smile as I remember all those years of basketball—the steals, the set plays, the rebounds and breakaways. I love this game. A forgotten piece of me finds its place as I warm up with Teddy. "Don't embarrass me, kiddo," he tells me when the other guys start to arrive.

That night I don't embarrass Teddy or myself. I'm not the best basketball player but also not the worst, and certainly not a liability. The guys who play are some of the nicest boys I've ever met, and definitely the nicest basketball players. When I brick a three and scramble back to get on defense, Eric calls over to me, "Just keep shooting!" And when I pick off a lazy pass, I hear Javon yell, "That's it!" Because I'm the only girl on the court, I can play as aggressively as I want and not have to worry that I'm going to hurt anyone; most of the guys are huge and laugh at my attempts to box them out. "Cute," Teddy says, lording the ball over me.

When we call it for the night, we all shake hands and the guys ask if I'll be coming around regularly. When I say I hope so, Eric smiles. "You better—you're so scrappy!" I haven't been this proud of myself in a while. Sometimes the best therapy is ninety minutes of hustle.

I join the game every Tuesday, and a few weeks later, Noah, the president's other travel aide, shows up to play. Noah is noticeably cute. He has shaggy brown hair, a square jaw, deep brown eyes, and those famous "kissable lips" Lisa had described. Unlike Cole, Noah is reserved, and he barely says hi when I introduce myself. And while Noah is intimidating, he isn't particularly tall, which is why we get paired up to guard each other. I can tell he's not happy about it by the way he barely acknowledges me, even though he must recognize me from work. But ten minutes into the game, Noah hits an outside shot right in my face and I involuntarily mutter, "What the fuck!"

under my breath. Noah hears it and cracks up. He's so busy laughing that he can't catch me as I sprint down the court, and the next thing he knows, I've scored on him.

"You've got to keep an eye on her, man," Javon says as he passes the ball into play.

"Or at least try to play defense," Eric adds.

Noah grins and looks at me. "That was your one for the night," he says.

After the game, Teddy drives Noah and me home. Before I get out of the car, I ask if they'd have any interest in going to a concert with me. Lucas, my fellow stenographer and friend, is playing at Rock & Roll Hotel on Friday. Sam was supposed to go with me but canceled his train ticket because of a campaign rally.

"Sounds cool," Noah says.

"Yeah, I'd be down," Teddy says.

I get their phone numbers, thank Teddy for the ride, and hop out of the car. I have two more friends!

AT THE CONCERT ON FRIDAY, NOAH IS NOTABLY QUIET. WITH HIS DARK features, deep voice, and pensive eyes, he seems like a British spy. *Still waters run deep,* I think, *or he's just stuck-up.* That's the tricky thing with quiet guys in D.C.—are they reserved or just not interested in talking to people lower on the totem pole? We get way too drunk after Teddy buys several rounds of shots, and some man in a suit stops Noah on the way out to ask him for his business card, which Noah reluctantly gives him. Then the three of us go to a falafel shop, and on the ten-minute drive home, Teddy passes out with his falafel nestled against his neck.

"Thanks for letting me tag along," Noah texts around midnight as I'm brushing my teeth. I use too many exclamation points in my response—Noah doesn't seem like an exclamation point kind of guy—but he texts back promptly and says we should hang out again sometime, that he's always down for a concert. "Think Teddy finished his falafel or is he saving it for breakfast?" he asks. I smile as I tuck myself in.

CHASING THE SUN

March

AFTER A POOL SPRAY IN THE OVAL OFFICE, HOPE AND I WALK TOGETHER back to the EEOB. As we cross West Exec, I see the Jeep Wagoneer in the parking lot and my heart melts.

"Do you know who owns it?" I ask Hope. "I die every time I see it."

"Really?" Hope says. "I'm ninety percent sure it's Jason's."

I scurry up to my office and am about to write a note to Jason to leave on his windshield, offering to buy his car with money I definitely don't have, but Peggy calls an office meeting.

"At the end of the month, the president is traveling to Israel, the Palestinian Authority, and Jordan," she says. "Beck and Lisa, you two will split pool duty, so figure out how you'd like to handle coverage."

"The other thing to consider is that POTUS is going to Petra the last day of the trip," Lisa adds.

Petra? *Petra?* Like *Indiana Jones and the Last Crusade* Petra?!

The day before we leave for the overseas trip, I find a picture of Jason's face and glue it onto a picture of Indiana Jones's body and then I stick my little creation on the windshield of the Wagoneer with some quote from the movie. He sends me a note that night saying that he loved the collage and he's excited I'm going on the trip.

Lisa stays with the press pool for Israel and Palestine, and I swap in when we arrive in Jordan on the fourth day. The morning of our big Petra field trip, I'm sweaty with self-consciousness as I wait in the motorcade. In the State Department guidelines, the dress code for Petra was "disaster casual," which means loose-fitting clothes you don't care about getting dirty and comfortable shoes you don't care about destroying. Lisa had advised me to wear green cargo pants, but as I dashed around D.C. trying to find a pair, I found only bright green slacks at the Gap. So now I'm sitting in the van looking like a preppy leprechaun.

To make matters worse, the Rattler already gave me a once-over. She saw my pants at the hotel breakfast buffet and I heard the disapproval in the rattle of her gold bracelets. For once, I knew she was right: I'm dressed all wrong for Petra. Indiana Jones would never wear kelly-green pants on a big adventure. All the other women on the trip are wearing khakis or cargos or black leggings. Like the awkward girl in middle school, I wrap my jacket around my waist, but instead of trying to hide a period stain, I'm trying to make my entire bottom half disappear.

A few minutes into the motorcade, as I look down into my stupid green lap, I check my work phone and discover Jason has emailed me on my BlackBerry: "Hey Indy, are you ready for this?!" I beam and forget all about my pants as I type back, "I'm like a bad penny—I always turn up."

It's so cool that someone as senior as Jason takes the time to write to me. We go back and forth over email until the helicopters take off, and then we're in the air. The views from the helicopter are incredible. We climb higher than we usually do, above the clouds and then between them and in them, and the ground disappears before it reemerges, and I feel as if I've traveled back in time to the age of the Nabataeans, who built Petra in the third century B.C.

We land and the choppers create a mini sandstorm before we

load into vans and begin our descent into the sandy desert mountains and into Petra. Tourists line the streets to watch the motorcade. We hop out of the vans and flit through warm yellow beams of sunlight that zigzag down the narrow pathways, like a child's drawing.

"Hi!" someone says behind me. When I turn around, Jason gives me a big hug, and as he does, he whispers in my ear, "Why are you wearing Lilly Pulitzer pants?"

I feel myself blush and am struggling to come up with a witty response.

"Hey! Jason!" the group of senior staffers yell. "Come take a photo with us!"

"Pardon me, little lady," Jason says, giving me a small bow before excusing himself.

As groups of staffers pose in front of the iconic Treasury, I pick out the popular group, the B group, the loners—it's as clear as it was in middle school. Nothing like a field trip to clarify one's social status. But before I feel like an outcast, Hope and Chuck Kennedy the White House photographer invite me to take a photo with them.

We're having such a fun time that I don't realize I've lost the press pool. I run down corridors of ancient sand and stone, watching my shadow race me along the walls, the desert sun illuminating the path before me. It's too incredible to be scary, but I can't find the press pool. Better to turn around and just to stick with White House staff at this point.

Before I go back to the Treasury, I remember to look up. How did I get so lucky?

I return to the White House staff group and join their walking tour. We see the ancient tombs and a bit of the irrigation system. Hope and I are like two stoned goons, our mouths hanging open as our brains try to process what our eyes can't believe. We see goats and camels and donkeys. We point and yelp and ooh and aah and take photos that will not come close to doing this place justice.

On the plane ride home, Hope is assigned the seat next to me. Jason stops by to tease me about my green slacks. He makes me feel like I'm in on the joke. Since Jason is slumming it with the stenographer and videographer, other staffers keep looking back at us, and I'm like, *Look! See! I'm cool! Jason thinks so!*

Skye stops by my seat—a first—and says, "Oh, so this is where the cool kids are." It's clear she means Jason.

"The kids don't get much cooler than Beck and Hope!" Jason says. The Rattler jangles by and shakes her head at the ground. Chad from the press office does a double take. He still calls me the steno, even though I work for him and he knows my name.

Jason seems oblivious to the looks and instead focuses on me. "Where is your boyfriend's campaign, again?" he asks.

"New Jersey," I tell him. "It's the worst."

"Yeah, my girlfriend is gone a lot, too," Jason commiserates. "Her family lives in Los Angeles."

"We should hang out!" I tell him, filling him in on Tuesday night basketball with the boys as I take out my phone to get his number.

"Definitely!" Jason says. "But only if I can put you in my phone as Bricklayer," he adds with a wink. "Noah told me you have a terrible jump shot."

Jason gets up to go back to the senior staff cabin. "See you Tuesday!" he calls out.

As we fly through different time zones, the sun sets, and sets, and sets. It's beautiful, the horizon on fire, and people lean out of their seats to take photos with their phones. Chasing the sun, I love everything and everyone. I love the bad movie Teddy chose, the fact that AF1 carries Bose headphones. "Stop laughing so loudly!" one coworker teases. We order celebratory glasses of wine, and we clink and toast, congratulate the speechwriters, pat the National Security rep on the back. The exhaustion settles into our bones and makes us giddy, goofy, honest. We're at altitude and have a temporary reprieve from the stress and pressure of our jobs.

This world is called the bubble for a reason, but as I look around, admiring each person in the staff cabin, I see the opposite of a container, even if we are on a highly protected 747 flying several hundred feet above the Earth. The thousands of people who enable the president to travel are far too expansive for a bubble, with webs and branches interconnecting in inexplicable ways. From the pilot, who can turn this plane on its side should we come under attack, to the local police officers redirecting traffic when we land, to the flight attendants, the embassies, the valets, the volunteers, the medical unit, the carpet guys—you won't hear about them at the rallies. The worker bees disappear when the bright lights come on and the music plays. But the infinite threads of endless work and invisible sacrifice are what I've come to appreciate the most.

No one knows it, but some of us are wearing the same underwear as yesterday, and some of us almost slept through the motorcade departure this morning because we set our alarms for 5 P.M. instead of 5 A.M. We're always just a few ticks, clicks, updates, and pings away from personal and collective disaster, but right now we're not our titles but our own selves—people with backgrounds and futures and exes and half-dead pets and crazy parents and broken hearts and big dreams; people who are listening to the president as he tells a funny story from two countries back, twelve hours ago, depending on which time zone you're counting in. We're so different, but we're swimming in this same punch-drunk delirium, and we have one major thing in common: We've found ourselves, shockingly, amazingly, how-the-fuck-did-this-happen crazily, flying halfway around the world on Air Force One. We are lucky. We are so goddamn lucky.

This is our shared life. There's magic in it, the joy of those living on a short leash, because the countdown is on, has been on, and the clock is ticking, and there is so much to do, too much to do, and the White Rabbit is yelling at us that we're late, but we're actually quite early once you set your watch to the right time zone. We've still got several hours in the air, and the Internet is down, and our phones are off, and the world is sleeping below, and here we are, flying on a luxury 747 capable of fighter jet defense mechanisms, so which movie should we watch next?

But here comes Dawn, the staff cabin flight attendant, laughing with us as she hands us hot towels. She has three children, and I don't know how she has the patience for all of us on these long trips. I offer a toast to Dawn, tell her she looks like a model with that glowing skin. She rolls her eyes, shakes her head, and tells me she just has new makeup, that's all. But when Dawn goes back to the kitchen she'll tell the others what I said, and on another trip, when we find the crew at a bar in Kansas City and drink $3 cocktails together until two in the morning, the other attendants will ask me if they look like models, too, because who doesn't like to be noticed?

Who doesn't want a compliment to level out the smell of the sweat that embalms our blazers, the dark circles under our eyes, the smeared mascara and blotted ketchup stains, the phones lost, pounds gained, the days without exercise, the decadent four-thousand-calorie meals we scarf down in the middle of the night? Who doesn't want a little light thrown in their direction when we've all had our focus on one man since we locked our front doors and loaded our suitcases into cabs three, four, ten days ago?

The hours pass, and Jason returns to the staff cabin to grab a Snickers from the candy tray in front of my seat. "Hope, don't let Beck hoard all the candy back here," he teases.

"Some of us have self-control," I shoot back, before draining my second sauvignon blanc.

"And some of us don't!" He shrugs with a wink, biting down on the chocolate.

Jason walks back to the front of the plane, and just as he's about to exit the staff cabin, he turns around and looks at me. It's electric. My face is suddenly hot: *It's just the wine,* I tell myself. That look was nothing. I'm exhausted and jet-lagged. After an overseas trip, we're nothing but loose wires and raw nerves. Whatever that jolt was, it wasn't real.

When we land in D.C., I drag my suitcase out to Pennsylvania Avenue and start my walk home. I turn on my phone and check to see if Sam has texted me during the fourteen-hour flight. He hasn't. Just as my heart sinks, my phone lights up with a new text. But it's not Sam. It's an unknown number. "Is this Bricklayer?" the message says, making me laugh out loud as I cut through Lafayette Park.

I go back and forth with Jason until I'm in my bed, teeth brushed, pajamas on. We text about cars, sending each other links to Wagoneers, and International Scouts, and Land Rover Defenders.

"You've got a thing for old guys, huh?" Jason teases after I send him a link to an '86 Jeep CJ-7 Renegade.

"Ew!" I text back, and he sends me a sad face.

"We'll have to go on a road trip someday," he texts as I turn out the light. I pause before I respond. This isn't good, is it? Texting Jason, who is not my boyfriend? Jason, who has a girlfriend? Jason, who is ten years older than I am, and a hundred times more important, and works where I work? "Someday soon, I mean," he adds.

I throw my phone across my bed like a hot potato. When I look at it again, he's texted a smiley face. I delete the conversation with Jason and open up my thread with Sam.

"I miss you," I write. I mean it. God, I miss him.

I fall asleep waiting for Sam to respond. In the morning, I still haven't heard from him. I step into the shower and wash Petra out of my hair, watching the sand circle the drain.

THE
KNOTS
IN OUR
LACES

April–May

"WISH ME LUCK!" I SEE OVER AND OVER AGAIN ON THE FACEBOOK WALLS of friends about to run their first marathon. I close my computer and head to work, remembering when my friend Kat ran the Boston Marathon in college and shat her pants during the twenty-first mile. "It's common! I swear!" she'd told me over the phone when I couldn't stop laughing.

That afternoon, we're proofreading Jay's press briefing—North Korean missile tests, hunger strikes at Guantánamo Bay, Prime Minister Fayyad of Palestine resigning, and the possibility of a Manchin-Toomey gun proposal—when Lisa gets a news alert on her phone: A bomb near the finish line at the Boston Marathon. Then a second.

We wait for the White House response as we crowd around the office television watching live footage, just as we did during Newtown. The press office calls up—POTUS will make a statement in the briefing room. "It's going to be a long night," Marie the press wrangler says to me over the phone. We wait and wait and wait.

We wait, but we don't pray. By that I mean we don't wait for a sign from any god, prophet, or spirit. Not with two terrorists on the loose and a twenty-four-hour news cycle. Not with a BlackBerry perpetually blinking red, perpetually in hand like an extra appendage. To pray is the privilege and the penalty for living outside this bubble. In a house underwater, on a shell-lined street in Chicago, in Baghdad, Crimea, or Homs—there you pray. But at the White House, when the sirens go off, officials are tasked with finding improbable solutions to impossible problems. Around the world, television screens get turned on and changed to the news as strategies at the White House are devised, passed up, knocked down. Over and over again. When first graders are shot to death, when families are blasted apart by a bomb, prayer alone will not prevent the next tragedy—but what will?

In the briefing room, television correspondents stop speaking into their networks' rolling cameras when the blue pocket door slides open. The president walks out first, and when he takes the lectern, he promises that we will get to the bottom of this and justice will be served. "I'm supremely confident that Bostonians will pull together, take care of each other, and move forward as one proud city. And as they do, the American people will be with them every single step of the way."

Within two days, the push for gun control again fails, and the Senate refuses to ban assault-style weapons or expand background checks. I feel as though I'm drowning in tragedy and simultaneously becoming anesthetized to it.

Demoralized, and desperate to talk to someone, I invite Hope over to Swann Street to drink beer on the stoop with Shilpa and me. We talk about the shootout with the Tsarnaev brothers, the failed Manchin-Toomey bill, the victims of Boston. At the end of the night, Shilpa and I collect the empty beer bottles and head inside. blasts DJ Khaled, and as we clean up the kitchen we friends, no new friends, no new friends."

I embrace the irony. If it weren't for my new friends, I wouldn't have any friends at all. Sam finally texts me right before I fall sleep: "Sorry, Cookie, long night—call you tomorrow?"

With Sam absent emotionally as much as physically, Tuesday night basketball becomes more important to me with each passing week. Sports have always been my outlet, and I'm not sure I've ever been so angry and frustrated as after the Manchin-Toomey bill fails. You'd think these "red-blooded" conservative congressmen who don't want equal rights for gays or the right to choose for women would be embarrassed to have the NRA so publicly cupping their balls.

I throw myself onto the court, playing as hard as I can and allowing myself to get roughed up when I go in for rebounds. "I'm sorry, but I told you to stay out of my house, kiddo," Teddy teases as I nurse a swollen eye.

Noah shows up for the Tuesday Department of Interior games about half the time, and I usually get matched up with him. By this point, we're comfortable trash-talking each other, and I've grudgingly given him props on his ankle-breaking crossover. At the end of each night, Teddy drops me off first and Noah waves from the passenger seat. "Same time next week?" Teddy asks, and I can't help but grin. Despite all the horrible news in the world, there are still moments of light.

RIGHT BEFORE MEMORIAL DAY WEEKEND, I'M WALKING ACROSS WEST Exec when I hear my name. It's Jason yelling, "Beck!" from across the parking lot. As I turn, I hear quick, heavy footsteps; he's jogging toward me.

Jason gives me a big, rib-clunking hug, wants to know how I am, what I've been doing—we haven't seen or spoken to each other since that night of texting after Petra.

Jason looks up to the North Gate and asks, "Can I give you a ride home?" His blue eyes shine in the May sun.

"Thanks, but I live in Dupont."

"So?"

"So that's way out of your way."

"That's all right," Jason says. "I like driving."

"I can't believe I'm riding in a Wagoneer again!" I say as I climb in, regressing to my seven-year-old self. The passenger side door doesn't squeak with rust the way my family's wagon does, and the backseat is not littered with decades' worth of book bag detritus: deformed paper clips, crumpled Wawa receipts, wads of melted gum.

"How's Sam?" he asks as he waves goodbye to the guards on West Exec.

"Great!" I tell him, as we make a right, and then another, and then are free, officially outside the bubble, driving north on Seventeenth Street.

"That's great!" he says enthusiastically.

"How's Brooke?"

"Oh, I don't know," Jason says, giving me Depression Dustbowl eyes at a red light. "I don't think it's going to work out."

"I'm sorry," I say, patting his shoulder.

He seems sad suddenly, and the silence is uncomfortable. I barely know this guy, and now he's not talking, and this is weird, and we work together, and he's breaking up with his girlfriend, and oh Jesus, he's so sad. I've only seen him happy and joking around. Did I do something? Am I Debbie Downer?

More from reflex than strategy, I do what Sam does for me when I'm down.

"Hey, can I play you a song?"

Jason smiles and hands me the adapter to plug in my phone as he stares straight ahead at the red taillights of D.C. rush hour traffic. I play him my favorite song, Dr. Dog's cover of "Heart It Races." It's only as I press Play that I realize I've envisioned this exact scene in my head during my morning runs. It's only as I sit back in my seat and wait for his reaction that I realize I'm not going to tell him this is Sam's and my song, that it's as sacred, as familiar, as the interior of an '89 Jeep Grand Wagoneer. Jason's thumbs thump to the beat on the 10 and 2 of the old steering wheel. I tell him about sitting in the way back for the thirteen-hour drive to Maine every summer, and Jason tells me about growing up in Wisconsin, rolling buckeyes with his family every Christmas, and guarding the candy from squir-rels as he watched the balls of chocolate and peanut butter freeze in the snow.

As we near my street, I realize there are so many more things I want to say. "Want to get Popsicles?" I ask in a last-ditch effort to stay in the Wagoneer. Jason hesitates but follows my directions over to Pleasant Pops on Florida Avenue.

I order Oreo; Jason gets chocolate. He puts a crisp twenty in the tip jar for our three-dollar Popsicles. Is he showing off? I don't know. But I'm showing off for him, balancing on the curb as though I'm walking on a tightrope. When I teeter, he puts his arm around my shoulders, but he doesn't let go when I've righted myself. He leans into me and says, "I've had such a crush on you."

I pull away and smile as I feel myself on fire. I pat him on the shoulder again, in an attempt to create some distance between us. The way he'd whispered into my ear to say it . . . It was practically a kiss.

"It's my roommate's birthday," I blurt out. "I should go home."

"Shilpa?" he asks. Of course he knows Shilpa. We all travel to-gether. He already knows so much about me. "Let's get you home!"

Back at the Wagoneer, Jason opens my door for me. While he walks around to the driver side, I lean over and unlock his door for him from the inside and push it open out of childhood muscle memory. But Jason has a funny look when he sits down, and doesn't immediately put the key in the ignition.

"What's wrong?" I ask.

"Nothing, it's just—Never mind."

"What?"

"That was very kind of you to open my door."

"No prob, Jim!" I tell him, giving him a big smile. It seems like forever ago that we were in Cambodia and I told him he looked like Jim Carrey. I don't know why he's suddenly bummed out.

Jason looks at his lap, his keys still in his hand. "I know I shouldn't be confiding in you, but Brooke never, ever opens the door for me. She just sits there and waits."

I want to make a joke about Brooke being Hollywood royalty but decide against it—maybe she's really nice. I'm sure she'd be mortified to hear Jason complain about her. A shiver runs down my spine—*Wendy's emails.*

When we drive up in front of my house just a few minutes later, Jason pulls over to the side but keeps the Wagoneer idling. "Well," he says with those Dustbowl eyes again. "Thanks for hanging out with me."

"Thanks for hanging out with *me!*" I say, happy to be so close to him, happy to be getting away from him. I lean over and hug him goodbye.

"You're so nice to me," he says quietly, looking at the steering wheel.

"I like being nice to you!" I tell him as I pat him on the shoulder. My hand is still on his shoulder when he leans over and in one deft motion puts one hand behind my head, the other on my cheek, and kisses me.

I'm not ready for it. I have a mini spasm, and he catches my nose with his mouth as my knee jerks up and hits the glove compartment so hard the drawer drops open and makes a loud buzz so you know something is wrong. The hand on my cheek leaves to close the glove compartment door as his mouth finds my mouth. The hand returns to my cheek. And now it's a real kiss, turning into real kisses, and for whole minutes I disappear from the world. For whole minutes, I am at the bottom of the Pacific Ocean in a deep blue Wagoneer with Jason. Starfish and sea crabs scuttle by. I do not need air. I will never need air.

Except I need air. And I need to go. It's Shilpa's birthday. I've got to go. So now I'm opening the door, catching his lips on my neck, hearing him say, "Tell Shilpa I say happy birthday," as I cross the street and stand on my porch to watch him drive away. As his taillights turn red at the end of my street, he hangs his head out his window and waves. I wave back. Stunned. *What the hell just happened?*

"Where have you been?!" Shilpa asks from behind me, walking out onto the porch wearing a pink paper crown and holding a margarita out to me. "Dinner reservation is for seven. Until then, we're drinking." I nod, dazed. "Beck!" Shilpa says, grabbing my arm, already tipsy. "Are you ready for this?!"

TRIANGLES
OF LIGHT

May–June

THE MORNING AFTER THE KISS, I WAKE UP IN SHOCK. *JASON LIKES ME*.
I can't believe it. As I brush my teeth, I look at myself in the mirror.
I'm not the kind of girl boys have crushes on. I'm the girl who
crushes until she's crushed. My entire life, I've fallen into that tragic
category of humans whose heart has not only been routinely broken
but pureed. Hammered. Hacksawed. T-boned. Punted. Wall-balled.
Kebabed. Clotheslined. Shanked. Flambéed. I'm the funny one, the
wing girl, Sporty Spice when all the guys want Posh.

As I walk to work, I feel a wave of guilt about Sam, but then I
remember Wendy, and I tell myself, "He had his secret, and now I
have mine." I have no idea what my end game is, but I play the scene
in the car over and over again in my head. *Jason has a crush on me*.

That night I text Jason to see what he's doing, but after twenty
minutes, he still hasn't texted me back. When Shilpa asks if I want

to watch a movie, I shake my head and continue to stare at my phone. Three hours later, I'm lying in bed, wide awake, freaking out. There's no way he hasn't seen my text.

It's not until 1 A.M., when I'm still staring into the glow of my phone, that I wonder whether the Wagoneer kiss wasn't the bottom of the Pacific Ocean for Jason. Maybe I'm just another notch in his belt. Maybe I just cheated on my boyfriend for the most shallow, briefest act of lunacy in the hope of feeling important. Maybe it was revenge, maybe it was about those emails. *Maybe,* I consider, not for the first time in my life, *I'm an idiot.*

More days pass, and in the hollow of my secret I grow lonely and then begin to panic.

As the days drag on in silence, I start to wonder whether I made the whole thing up. Did I imagine what he whispered in my ear? Have I gone completely mad?

That weekend, in an effort to distract myself, I ask Shilpa if she wants to go to Lucas's show.

"Thanks for coming!" Lucas says when he sees us, giving each of us a hug. Lucas is abandoning me in the stenographers' office to pursue music full-time. I miss him already.

"There's a bar in the back—watch out for the punch, that stuff is whack-strong."

Shilpa and I go for the punch.

On the stumble home through Adams Morgan, I'm in the middle of telling Shilpa about the black-and-tan coonhound my parents are rescuing from Alabama when she cuts me off: "Is something going on between you and Jason?" she asks.

I'm literally holding a photo of a puppy up to Shilpa's face when I freeze. But the "whack-strong" punch tells me to trust Shilpa, that this isn't a big deal, and obviously she already knows if she's asking.

"I thought there was," I say, "but I guess there's not."

"Huh?"

"He kissed me in his car, and he said he had a crush on me, but that was last week, so I don't know."

"Were you guys drunk?"

"No! We had Popsicles. On your birthday. And then he kissed me in the car. But he hasn't texted me, so I'm pretty sure I'm crazy and made the whole thing up."

"Wow," Shilpa says.

"Yeah."

"I think this is what we need to do," Shilpa says gently. "I think we need to get jumbo slices from Duccini's, and then you need to tell me what's been going on."

Around 2 A.M., the glow of my phone wakes me up. Before my eyes can focus, I realize I'm in the living room, sprawled on the couch and still gripping a jumbo-slice pizza crust. I definitely can't make fun of Teddy for that falafel incident ever again. "Hi!" Jason texted just a minute ago. "I'm driving by your house—are you still awake?"

Ten minutes later, in the middle of the night, I close the front door behind me, walk down the porch steps, cross the empty street, and open the passenger side door of the Wagoneer. "I've missed you," Jason says, pulling me toward him. We sit in the Wagoneer and sink back to the bottom of the Pacific Ocean. Between long, luxurious kisses, Jason says he hasn't stopped thinking about me since last week. We talk about everything—our childhoods, our families, our favorite episodes of *The Office*, exes, future plans. Around 4 A.M., he says I'm unlike anyone else at work, that I'm smart, and friendly, and interesting. He describes me as "magnetic." When we aren't kissing, we're laughing, learning about each other's best and worst days. The night melts away and before I know what's happening, my neighbors are outside in bathrobes, walking their dogs and grabbing their newspapers as the sun comes up.

"It's been a while since I made out in a car all night," I tell him before opening the door of the Wagoneer.

"Are you going on the California swing next week?" Jason asks.

"I think so," I tell him, trying to remember whether it's Lisa's turn for a trip or mine.

"I hope so," Jason says, grabbing me by my T-shirt collar and kissing me hungrily before whispering in my ear, "We could have some fun."

What the hell am I doing? I ask Shilpa if we can go for a walk, and in the sobering sunlight, my eyes burning from not sleeping, Shilpa is more concerned than she was the night before. "Do you think this is going anywhere?" she asks through big sunglasses. She's met Sam and likes him—and I definitely still love him. As our iced coffees sweat in our hands, I tell Shilpa that Sam really knows me, but Jason really *wants* me.

"It just feels so urgent," I explain. "Like it's not a choice when we kiss."

"Isn't that the definition of lust?" Shilpa asks.

I know I should feel terrible, but I'm in such a good mood after talking to Jason all night. *My crush has a crush on me.* I'm light-headed from his attention. If only I could tell Teddy and Cole and Noah— they worship Jason like a cool older brother. On the road, they follow him around, as cute and loyal as puppy dogs.

With him I feel like my most honest self—I told him things in the Wagoneer I'd never told anyone. I lost count of the number of times he started off a confession with "I can't believe I'm telling you this, but . . ." The kissing was secondary to that unabashed honesty.

I can tell Jason is a good secret keeper—it's part of his job, after all, which is a whole other factor in this. I know we need to be discreet. But is this just some silly flirtation for him, or might there be more? The stakes seem too high for both of us to casually put so much at risk.

Lisa lets me cover the California trip, but when I text Jason to tell him the good news, I don't hear back from him. This time, however, instead of getting upset about his nonresponse, I remember what he told me in the Wagoneer: that one of the reasons he likes me is because I'm "so cool" and "such a free spirit." Cool girls don't overtext. Free spirits aren't needy.

The week drags by. Finally the bubble flies to San Jose to attend two Democratic Senatorial Campaign Committee events. On the cross-country flight, Jason comes back to the staff cabin and sits with me during takeoff. Normally he has to work on flights, but we continue to talk as the plane climbs higher into the sky, and he's still next to me when we're at cruising altitude. I pretend not to notice everyone else noticing that Jason is still sitting with me, but suddenly it feels as if everybody in the staff cabin is staring at us.

"Jason, let's go," the president says. My stomach bottoms out as I look up and there he is, POTUS himself, standing over us and look-ing even taller than usual. And annoyed.

I give a tight-lipped smile, mortified. Jason made POTUS wait.

"Sorry to interrupt," POTUS says to me in a gruff tone I haven't heard before. My face is so hot it might explode. We're on this plane to work on the president's behalf, not flirt like middle school stu-dents on a field trip.

As we fly over Nebraska, Cole sits down in the empty seat next to mine to watch TV on the big screen. When the news anchor says a new study shows funny women are less likely to get promotions at work, Cole nudges me. "Uh-oh, Beck," he teases, "looks like you'll need to tighten up if you're going to be director of stenography someday."

I know Cole is kidding, but I hate that he thinks—or that anyone thinks—I want to be a career typist. I also hate this study, which seems so ass-backward it's probably true. When we land and motor-cade to Silicon Valley for a bunch of fundraisers, Jason and I text back and forth, but at the end of the night, back at the hotel in San Jose, Jason stops responding and I succumb to feeling dumb and crazy yet again. I can't sleep, I'm so angry at myself for messing up my relationship with Sam. What am I going to do about him? What am I going to do about all of this?

As my mind spirals, my phone lights up. "Hi! I'm sorry—I fell asleep!" In spite of myself, I let out a deep sigh. He does like me, and in this moment, that's all that matters. "Can I come say good night?" Jason asks. I say yes, and he asks me to prop open the door for him. A few minutes later, there's a gentle knock on the door. As Jason enters my hotel room, I hold my breath and watch a triangle of light grow across my ceiling. When he closes the door behind him, the triangle shrinks back to nothing.

"Hello?" he whispers in the dark, as if he might have walked into the wrong room. I'm standing on my bed like a little kid so that we're the same height, and he picks me up for a hug before putting me down and kissing me, cradling my face with his hands. "Is this okay?" he asks. I start to answer, but his mouth is on my neck, his hands are all over me. It's so much better than okay, and so much worse.

DON'T DRINK THE WATER

June–July

"BE CAREFUL," MY MOM TELLS ME RIGHT BEFORE I TURN OFF MY PHONE. We're on our way to Africa for a ten-day swing—Senegal, South Africa, and Tanzania. I'm starting to feel comfortable, like a regular, as if I belong in this bizarre bubble. I know what I'm doing, and nothing is scary when the Secret Service is around you.

The only problem is Jason, whom I haven't seen or spoken to since San Jose three weeks ago. On the flight back from California, he didn't come back to say hi, and he hasn't texted once since we landed in D.C. I decide that it's over; that enough is enough; that I'm going to tell Sam, but I want to wait until I see him in person. He'll be hurt, but he'll forgive me. Maybe my Jason mistake was a good thing—for the first time, I get how Wendy could have happened.

As I board Air Force One, I put on my game face. It will be hard to avoid Jason for a whole overseas trip, so I've been giving myself pep talks and I've been writing a ton of notes in my journal about all the things I will and won't do. (I *will* say hi and smile. I *won't* say anything about what happened in San Jose.) Even though it shouldn't matter—it was clearly a one-time thing, a quick and easy California conquest—I still want Jason to think I'm a cool girl, a free spirit who knew what she was doing and isn't worried about it, hasn't thought twice about it.

I've been drowning in guilt and self-loathing ever since San Jose, especially because Sam has been calling more and making an effort to be a better boyfriend. Jason hasn't reached out once, not even for my birthday, so I'm done with him. Shilpa was right: It was just lust, nothing more, and it's all in the past now, buried in the backyard with the family pets. Jason's disappearance only highlights the difference between him and Sam. Sam and I are real.

When I enter my room at the Radisson Blu in Senegal, I grab the water glasses in the bathroom and turn them upside down over the hot and cold faucets of the sink so I won't use them. Even though we're staying in a nice hotel, the medical unit warned us not to drink the tap water, or even use it to brush our teeth. By putting the water glasses over the knobs, I'll think twice about what I'm doing. The last thing I need is to get sick on a trip. Rumor has it a Fox News reporter is already violently ill in her room at the press hotel.

But the physical risks of traveling are nothing compared to the emotional ones. International trips sometimes feel like college orientation, where everyone is smiling on the outside but dying on the inside. I feel isolated, despite being surrounded by friendly faces. Everyone else seems just fine, which makes me feel even worse. "Have you seen the buffet spread?" a girl from advance asks cheerfully in the elevator. "The food here is amazing!" It's a survival strategy, of course—fake it till you make it—but I've never been good at faking it.

The first night in Senegal I go outside to the hotel bar and find Hope, Shilpa, and Teddy. We're right on the ocean, on a gorgeous patio with string lights and comfy chairs surrounding firepits. I'm having the best time . . . and then Jason appears.

"Jason!" Teddy shouts. "Over here!"

Before Jason comes over, he orders another round for our table, and Teddy toasts: "To Jason, everyone's favorite guy."

I play it cool. I smile, say hi, thank him for the Cape Codder, but don't meet his eyes when I feel them on me, especially after the second round. I tell myself my face is hot from the fire.

At the end of the night, after brushing my teeth with bottled water, I set my alarm and check my email one last time to make sure they haven't changed the morning's motorcade departure time. And while there is no update from the trip coordinator or scheduler, there is a new message from Jason, from five minutes ago. He's sorry he hasn't been in touch, but he's really missed me. My phone pings again: Apparently he can't get something I said out of his mind . . . Can he apologize in person?

I open my door and let it rest on the bolt. I get ready for bed and write in my journal, putting down everything I think but can't say. (I *will* ask, "How are you?" I *won't* say, "I thought you had a crush on me.") Soon enough, I hear the hinges yawn and that familiar "Hello?" I think about where I want to sit or stand. The room isn't particularly big despite how fancy the rest of the hotel is. Jason enters and we dance around each other awkwardly before I tell him he can sit down on the bed, and I stand, leaning against the bureau. I ask him what he can't get out of his mind. He says there was this moment back in San Jose when I turned and looked at him and said, "Don't fuck with my head." He says he kept thinking about texting me but then he'd think of that, and then before he knew it, it was two and a half weeks and he hadn't reached out.

I stay strong, thinking of Sam and his green eyes, and tell Jason that this is helpful and I appreciate the explanation. He assures me he's thought about me, and I sprawl out next to him, and we talk. He tells me a story about the secret swimming hole he discovered the summer he turned fourteen, his blue eyes blurring my vision, and I untie his shoelaces. I measure his hand against my hand, and then I hold his hand. Have you ever wondered where the ocean begins?

We stay up all night, just like we did in the Wagoneer, and the talking is as fun as the hooking up. He bathes me in compliments, but when he compares me to Brooke, and reiterates his plans to end the relationship, I think of Wendy's emails and change the subject.

"The Rattler certainly likes you," I tell him. She'd come over during the firepit powwow but had spoken only to Jason.

"The Rattler?" Jason says. "Oh! Her!" He starts laughing, shaking his head. "I've never heard her called that before."

"I made it up," I tell him. "Her gold bracelets rattle like a warning that she's full of venom."

"Ah, well, that's too bad," Jason says.

"Hey, she's earned it," I tell him, feeling empowered.

"She's probably just threatened by you," Jason says, squeezing me.

"Yeah, I get that, but I bet that if she really puts her mind to it, and works super, super hard, in a couple of years she could probably be a stenographer, too."

"You know what I mean." He laughs. "Actually, before she took this job, you guys were kind of similar."

I swat at him. "You shut your mouth!"

"She was cool! I swear!" Jason says, dodging the pillow I'm trying to smother him with. "This place can do bad things to you if you're not careful."

"Tell me about it," I tell him, kissing my way back to oblivion.

When Jason gets up to go to the bathroom I get nervous he's going to forget that he can't drink the water, so I grab his button-down, wrap it around me, sprint over, and bang on the door. He slides it open, looks down at me, and gives me this gentle smile of pure affection.

"What did you say?" he asks.

"Don't drink the water!"

He scoops me up, holding me as I hug his neck, and carries me back to bed. He leaves at dawn to beat the foot traffic in the hallway. I watch the triangle of light grow bigger on the ceiling and then shrink back to black.

AND SO THE TRIP BEGINS. AT BREAKFAST THE NEXT MORNING, I SIT down across from Shilpa and next to Hope.

"That was a fun night!" Hope says.

"Sure was."

"Did you go right to sleep?" Shilpa asks, locking eyes with me over her orange juice. She knew how nervous I'd been to see Jason, and how committed I was to Sam and never cheating again.

"Sure did," I lie.

Shilpa, however, is not fooled. After breakfast, she links arms with me as we walk to the motorcade.

"Two things, B," she says. "One, step up your lying game. And two, I get that this is really hard for you." I start to thank her, but she cuts me off. "I think you need to think of avoiding Jason as being on a really intense diet."

"Huh?"

"You're trying not to indulge, but sometimes you might crack."

"And that's okay? I don't get what you're saying."

Shilpa shakes her head. "Just because you sneak a doughnut doesn't mean all the hard work is lost and you should just give up on a healthier lifestyle."

"Oh, gotcha. That's good. Thanks, Shilp."

But as we load into the motorcade vans, I'm already wondering when I can see Jason again. Will he visit tonight? Tomorrow night? Every night for the rest of the trip? Every night for the rest of my life?

I'M COVERING AN INTERVIEW OF POTUS ON THE FLIGHT TO SOUTH AF-rica when I start to get nauseous. When we stop at the embassy, I puke in the bushes. *Shit, shit, shit. I'm sick on a work trip.* By the time I get to my hotel room in Johannesburg, I'm a disaster. The president's doctor and nurse come to my room at midnight to hand-pump an IV, which takes over an hour to administer. I tell them about my water-glass trick, and the doctor explains it could have been something as seem-ingly benign as a drop of water on a lettuce leaf. As soon as they leave, I vomit the IV all over myself and the bed, and spend the entire night hunched over the toilet, dry heaving until dawn.

By 7 A.M. I'm delirious with a fever and hallucinating in my hotel room. I call Sam to tell him I'm dying—not because I'm being melo-dramatic but because I see the doctor standing in my room, who tells me I'm not going to survive this.

"The doctor says I'm going to die here," I tell Sam.

"Cookie, wait, tell me what—" but I hang up on him and pass out, the fever ravaging my body. I wake up eight hours later to a knock on my door. My shirt is soaked through with sweat. I crawl across my floor and reach up, turn the knob. The doctors and nurses are still out with POTUS and FLOTUS, but Rachael the nurse had asked a Secret Service agent to check on me. And here he is, my knight in shining armor, tall and saintly and holding out a red Enervit, the South African equivalent of Gatorade, which I'm pretty sure saves my life.

I email Jason after my fever breaks and tell him I'm sick, and he comes over late that night after a full day of helicopter rides and bilateral meetings to take care of me. When he enters my room, I wrap my arms around his waist, dig my chin into his chest, and look up at him. I like him too much. He looks down at me and sighs loudly.

"What?" I ask.

"You're pretty adorable," he says and shakes his head before squeezing me tightly. I ask him to tuck me in and he cocks his head, clearly amused. "I don't think I've ever tucked anyone in before," he says.

"Liar," I tell him, thinking of that propped-door move, the way he flirts with everyone on the road, even the hotel advance associate, who is eight months pregnant. He's done more than his fair share of tuck-ins.

"I'm serious," he says, touching my nose with his nose and staring into my eyes. When he looks at me like that, and gets so close to me I can smell his mint gum, nothing matters beyond the moment.

Jason accepts my request with an almost comical earnestness, straightening the sheets and puffing the pillows before letting me approach the bed. He double-stacks the pillows and I toss one aside. "Only one pillow," he says. "That's good to know." When I lie down, he makes sure the covers are up to my chin. He leans down and kisses me. "This is nice," he says. "I like tucking you in." It feels a lot like something, though there's a part of me that questions everything about him, distrusts each word and kiss that falls from his lips.

"I should go, but you have the prettiest mouth," he says, pulling my face toward his.

"The prettiest mouth?"

"Mm-hmm."

"Sometimes," I say, dodging his kiss, "you say these nice things, but it's like you've used them before—like you have this cardboard box of compliments you found at a yard sale, and you just dig around and pull something out."

Jason's eyes twinkle. "Oh, you smart girls," he says, pushing my hair out of my eyes. "You smart girls kill me. You're always thinking. I can see it now."

If we both know he's a liar, doesn't that make this thing between us honest?

"Have a good sleep," I tell him before he leaves.

He chuckles, his silhouette backlit from the hallway lights. "You have a funny way of speaking," he says. "But you, too, babe. Have a good sleep."

It takes me three days to recover. I can't eat or even sit up for extended periods of time, and I miss all the events in Johannesburg and most of Cape Town. Lucas, Lisa, and Margie, who are with the press charter, take turns swapping in to cover my role as pool stenographer. It's Lucas's last trip, and he writes a funny song about abandonment to cheer me up while I lie in bed recovering. Even though my getting sick increases their workload an exorbitant amount, Lucas, Lisa, and Margie are gracious about it. "Just get better," Lisa writes to me.

Before we fly to Tanzania, I eat a piece of toast, give myself a pep talk about not puking on the president, and travel with POTUS and the pool to see Archbishop Desmond Tutu's HIV Foundation, and also to visit Robben Island.

The entire Obama family travels to Robben Island, and as POTUS stands in the limestone quarry, hands on hips, in full dad-in-khakis mode, I realize that Sasha and Malia stand the exact same way as their mother: weight on one leg, arms crossed, intently listening to the tour guide explain how prisoners were forced to break up the limestone into rocks and cart it from one end of the quarry to the other for no reason other than to keep them busy. Sasha leans into her mom, who puts an arm around her. They're a family learning about an all-too-recent period of history with two hundred of their closest agents/reporters/staffers/photographers in tow.

"How are you feeling?" Jason whispers. He must have just crept over to ask me that—the other senior staffers are on the other side of the quarry, far from the press pool and me.

"Better," I tell him, feeling my face flush as reporters notice him and head over to say hi. Hope was right—he's the best ambassador we have.

"Glad to hear it," Jason says in my ear, in that whisper-kiss he must have mastered long before he met me, right before he bends down to hug a female photographer.

IN TANZANIA ON THE LAST NIGHT OF THE TRIP, I FIND JASON OUTSIDE the palace, chatting with a guard. I smile to myself as I approach. This is why Jason is irresistible—because while all the D.C. creatures are inside, trying to impress POTUS, he goes elsewhere to seek out the least important people. Money and titles do not impress him. He keeps an eye out for the quiet cogs and underdogs.

"Hey there," Jason says, calling me over.

I ask him his favorite part of the trip.

"Right now, being with you," he whispers.

I choose to believe him.

ON THE FLIGHT HOME, JASON COMES BACK AND SITS NEXT TO ME. "CAN I play you my favorite song?" he asks. I nod. The Rattler looks up from her *Cosmo* as Jason hands me his earphones. I hear her bracelets before Jason presses Play, but with him by my side, her sleeve of gold hisses with nothing but empty threats and insecurity. As the song plays, it's hard not to reach over to hold Jason's hand.

"Like it?" he asks.

"Of course I like 'Obvious Child,'" I whisper the way we did this morning in Dar es Salaam. Everything between us is a secret. Everything between us is sacred.

Standing up to go back to the senior staff cabin, Jason says I look cold and asks if I'd like a blanket. Before I can answer, he tucks me in with a blue Air Force One fleece throw. "Have a good sleep," he says, squeezing my hand under the blanket.

WHEN I GET BACK TO D.C. I TAKE A TRAIN UP TO SEE SAM IN NEW JERSEY, who's fully immersed in the Buono campaign. I feel like an outsider, like I don't even know him, or maybe I'm so racked with guilt I don't recognize myself. It's hard to tell what's real anymore.

Sam is the boss of a bunch of twenty-two-year-olds whose jaws drop when I make fun of him at a bonfire, as we swig cheap beer out of cans. They freak out over my Sam impression, but Sam laughs and explains that's why he calls me Tough Cookie. Our eyes meet across the fire, and there he is, that guy I love who always encourages me to have more desserts, more drinks, more fun; the guy who will sit with me in a dog park for the better part of a Saturday. Or at least, that's who he was when we lived and worked in the same city. In quiet moments, I catch glimmers of what Sam and I once were— the way I feel safe as soon as I nuzzle into his flannel, the way he can finish my sentences. But there's also this guy who's standing around talking about Chris Christie on a Saturday night and introducing me to people as "Beck, my girlfriend, who works at the White House." He's proud, but then I have to backpedal and say, "Well, just by accident, I don't actually like politics that much." The girls try to impress me with their knowledge of Obama's policies (they're all Obama campaign alums), and I get the sense they're trying to network. I want to tell them they're wasting their time—I may work at the White House, but Smokey the stray cat that lives on West Exec has more clout than I do.

I don't let myself think about Jason when I'm in New Jersey. Instead, I throw more wood on the fire and try to bond with Sam's campaign colleagues. But I feel the distance of long distance between us, even as I sit by his side.

BLOOPERS

August

JASON NEVER CALLS, HE ONLY TEXTS ME, EVEN WHEN BROOKE IS OUT OF town. The rational part of me knows this is bad. But, as pathetic as it is, I like getting texts from him because then later, when he ignores me, I have proof right in my phone that only two hours or two days or two weeks ago, he said some pretty sweet things to me. Well, typed them, anyway.

The air-conditioning on Swann Street fights through the thick humidity of another August night as Shilpa and I host Teddy, Noah, and Cole for a viewing of *Frances Ha*. The goofy protagonist is twenty-seven years old and so are we, and none of us have any idea what we're doing. I'm basking in the television light, enjoying my newfound friend group, and then there it is. My phone illuminates in my lap and I try not to get excited.

Hi!

My heart thumps at the sight of the familiar unfamiliar number. I've deleted those digits a dozen times so I won't be tempted to text Jason when I'm drunk, or happy, or sad, or angry, or, basically when I'm feeling any feeling. Cool girls don't overtext. Free spirits aren't needy.

But with those two letters, a billion fizzy bubbles rise to the top of my rib cage.

Wanna go see a movie with me?

"Where are you going?" Shilpa asks as I jump up to put on my shoes.

"Sam's old neighbors need me to babysit—some kind of emergency," I improvise. "They're in a total jam if they're asking me." I sigh, exasperated by other people's parenting, tying my sneakers with dramatic urgency.

"Really?" Shilpa asks, locking eyes with me, suspicious. I've had to lie to Shilpa repeatedly since that first lie in Senegal, and now I'm in too deep to come clean. Besides, she's made it clear she's Team Sam, that Jason is just a cad with a girlfriend. I tell myself that I'm protecting her and myself by not keeping her in the loop.

"Bummer," Noah says, hitting Play and turning up the volume to emphasize his apathy. I suspect he knows I'm lying, but who knows what they know? Do the guys talk about this stuff? Noah, Cole, Teddy, and Jason are deep inside the concentric circles of power. They work closely together and directly with the president, and they genuinely get along well. Noah, like No-Drama Obama himself, prefers to evade crises and avoid hysteria. I can tell from a furtive side glance that Cole is taking his cues from Noah, and Teddy is oblivious to everything because he's playing Clash of Clans on his phone, determined to get to Town Hall 11. That's the beauty of guy friends—mostly they're clueless, and even when they're not, they'd rather not get involved.

Jason picks me up two blocks from Swann Street, and we drive forty minutes to Baltimore in the woody.

"Where's Brooke?" I ask.

"Where's Sam?"

"New Jersey."

"Let's just say Brooke is in New Jersey, too," Jason says, squeezing my knee as we stop at a red light. I know Brooke is at her family compound somewhere out there in Beverly Hills, maybe attending one of her father's film premieres. Sometimes, when I'm feeling particularly low, I wonder if Jason would already have broken up with Brooke if she weren't so well connected.

We listen to Paul Simon the whole drive up.

In the darkened theater Jason lets me put my head on his shoulder and takes my hand. The movie begins—it's an action flick neither of us is that excited to see—but I don't want it to end.

Of course, it does end. When I start to stand up during the credits, Jason pulls me back down. For a moment I think he, too, wants to linger in this moment for infinity, but then he says, "Let's wait to see if there are bloopers."

"Bloopers!"

"Yeah, the funny outtakes," he says with an unmistakable air of authority, as if only the cinematic elite would know about bloopers.

I let it slide. It's still a magical night in a Baltimore movie theater with Jason. He leans over and kisses me on the cheek, throws his arm around me as if I'm his, and whispers, "The best parts usually come after the big show," as he puts my hand on his crotch.

"Wow," I say, "you really *do* get excited about bloopers!" He laughs, and I think, *Does she make you laugh the way I do?* But funny girls make good friends, not successful women—that's what the new study shows. I bet the new study also shows that funny girls make good slutbags and not respected girlfriends. But tonight, as we laugh together at the outtakes, I pretend I'm Jason's girlfriend.

"YOU'RE NOT A SOCIOPATH," HOPE TELLS ME AS WE FLY TO L.A. ON AIR Force One for a taping of *The Tonight Show with Jay Leno*. I lasted an hour into the flight before dumping the entire Jason saga right into Hope's lap. Shilpa is over the ups and downs of the affair and has made it clear she thinks I need to either break up with Sam or stop cheating on him, so we've stopped talking about it. I don't blame her, but I need someone on my side who can listen, because I'm a disaster and hate myself but won't change my behavior, which makes me hate myself even more.

Hope's reluctance to judge anyone or anything makes me confident she'll be supportive. She's seventeen years older than I am, so she has an aerial view of affairs. And I need her to calm me down, because I've only just realized I'm a sociopath.

"You're figuring it out," Hope says, giving me a gentle smile that makes me relax a little. "It won't always be like this," she assures me as I thank Rob the flight attendant for the lunch tray he's handing me. "Just remember, Beck, change is the only constant," she says. Sometimes sitting next to Hope feels like attending a Zen yoga class. I think of her as my soul Sherpa.

"If you were a sociopath," Hope says, "you wouldn't be upset about this, and you'd definitely be sleeping." It's true. I haven't been sleeping, and when I do, it's a swirl of nightmares that jolts me awake in a sweat of panic.

Hope makes some valid points, but I'm not convinced. When we return from L.A., I go up to Philly for a return-to-my-roots weekend. Work has been so busy, I've barely been home, and as I stand on the platform at 30th Street Station, waiting for the R5, I bite into my still-warm soft pretzel and bop along to my music. Compared to D.C., Philadelphia is grittier, but it's also better. I love how authentic Philly is—which is part of the problem, because my parents see right through me when I walk in the back door.

"You look terrible," my mom says. When I give her my best smoldering stare, my mom responds by doubling down. "No, I'm serious, you look just beyond awful, like someone has been punching you for fun." She has a real way with words.

I've barely put my bag down when everything starts tumbling out of my mouth—all the lying, all the secrets, all the bad things I've done and kept to myself. My parents are horrified. "Well, you always have been a great liar," my dad says, sighing, "but I don't think you're a sociopath."

My mom nods solemnly. "I think we can cross out sociopath, but you should probably talk to someone who is less biased."

"What are you going to do about Sam?" my dad asks, his eyes full of concern.

I realize I've just implicated my parents.

"Let's hold off on telling your siblings about your lying, cheating ways," my mom says, teasing but not teasing. "At least until you figure out how you want to handle all this going forward." And as shitty as I feel, somehow I feel better. That's the incredible thing about parents: They'll love you even after you've told them flat out that you're a terrible human being.

That said, my parents are worried. In a Hail Mary attempt to get me back on track, they suggest I call a highly regarded therapist in Philadelphia for an emergency session. He hears my SOS and squeezes me in the very next morning.

I've barely shaken the therapist's hand when I start confessing everything—the events, the lies, the travesties. He scrunches his nose at my stories as if they're lunch meats that went bad weeks ago.

When I take a breath and finally conclude for him that I'm pretty sure I'm a sociopath, he shakes his head and explains no, I'm not a sociopath, but it does sound as though every time I say I want to disappear, I disassociate.

"You're disassociating with Jason, and also when you're with Sam," he says gently. "It's a defense mechanism people employ when they're under severe stress, and you'll keep doing it until you figure out where your real self is."

"So do I choose Sam or Jason?" I ask, desperate for guidance.

"This isn't about Sam or Jason," the therapist says. "This is about you figuring out what you want and who you want to be."

At the end of the session, the therapist pats my back as he walks me out. "I can tell you really love this Jason guy," he says. "But do me a favor, Beck."

"What?"

"Next time he comes for you, and there will be a next time, do not walk in the other direction." He pauses, looks me in the eye. *"Run."*

When I get back to Swann Street, I look forward to writing in my journal to sort out the intense therapy session. Who am I? Who do I want to be? But when I turn the key and open the front door,

Sam is in my living room, waiting to surprise me. "See!" he says, "New Jersey isn't so far away!" As he pulls me in for a kiss, I realize I'm not only disappointed that my boyfriend is here but also that I'm disassociating as I ask him what he'd like to drink. I'm playing a role in my own life rather than living it. I smile up at Sam and disappear.

A WEEK BEFORE THE ANNUAL TRIP TO MARTHA'S VINEYARD I FINALLY screw up the courage to tell Sam we need to take a break. Okay, so asking for a break requires significantly less courage than actually breaking up with someone. I tell Sam it's because I'm sick of his frenetic campaign life and I fail to mention that I think I'm in love with someone else.

Sam is devastated. Crushed. Obliterated. He's been oblivious to the depth of my dissatisfaction, in part because he's been completely absorbed in the campaign and in part because I gave up communicating with him. Instead, I started a relationship with someone else. I have never felt so lost or messed up or slimy, but at least now that we're on a break, I'm free to misbehave.

Just the thought that Jason and I could have a future together sends me hundreds of feet up into the air, flying on red balloons and Van Morrison songs. And then I realize I'm getting ahead of myself. I have no idea what Jason's response will be to this "break," but the Philadelphia therapist probably has a point—isn't this about me? Even if Jason doesn't immediately split up with Brooke, the idea of not cheating on someone, of being free to behave badly and hurt only myself, is liberating.

The first night on the Vineyard, when Jason predictably comes to my room after several hours of dancing together at the Seafood Shanty, I tell him I've broken up with Sam.

He says something like, "Oh, really?" and then instantly seems to fall asleep. The sun is still hours from rising when he leaves without a word.

I go for a long run to clear my head and then call Hope, but she doesn't pick up. She chooses not to cover POTUS's vacation trips unless there's a public event planned, and instead uses that week to have a little time to herself. Knowing Hope, she's probably at a picnic with a bunch of strangers in Dolores Park or at a gallery opening in Chicago or teaching a film class in New York. The mysteries of a brilliant hippie left to her own devices.

I take a deep breath and call Shilpa. She picks up on the second ring and offers the most sympathy she can. "He's tricky, B," she tells me as she talks over the phone on her walk from Swann Street to the White House. Even while the First Family is away, Shilpa is still responsible for helping compile and proofread the memos for the president's briefing book.

Jason is right outside my window talking to an agent who is dressed in the standard Secret Service Vineyard–casual uniform—black sunglasses, khakis, and a short-sleeved button-down shirt.

"I wish you were here, Shilp."

"Me too, but it's only the second day of a weeklong trip. Maybe he'll come around!"

Jason doesn't come around. In fact, he avoids me.

Staff stay at Kelley House, a small inn right by the water in Edgartown, so it's hard for him to elude me entirely. My job is to be on call in case anything happens, so I spend my days by the pool behind the inn, writing. One afternoon, Jason comes out to the pool as a cut-through to get lunch at the Quarter Deck. I'm the only one there, so he stops and says hi. On my laptop is the whole story of us—how quickly it started, how quickly it ended.

"Hey! How's it going?" he asks, surprising me by sitting down.

"Fine, thanks," I tell him, my whole body tense.

"So, about your recent decision . . ." he starts to say.

We both hear the rattle before we see her.

"Jason! There you are! Slow down!" She clip-clops out of Kelley House in sky-high wedges, a low-cut beach cover-up, and a gigantic sun hat.

I sit up straighter. Maybe, if nothing else, Jason will formally introduce us at last. I look at her and wait for her to look at me, but she doesn't. Instead, the Rattler hovers over Jason and scolds him for getting sunburned.

"Jason, honey, look at those red cheeks!" she says in a saccharine voice I've never heard before—like she's the concerned mommy and he's the son she wants to care for . . . but also sleep with? I suddenly feel like I'm intruding on some intimate moment. I look back at my laptop and pretend to read the words on the screen.

"Let's get you covered up," the Rattler says, fishing sunscreen out of her Louis Vuitton bag. She squirts sunscreen into her palm and begins to dab it on his face, slowly rubbing the white liquid into his red cheeks.

"Are you going to the Quarter Deck?" the Rattler asks Jason. He nods, his eyes closed as she continues to smother him in sunscreen. "I'll come with you," she says. As Jason stands up, he gives me an apologetic look and asks if he can get me anything. I shake my head. I'm humiliated, which is secondary to the disgust I feel toward Jason and the Rattler. They deserve each other.

As they leave for the Quarter Deck, the new White House photographer, Amelia, appears with a book in hand. Amelia is attractive and tall and sporty, like a spunkier, tougher version of Jessica Alba. Noah, Cole, and Teddy told me earlier in the week that she's "really cool," too, so naturally I'm really intimidated. I wave and she waves back before walking over and plopping down at the table next to me, in the seat Jason has just vacated.

"What are you reading?" I ask her.

"*Wild*," she says. "This woman hits rock bottom and decides to hike the Pacific Crest Trail by herself."

"Any good?"

"I'm obsessed," Amelia says with a big smile. She leans back in her chair, as if she's happy to hang out with the stenographer. "This writer just nails it, you know?"

"I love when that happens."

"I'll probably finish it tonight if you want to borrow it."

And just like that, I have a new friend. Amelia and I hang out the rest of the week and slowly get to know each other. Unlike Hope and Shilpa, Amelia is quiet, more reserved. Sometimes I feel I'm talking her ear off, but she's always willing to listen. When we lounge by the pool behind Kelley House, I ask her why she never wears a bathing suit; she's always in khakis and a polo while I tan in a bikini.

"I didn't pack one."

"We're on an island for a week!" I say in disbelief.

"It's a work trip," Amelia says earnestly.

"You're making me feel bad."

"Maybe you should," Amelia says, her eyes smiling through her sunglasses. She has a dry sense of humor, like Noah, and I find myself trying to show off for her in an attempt to get a reaction. It's funny how fast a stranger can become a big sister in this bubble. Traveling with the president is like summer camp on steroids—a week on the road is like a year at home.

Even though my stomach drops every time I hear Jason's voice down the hall, Amelia entertains me through the week as we go on hikes and bike rides and ridiculous adventures to find the best coffee on the island. I tell her that my boyfriend and I are on a break, but I don't tell her about Jason. I want her to like me, and no one likes a cheater.

"Just remember, if you get back with Sam, don't let your own dreams get lost while he's chasing his," Amelia says over dinner at the Port Hunter. "You sure you don't want one?" she asks, pointing to her plate of oysters.

"Definitely not touching those."

"You're nuts," Amelia says, shooting the oyster and grinning as she slurps the leftover juice out of the shell. "It's like tasting the ocean," she says, her eyes half closed in bliss.

"Have you met Hope the videographer yet?"

"Just briefly—why?"

"Something tells me you two are going to get along great."

THE LAST NIGHT ON THE VINEYARD, JASON COMES TO MY ROOM. HE SAYS he can't give me what I deserve. He's decided he's going to make it work with Brooke.

"You're a good person," he tells me.

"Are *you*?" I ask.

"I'm trying to be—by making things work with Brooke," he says.

I nod. Okay.

He kisses me one last time on the mouth, then on the top of my head. After he leaves I can't stop crying. It's like being a little kid again: The more I tell myself to calm down, the harder the tears flow. I was so wrong about him, and us, and everything.

LIVING
THE
DREAM

September–November

IN THE FALL, WE'RE SUPPOSED TO ATTEND SUMMITS IN ASIA, BUT WE can't go because Congress is a bag of dicks and shuts down the federal government.

"It's like not showing up to my own party," POTUS says about missing meetings in Brunei, Malaysia, the Philippines, and Indonesia. "I think it creates a sense of concern on the part of other leaders."

Because of the shutdown, a lot of people at the White House are required *not* to work, but because I'm a contracted position, I still have to go in every day, even though most of the press office is gone. Josh Earnest, future press secretary and current principal deputy press secretary, is forced to act as press wrangler when we go on an in-towner so that POTUS can publicly scold Congress for holding the country hostage as they throw a temper tantrum. I love it when he quotes Mark Wahlberg from *The Departed* to tell Congress: "I'm the guy who does his job. You must be the other guy."

Meanwhile, Sam sends me an email from New Jersey asking if I've been listening to as much Haim and Dawes as he has. Yes, the answer is yes. I love him. He's my family. He's my thunder jacket. Whatever I felt for Jason wasn't real, couldn't be real; it was the circus, a confection, a dog-eared daydream, a Molotov cocktail of jet lag and alcohol and five-star hotels. But Sam is real, and I want to make it work. So I tell him we're back, I'm back.

The shutdown finally ends in mid-October. Joe Biden brings in doughnuts. Shilpa stops pressing green juices and comes back to work with the rest of the "nonessential" White House employees. And a week later, we prepare for some good news: the launch of HealthCare.gov.

"Epic fail" doesn't begin to cover how awfully the launch goes—or, more accurately, doesn't go. Even in background briefings with press, POTUS can barely contain his anger as he assumes responsibility for the botched website. After all the hell he went through to get the ACA passed, the website launch should have been the easy part.

The silver lining—or, rather, the "but the good news is" pivot—is that the failed launch showcases how behind the federal government is when it comes to technology. POTUS won in 2008 in large part because of a tech-savvy grassroots organization, so he recruits the brains behind Facebook and Twitter and other major online platforms to volunteer in the ultimate community service project: bringing the federal government into the digital age. In a few months, not only will the website be up and running, but there will be a bunch of Silicon Valley dudes walking around the West Wing in jeans and flannel shirts.

POTUS rallies, and in November he plane-hops from Maryland to Texas to Louisiana to Miami to advocate for an infrastructure bill.

It's Skye's birthday the night we RON in Miami, and she shows up at the hotel bar wearing bright teal sparkly spandex pants, a crop top, and stilettos. Everyone orders drinks, and after the second round I go upstairs to get a sweatshirt. I'm wobbling down the hallway when I see my favorite Secret Service agent, and I show him that I can finally do crow, a yoga pose I've been working on. I'm upside down, my knees on my elbows, when he says, "He's behind you," which of course means POTUS is behind me. I look between my legs and see him and his entourage—Marvin, Noah, Jason, Cole, Teddy, the doctor, the nurse, the Secret Service agent Mike White—walking down the hall.

I jump up and POTUS says hello as if he hadn't just seen me upside down, balancing on my hands. I'm way too drunk to be talking to him. "Looks like somebody might not make it to the gym tomorrow morning," he says with a quick wink.

When I go back to the bar, I pound several glasses of water and tell everyone good night. I'm going to prove POTUS wrong and get to the gym before him tomorrow. Skye, of all people, insists I stay because it's her birthday. In spite of myself, I'm flattered and say okay.

And then Jason shows up and gives Skye a big birthday hug. As I sit in a corner booth with Teddy, Cole, and Noah, Skye flirts with Jason at the bar, falling into him after he recites the joke about his eighth-grade math teacher that he'd told me on the flight to San Jose.

"I guess that's on again," Cole mutters with an eye roll. My stomach drops.

Teddy shrugs. "It's not his fault he's irresistible." Noah fidgets next to me as Teddy continues. "Actually, I find myself in a similar conundrum—no one can resist a Teddy bear, am I right, Becky?" The boys laugh and I muster a smile.

Jason summons us over and while everyone listens to his stories and laughs at his punch lines, I see why I fell for him—because everyone falls for Jason. I feel like the world's biggest idiot for thinking I was special—and that's before I realize that my room, as luck would have it, is between Jason's and Skye's.

We all say good night, and as Skye pulls out her key card, she goes, "This is me," in a voice usually reserved for the first five minutes of a late-night Cinemax movie. I go into my own room and crack the door, waiting to see if Jason is going to walk by my room to go to Skye's. It's a game of midnight Whac-A-Mole in a Miami hotel.

We're on a secure floor, so a hapless agent stationed in the hallway witnesses the whole thing. I don't see any movement, but I suspect that Jason has gone the other way, up the stairs, along the hallway, and down the opposite stairwell so that he can avoid my door and duck into Skye's room from the other side.

I'm so angry I see white as I charge down the hallway. Has he been with Skye this whole time? Before me? During? I blow past Skye's propped-open door and go into the stairwell next to her room and wait. Before I can wonder if I've gone crazy, I hear Jason clamber down the stairs above me. As he rounds the corner and sees me, his eyes bulge, but then he puts a smile on.

"Hi!" he says, like this is nothing strange.

I can hear my heartbeat in my ears. "Hi."

"What's going on?" Jason asks. You'd think we'd bumped into each other at the coffee shop across from the White House, not a hotel stairwell at two in the morning.

"Just living the dream," I tell him, and before I know what I'm doing, I punch Jason as hard as I can in the shoulder and walk back to my room. Behind me, I hear Jason walk into Skye's room.

When we get back to D.C., Jason and I avoid eye contact and any acknowledgment of each other. Even though I'm back with Sam, I reserve the right to hate Jason for lying to me. He didn't want to "make it work" with Brooke; he just didn't want a high-maintenance sidepiece who stood up for herself.

Weeks go by, and as the leaves change, we fly to Seattle and California for DNC fundraisers. *Be cool*, I tell myself as the carpet vans navigate Joint Base Andrews and drive onto the tarmac.

Traveling with Jason for the first time since Miami Whac-A-Mole is only the second reason I need to stay cool; the real reason I've spent the past forty-eight hours practicing my don't-lose-your-shit face is because David Remnick, editor of *The New Yorker*, is traveling with us.

Just. Be. Cool.

And there he is, getting his bag from the back of the other white carpet van while chatting with Hope and looking badly in need of a meal. There's only a handful of us on the plane who read *The New*

Yorker regularly, but that relatively small club includes the president, who can read feature pieces while playing cards and between making phone calls to foreign heads of state.

I say hi to Daniel, the Air Force Raven, at the bottom of the airstairs, and he teases me not to start any trouble as he crosses my name off the manifest. Behind me, I hear David Remnick spell out his last name.

Right before Jay starts to gaggle, he comes back to the press cabin with Remnick. I watch the reporters ID him. A few say hello, while others bristle because if the editor of *The New Yorker* is here, it means that he's getting one—and possibly several—exclusive opportunities to speak to the president, which I'll be covering.

With Remnick attending the gaggle, I feel more self-conscious than ever and try to seem like a dedicated stenographer but also a bona fide badass with obvious writing potential. (Don't ask me what that looks like, but let's just pretend I nailed it.)

Teddy just got promoted to trip coordinator, which means he's now traveling with Noah, Cole, Amelia, Shilpa, Hope, and me, rather than ahead of the president with the advance team. I have more friends in the staff cabin on the way to the West Coast than I could ever have imagined. When the Rattler walks through, I'm too busy laughing with my motley crew to hear the clink of her bracelets.

In Seattle, I wake up at 4:30 A.M. in a cold sweat from a swirl of nightmares. It's Sam and it's Jason and it's me and it's Wendy and it's Skye and it's every lie that's taken over my life. I know Teddy is up because he's organizing baggage call, so I text him to ask if he wants to go see the guys tossing fish at the famous fish market.

TEDDY: Thanks but no thanks, kiddo. Why are you up, anyway?

ME: Can't sleep.

TEDDY: So you're *Sleepless in Seattle*?

Alone in a dark hotel room, I burst out laughing.

The next day in San Francisco, I swing open the Press 1 van door and David Remnick looks up from his laptop. "Are you Beck?" he asks. My heart stops, my head nods. I must have totally nailed that potential-writer face on the plane. "My assistant knows you from school—Emily Greenhouse?" Emily, David Remnick's assistant, was a TA in a class I took. "She recognized you from the photo I took of the gaggle," he says. "Oh, also, I'm David."

As we shake hands, I try to think of something clever to say but draw a blank.

"I hear you're the stenographer. Think I could get the transcript of my interview?"

Oh, to be wanted.

"Absolutely!"

The next night, our last stop is Magic Johnson's house for a fundraiser. Magic and his wife, Cookie, live in a gated community in Beverly Hills, and while POTUS stands in the finished basement with Magic, shaking hands and taking photos with big-ticket donors, I lean against a wall with staffers. David Remnick, not sure where to go, sidles up to me like a nervous wallflower at a high school dance.

"You must be pretty good at being inconspicuous," he whispers.

"I can find a corner in any room," I tell him. Together, we ogle one of the donors, who appears to have half a bird in her hair.

In a sudden swoop of fairy dust, Magic's assistant appears out of nowhere and invites us to take photos with Magic himself in the trophy room. I'm stunned and wait for Chad, the most senior staffer, to lead the way. Instead, no one says anything. No one even acknowledges this gracious offer. What is wrong with these people? Chad leans against the wall with his hands in his pockets and the disdainful look that is, sadly, his resting face. He sets the tone, and his tone is we're not here to do pictures, so we will not do pictures. The assistant's smile fades into a frown of confusion. I bet she's never gotten this reaction when offering photos with her boss.

As I see my opportunity with Magic disappear, I catch Jason looking at me from the other side of the room. Suddenly, I don't care about the hierarchy. Screw seniority. It's like that quote I always hear in Katharine Hepburn's voice: "If you obey all the rules, you miss all the fun." Sorry, padre, you're forgetting that this Magic moment won't happen again. I pass all senior staff and tell the assistant, "That's amazing! Thank you!" David Remnick follows me, and Chad and the rest of the boys fall in line behind him.

Magic's assistant leads me down the hall to a room with the

waxed wood floors of a basketball court, trophy cases lining the walls, and the roar of a cheering stadium blasting from surround-sound speakers. Across the hall is Magic's workout room, and I wonder if he powerlifts to his fans' cheers, because I definitely would.

Magic is ready to receive me in the trophy room. He's as kind as I'd hoped, and my fingers disappear in his boat of a hand before we smile for the camera. It's just like my old basketball coach used to say: "You miss a hundred percent of the shots you never take."

On the flight home, I follow Remnick up to the president's office on Air Force One and move the mic back and forth as they speak, trying to focus on their discussion and not on the fact that my job is embarrassingly easy and David Remnick most likely thinks I'm pathetic. Afterward, I send the audio to Peggy and Lisa, then join Hope and David Remnick in the guest cabin.

Just as I sit down, Hope leans forward and says, "I need to tell you, David, that Beck is a great writer." My face heats up faster than a Hot Pocket. *Why, Hope, why?* This is David fucking Remnick. You don't tell Gregg Popovich your twelve-year-old brother is a great basketball player, and you don't tell David Remnick the White House stenographer is a great writer.

"I'm happy to hear that," Remnick says graciously. "You have an interesting perspective here," he says, looking at me. "Keep notes," he adds.

I nod.

AFTER TOUCHING MAGIC IN CALIFORNIA, REALITY SETS IN ON THE EAST Coast with a hard landing. The campaign Sam spent eighteen months working on in New Jersey had ended as we all knew it would. Despite Sam's best efforts to tell people about Bridgegate months before it breaks on the national stage, Chris Christie decimates Barbara Buono. The loss had come before the California trip, but when I return from the West Coast, I find Sam lying on my bed, staring at the ceiling, his life stacked up in cardboard boxes in the corner of my room. "I feel so lost, Cookie," he says, his eyes glazed over. Sitting down next to Sam, I put my arm around him and rest my head on his shoulder. I tell him we'll figure it out. I don't tell him I feel lost, too.

WE JUST
TRY TO
GET OUR
PARAGRAPH
RIGHT

December

A FEW WEEKS AFTER CALIFORNIA, DAVID REMNICK IS GRANTED A follow-up interview in the Oval Office, and I'm excited to cover it. POTUS and Remnick delve into a variety of subjects, but POTUS grabs my attention when he says the narrative of history is long, and "We just try to get our paragraph right." Life is short and this world is big. *Get your paragraph right.*

And if you're not sure what's right, *write.* I draft a letter to Jason to close the door on the whole affair. He's shocked to see me waiting for him at his desk, and I'm shaking like a wet dog in winter. I hand the piece of paper to him and say, "Thanks so much," and he says, "No, thank *you*," and we smile at each other like bad actors, which we are. But it doesn't matter—it's over now.

Peggy asks me if I'd like to cover the First Family's annual Christmas vacation in Hawaii. I've never been to Hawaii, but I have seen *Blue Crush*, so I immediately say yes. I'll spend two weeks living that montage in which Kate Bosworth does a million pull-ups and shows off her six-pack abs as she gets back in surfer shape.

"Want me to come visit you on Oahu?" Sam asks one night on our walk home from dinner. Sam is going home to L.A., and he explains that Hawaii is the West Coaster's Florida.

Ever since Sam returned from New Jersey a month ago and set up his travel suitcase in the corner of my bedroom, I've been agonizing over whether I should tell him about Jason so we can move forward together, or whether I should break up with him because I've broken us.

"I actually already looked up tickets. It's not cheap, but you're worth any price, Cookie," Sam says with the cheesy wink of a game show host. When he takes my hand in his, I know I need to confess.

"I have to tell you something," I say, feeling myself separate.

I watch the scene unfold from the other side of the street. I hear myself tell Sam that I cheated on him with Jason, just a couple of make-outs in a car, and I watch his mouth fall open, his eyes well. He is devastated, but he blames himself for being too absorbed by the campaign in New Jersey. He's so upset by the make-out confession that I can't bring myself to tell him about San Jose and Africa and Martha's Vineyard. I can't stomach watching him cry and causing him pain. No one tells you how bad it is to be the bad guy.

Sam looks up at me, but instead of telling me it's over, he acknowledges right there on the sidewalk that he's been an absent boyfriend. He reaches for my hand again.

"It must have been hard for you to keep such a big secret from me," he says with a compassion that makes me dizzy. "I still want to come to Hawaii. I want to make this work."

Is a half-truth any better than a full lie? Why couldn't I have been brave enough to tell him just how serious an affair it had been so he could make an informed decision? Without the whole truth on the table, I'm no less confused about what I want, and Sam doesn't know enough to know what he wants. We walk home, with Sam's eyes on the sidewalk as if someone just ran over his dog, and both of us knowing it was me.

The day Air Force One takes off for Hawaii, I wait at the North

Gate with my suitcase and the three-foot-tall Santa lawn ornament I bought for $5 at a grocery store when I was fifteen. My mom calls it tacky, but I've taken it to college, to boarding school, and now on to Oahu. I plug in Santa before wheels up, much to the chagrin of the Rattler, who scowls from across the cabin.

As we level off in the air, POTUS strides through the staff cabin, and his face suddenly lights up. "Santa's here!" he exclaims. Marvin gives me a big thumbs-up. The nurses and doctors come back from the medical cabin to take photos with Santa. And then a few minutes later, Jason walks through, sees the Santa, then looks at me. I don't say anything. I give him the same death glare I've been giving him since November. We haven't spoken for weeks, except for when I gave him my letter, to which he never responded. Not that I expected him to. Well, maybe I did.

Ten hours later, we arrive in Hawaii and I haul my bags and lawn ornament Santa up to my room at the Moana Surfrider. My balcony overlooks the ocean, and even though it's nighttime, I know this is the most wonderful place I've ever been. I grab my phone to text Sam about our room with a view, but as I do, an all-too-familiar unknown number appears on my screen.

> I'm sorry for everything that happened, but I wanted you to know I loved your letter. It's the best thing I've ever received.

I glare at my phone.

> I hope we can be friends.

Still glaring.

> I never wanted to hurt you. I care about you.

Still glaring.

> I tried to talk to you that last day in LA, when you were alone on that bench, but then Teddy showed up.

Liar.

Only you would bring that ridiculous Santa on AF1.

No shit.

I miss you, Beck.

Still glaring.

I hope you'll think about forgiving me. I'd like to be friends with you.

I throw my phone, and then I pick it up, because that's actually a bunch of nice texts, and he did apologize, and I'm sure Skye meant nothing, and she probably initiated all of it, and before I know it I've typed back, "We can be friends."

I've forgiven Jason.

"You know my favorite part of your letter?" he asks. I watch the three dots as he types. It goes on for minutes. He types an entire paragraph.

I can see him splitting wood, resting the ax only to retrieve the pipe sitting on a nearby stump. He is hunched over blueprints, or bending down at a picnic table to tie a little boy's Ked. I can see him folding his suit, mapping out the next day in his head. He waves to the grounds crew, the cleaning staff, and the movie stars in a brand-new Lexus he didn't buy and doesn't want. I can see him eating a Whopper by himself in the Wagoneer late at night, inhaling the brief respite of solitude. I see him lumbering down a sidewalk in a strip mall in Mobile, Alabama, with a boxful of abandoned kittens and that look on his face like, "What am I going to do with a boxful of kittens?" He is the perfectly rolled buckeye in the snow, the secret swimming hole in the summer. He is the only one I want to tuck me in, wish me a good sleep, and make me laugh so hard that tears roll down my cheeks.

It's the one paragraph in a three-page letter that barely includes me. It's all about him. Of course it's his favorite.

A few days later, on Christmas Eve, I borrow an advance associate's car to pick Sam up from the airport. Sam isn't especially happy to see me; he's the only person more aware of Jason these days than I am. Guilt and anger chase each other in waves as I think of Wendy's emails, and how I've behaved so much worse, but how maybe I wouldn't have done this at all if the Wendy thing hadn't happened, or Toledo, or New Jersey. But those are excuses, and now we're in Hawaii—just my boyfriend and me, and the guy I cheated with, and the First Family, and a dozen staffers, and several dozen Secret Service agents.

But the next morning, on Christmas Day, I wake up next to Sam and realize this could be the start of a new chapter. We spend the morning opening the presents we've hidden from each other, and then we go downstairs to the Banyan Tree Christmas buffet. Charlize Theron and Sean Penn are having breakfast on the veranda, a hundred feet away. After stuffing ourselves, Sam and I rent surfboards and spend most of the day on the water.

As night falls, we get ready to attend the traditional White House staff White Elephant party. We're each supposed to bring a small gift, so I wrap up a hot-pink fanny pack full of Hawaiian-themed tchotchkes. When we arrive at the party room, I immediately lock eyes with Jason. He starts to stand up, but I shake my head. I've never felt more protective of Sam. The night devolves from there. Jason chooses my fanny pack during the gift exchange, and Sam practically growls as he watches Jason parade around in it.

A few days after Christmas, I receive an email on my work phone that there's a luau at the president's friend's house. I'm so excited, but there's a hitch: Sam isn't allowed to come.

West Coast chiller that he is, Sam makes the best of it and prepares to go golfing as I figure out the appropriate outfit for a luau with the First Family. Not five minutes later, Jason texts me, asking for Sam's number.

ME: Why?

JASON: Because we were just stuck on the elevator together and I want to invite him to the luau.

Jesus Christ.

Then I get another message, this one from Sam:

> SAM: You're not going to believe this. I'm about to get in Jason's car and
>   drive with him to the luau.
> ME: But it's on the North Shore—it's a 40-minute drive.
> SAM: Yeah, Cookie, I'm aware.

The drive to the luau nearly kills me. When I finally arrive, Sam and Jason are already there. Apparently they smoked cigarettes together and Jason apologized for hitting on me and said it was nothing. The fact that Jason told Sam our tryst had meant nothing to him cuts me to the core, even though it's *my boyfriend* telling me this. I need to get a grip on my emotions, and fast. After Sam and I have a quick recap in the kitchen, POTUS comes over to Sam (POTUS loves big, athletic dudes), so Sam is in heaven and proudly tells him he worked on both of his presidential campaigns.

"Really?" POTUS says. And before Sam confirms, POTUS pivots and yells over his shoulder, "Hey, Jason, this guy worked on both my campaigns—how great is that?"

I make a beeline to the cooler and pour myself a huge cocktail.

Sam and I go for a walk on the beach and we encounter a monk seal, who is waiting for the tiger sharks to go farther out before getting back in the water. As we watch the seal, Sam tells me Jason is a cliché and a creep and stupid and transparent, and he's disappointed I would fall for his shtick. I am, too.

We go back to the luau, where everyone is in full party mode. It's a perfect day in Hawaii. Fun music rides the soft breeze and provides a soundtrack to the annual beach volleyball game. After the president's team wins the match, I ask him if he saw the seal down on the beach. "I saw her first," POTUS says, competitive as always. For a second, I forget about Jason and Sam, and revel in the moment. I never thought I'd find myself casually chitchatting with the president of the United States on the North Shore of Oahu while his daughters read in a nearby hammock and FLOTUS holds court with her friends, cracking jokes and sipping fun drinks through straws. But here we are.

POTUS wants to know if Sam tries to run with me, and what my splits are on the treadmill. After I tell him, he walks away to tell Mike White, his agent, because they'd been betting.

As I look out at the ocean, I realize I've never felt more alone. Like the monk seal on the beach, I can't stay where I am much longer. But the tiger sharks are waiting. If only I could go for a long run—not just away from the luau, but far away from me and this person I've become: a D.C. creature with a duplicitous heart. I'm in love with two men. Caught between them, I'm drowning.

Act III
2014

*In a world of complex threats, our
security and leadership depend on all
elements of our power.*

PRESIDENT BARACK OBAMA,
STATE OF THE UNION ADDRESS, 2014

SPLIT RIGHT DOWN THE MIDDLE

January

THE YEAR BEGINS WITH POTUS STANDING ABOVE ME, ARMS CROSSED, like an amused father. He's in the staff cabin of Air Force One, and as we take off from Oahu en route to Washington, he looks around at our forlorn faces. "All the adults around here are acting like Charlie Brown," he says. "Everyone is just so sad!" He flashes that famous grin as he takes inventory of each of us, landing on me. "Hey, you got a nice tan!" I blush and he keeps going. "All right, here we go, people," the president says as he heads to the guest cabin. "Back to work."

Home again on Swann Street, I pull my suitcase through the front door and up the stairs to my room. The house is empty. I lie down in my bed and look out the windows. I hate winter. I hate the black ice and dark mornings and darker evenings. I hate the cold that sits in your bones and makes you want to stay in bed all day. I hate that Jason lives with Brooke, sleeps with Skye, and is indifferent toward me. I've always hated winter, but I hate even more this snow globe of self-destruction I've created for myself.

Fuck that, I think, sitting up and reaching for my sneakers. I'll stick it to Old Man Winter.

Inhaling the icy air up the Adams Morgan hill feels like chugging a tall glass of sharp knives. As I descend into Rock Creek Park, I run fast and hard so I don't have to think, so I'm too tired to worry about my reality.

This becomes my blueprint for survival. Hours before sunrise, before automatic coffeemakers switch on, before Paul Ryan begins toning his delts and figuring out how to screw over poor children and the elderly, my feet hit the pavement, unclear whether I'm the chaser or the chased. I set my alarm for earlier and earlier, and my runs get longer and longer. The fog coming off the creek reminds me of the opening scene in *Hamlet* as I try to outrun my ghosts. Surrounded by nocturnal scavengers and strange shadows, I'm not a stenographer, or a cheater, or a phantom of my former self. I am just here. I fly through the darkness, away from the past, under the bridge and toward the unknown, all the while trying to keep up with the drums beating, the trees whispering, the forest creatures chanting that ancient hymn of the hunted: *Go faster. Go faster. Go faster.*

"YOU OKAY, KIDDO?" TEDDY ASKS. IT'S A TUESDAY NIGHT AND I'M FLAT on my back, looking up at the basketball boys, who stare down with varying levels of concern. Something is wrong, so wrong. I heard the snap before I felt it in my foot as I came down from a rebound. I blink back tears as I tell the guys I should probably call it a night. Noah and Teddy offer to take me to the emergency room, but I'm embarrassed to have made the game stop. I tell them I'm fine, crack some jokes, try not to limp as I walk off the court.

It's windy and freezing as I wait for a cab on the stone steps outside the Department of Interior. I wish Sam was here, but he's spending this week at home in L.A. since he spent Christmas in Hawaii with me. None of my girlfriends have cars, and I can't call Jason, obviously. Shilpa is still at work, compiling memos for the president's briefing book tomorrow, and she doesn't even get cell service in her cubby office. The cab drops me off at home and I hop on one foot out of the car, up the steps, and into the house, where I crumple up on the couch and cry. Nothing has ever hurt like this.

The next morning, an orthopedist does an ultrasound on my foot and tells me I've torn my plantar fascia—the thick band of ligament that runs the length of my foot. "You see that?" the orthopedist asks, tracing the line on the ultrasound screen with his finger. "You're split right down the middle. You're not supposed to run through that kind of pain." He sounds both appalled and impressed when I tell him I've been experiencing this pain for months but haven't stopped running.

The orthopedist shakes his head. "Normally the only idiots who ignore all the warning signs are NBA players."

I can't wait to tell Teddy and Noah how tough I am.

He orders me not to run for six to eight months. "I'm not kidding—do not try it," he says when he sees my face. "It's not about how strong you are or how much pain you can handle. You've already proven yourself. Give yourself time to recover."

Sam returns to D.C. the following week to start his search for his next job. He cooks me dinner most nights and massages the scar tissue as my foot slowly begins to heal. It makes me wonder, *Can I be better? Can't I work harder to love Sam in the way that he clearly loves me? Why can't I erase my mistakes? Why is there so much scar tissue?*

Though Sam is physically present and taking care of me, he's also back in the political game and drinking the D.C. Kool-Aid. In order to find the next campaign job, he goes to the networking happy hours I despise and comes back name-dropping staffers from Capitol Hill as if I care. He's back in my room and seems depressed again, just like he is every time he comes back to me after a campaign.

Within a week of establishing our new routine, I'm losing my mind. I feel trapped. Work has turned from sometimes tedious to entirely insufferable. I can't travel. I can only type. And unfortunately, I realize I truly hate typing. The office, always small, suddenly makes me claustrophobic.

As Lisa and Peggy pack up the steno backpack and alternate presidential trips, I sit at my desk and stare at the screen, as lonely as when I first started. I don't even have Lucas to keep me company in the office. I'm stuck transcribing other people's thoughts for a living. When Shilpa texts me, "Miss you, B!" with a photo of her and Hope and Amelia at a bar in Milwaukee, I grind my teeth as I continue proofreading the transcript from some off-the-record background briefing no one will ever read.

One night, after another boring day at work, I return to Swann Street, where Sam has made dinner. I complain about the spice level, and he slams down his fork and yells, "You're not going to let your foot break us up!" I think he's going to walk out the front door and never come back, but instead he storms upstairs and returns with my laptop. As our dinners get cold, Sam makes me go online, buy a bathing suit, goggles, and a swim cap, and even splurge for a waterproof iPod and earbuds. The next morning at six, he drives me to the local pool.

I start swimming regularly, hating every minute of it. Six-year-olds lap me without even trying. My anger explodes into each stroke, and I come up gasping for air. But after forty minutes of fighting the water, I feel better. Swimming isn't running, but it's better than nothing.

Sam isn't the only one helping me. Hope brings over wine, and Shilpa does my dishes. Even Noah, Cole, and Teddy step up. When they're not on the road with POTUS, they drive me to and from work. They text me every morning and before they leave the White House every evening to make sure I have a lift. It's as if I have three big brothers. We are at the point in our friendship where we can drive in silence. We are comfortable. We are real friends.

Yet despite all the support, I'm angry. Because the truth is that without being able to run myself into a trance, I am drowning in a year's worth of ingrown lies. It's not just that I can't travel with POTUS, or dance in my room, or walk to work. It's not just that I'm hostage to the banal back-and-forth between Margie and Lisa as I sit in my office. I'm quietly furious and secretly seething that throughout this injury, Jason has disappeared.

POTUS asks me if I'm okay when he sees me limping down the hallway in a boot, but Jason never reaches out. I'm sure the boys have filled him in during one of the many trips I've missed—even an Air Force Raven has emailed me to wish me a speedy recovery. It's hard to swallow the fact that I've run hundreds of miles away from my own life and straight into a debilitating injury because of a guy without the basic human decency to send a stupid get-well text.

I'm too ashamed to discuss any of this with Hope, let alone Shilpa, so I start to write. The pool opens at six, and I'm back home and showered by seven, which means I get in two solid hours of writing before Noah, Cole, or Teddy picks me up.

When Skye announces that she'll be leaving in a few months before starting business school in the fall, I wonder if I should consider applying for a position with the travel team. The job would guarantee even more time on the road, and it would help me integrate more fully into the White House staff. Unlike stenographers, who are lone wolves on trips, the advance office serves as the liaison between the military, the schedulers, and foreign officials. I would be good in that position, I know it. I write to the travel director and travel manager and let them know I'd appreciate the opportunity to interview for the job.

"Great!" the director writes back. "We'll keep you in the loop."

When I tell Cole and Noah that I've applied, they agree I'd be a good fit. Maybe this will be the answer to my personal stagnation.

At the end of January, the president promises in his State of the Union address that 2014 will be a year of action. Standing before Congress, President Obama declares, "I've got a pen, and I've got a phone." As I type up his words late at night in the stenographers' office, I realize I'm ready to act, too.

SCAR
TISSUE

February

"I THINK YOU'RE GOING TO LOVE MY NEW BOSS," SHILPA SAYS ON WEST
Exec.

"Why?" I ask.

"Well, she's very friendly, honest, calls everybody honey, and is
pretty anti-D.C. bullshit."

"Introduce me this second."

I follow Shilpa into the West Wing and we say hi to Matt, a high
school star quarterback turned Secret Service agent who travels with
us. "See you Wednesday morning, Hopper?" he asks me with a
wink.

Tomorrow the bubble is overnighting in New York, so on Wednesday morning Matt will follow POTUS to the gym for an early workout. Normally, if I weren't confined to my office, stuck in a stupid
boot with a foot torn in half, I'd be running on the treadmill when

the entourage arrived. Matt told me last summer that Hopper is my Secret Service nickname because apparently I "have a hippity-hop" when I run.

"Yeah! See you Wednesday morning!" I say facetiously, playing along. Just the fantasy that I could run the day after tomorrow makes me smile.

And then I hear a deep voice behind me: "Wednesday morning? What do you two have cooked up for Tuesday night?"

It's a familiar voice but I can't quite place it. Shilpa is staring at me with such big eyes I'm scared to turn around.

I should have known. It's Vice President Biden, now laughing at his own joke, his blue eyes sparkling as he winks at me before putting on his famous aviators and heading out to West Exec. His teeth are so white I squint when he smiles. Any White House staffer will tell you: Uncle Joe will get you every time.

"Oh. My. God," Shilpa says, her jaw still hanging open.

"Way to go, Hopper," Matt teases. "My wife is going to kill you!"

Matt's wife is also a Secret Service agent. She could strangle me with her pinkies if she wanted.

I follow Shilpa to her tiny cubby of an office, which is more like a four-foot-long hallway between two other West Wing offices. There are no windows. Suddenly a tall woman with long chestnut-brown hair, freckles, and a gigantic smile appears in the doorway of the staff secretary's office. She looks like a Patagonia model crossed with a fun camp counselor, in a black skirt suit. It's like Heidi went corporate.

"Hi! I'm Tess. What's your name?" she says, extending her hand.

I introduce myself and Tess immediately invites me into her office, which is full of unpacked boxes. Shilpa shoos me inside, as Tess lifts a carton off the couch and invites me to sit. "So when did you start here?" she asks, as though she had planned to meet me.

It's all a little confusing—Tess is new, but as staff secretary she's also quite senior, and yet she's also taking an interest in me, even though I've already told her I'm a stenographer. Maybe she misheard me. No one invests in the stenographers. I tell Tess my Craigslist story and she tells me that she fell into this world by accident, too, that she'd actually spent two years living in a tent while she worked for AmeriCorps.

"I never wanted to be in politics," Tess continues, "but Barack Obama changed that. My husband is a tugboat captain and a registered Republican, but he was the one who pushed me to volunteer for the campaign in 2008."

"That's so crazy!" I respond, looking out Tess's big window. Unlike Shilpa, Tess has a real office, complete with a door that closes and a view of West Exec parking lot, which is basically the Walk of Fame of parking lots. Anybody who is anybody has been on West Exec—from Charles Barkley to Bill Murray. This window offers perhaps the best people-watching on earth.

"Yeah, so I worked on the campaign and then actually did Shilpa's job at the start of the administration," Tess explains. "Then I moved to the Department of Agriculture because I'm interested in sustainable food systems, but then I got a phone call asking if I could take this job, so here I am!" Tess leans back in her office chair and stretches out her legs, which are really, really long.

"Did you play basketball?" I ask her.

"Yes!" Tess says. "Did you?"

I'm about to answer when I glance outside the window, and there is Jason, hands in pockets, bending down to talk to someone. I can see bright red stilettos and know only one person who would wear those in February, when West Exec is a sheet of black ice. He shifts his weight to one leg and I see Skye. I watch to see if they go into the EEOB, but they head to the Wagoneer instead.

"Beck?" Tess says, smiling as I swallow bile. "Were you a point guard, honey?"

WHEN I GET HOME, SAM TELLS ME THAT HE'S LANDED A JOB WITH SENAtor Mark Warner of Virginia, which means he can live in D.C.

"Do you want to move in together?" he asks.

I have my answer ready: "You're just going to move again when the campaign ends in November," I tell him. "In nine months, I'll be stuck trying to find a new roommate or a new apartment. You'll be who knows where, and I'll be pissed."

Sam doesn't say anything. He knows these are valid points, but we both know that two years ago all I wanted was to live with him. Between his moves to Ohio and New Jersey, I'd begged him to stay in D.C. He hadn't. So now I'm the one backpedaling from our future. "It's just, for the first time in a long time, I actually like my living situation."

He nods. "I get it," he says quietly.

That night, I'm half asleep when Sam asks in the dark, "When do we get to start our life together?" I can feel the bulk of his sadness, the very weight of it a third body in my bed.

"I don't know," I respond. What I don't say is that I don't know whether we will have a life together.

SAM RENTS AN APARTMENT ON H STREET, WHICH IS ACROSS TOWN FROM my house. The bus ride takes close to an hour, and there's no metro stop nearby. Even though Sam has a car and I'm still in a boot, most nights I find myself making the trek to H Street because Sam works later than I do. I know I was the one who didn't want to live together, but I resent living this far apart as I hobble in my boot to the bus stop.

Only Sam would get an apartment in a different city quadrant than his girlfriend, I think as I sit in bumper-to-bumper traffic for ninety minutes on a Friday night. It's like we're still doing long distance even though we're in the same city.

One night after Sam walks into his H Street kitchen and helps himself to a beer, I remind him to make me a key. More than once, I've gotten to the apartment before him, and then I'm stuck outside.

Sam rolls his eyes, sips his beer.

"Or do you not want me to have a key?" I ask.

"Of course I want you to have a key, Cookie. I'm just busy. I'll do it this weekend."

I try to believe he means it, even though it feels as though optimism leads to nothing but pain. I learn from Cole that someone else has filled Skye's position on the travel team. I was never even contacted about an interview. Someone senior must have made the call,

Cole explains, which means the schedule and advance team skipped the whole democratic-process thing.

A couple of weeks later, I still don't have a key to Sam's apartment, and when I arrive before he does, I'm stuck outside on his stoop—again. Just as I'm about to take out my phone and lay into him, the sky opens up, and within seconds I'm drenched.

Maybe my parents were right, I think. They love Sam, but they've been concerned. They see the key as a sign that Sam isn't ready to fully commit. I've explained he's just super busy and maybe a little preoccupied with the campaign, that it's nothing personal. After all, Sam was the one who wanted to live together. But now, as my clothes stick to my skin and the bolts of lightning creep closer and thunder growls above my head, I think maybe my dad had a point when he said, "Sometimes it's what people don't do that hurts the most."

By the time Sam shows up, I'm soaking wet and shivering on his front steps like a pissed-off cat. I wait to hear the profuse stream of apologies as soon as he gets out of his car, but when I look up at him, he's typing on his phone. "Are you fucking kidding me?" I yell, the thunder adding a roar of punctuation. Sam, who is hungry and tired and stressed, yells back. We fight all night, prowling around each other like caged panthers.

In the morning, we don't speak, let alone apologize. But that night, Sam shows up on Swann Street unannounced and slides a key into my hand as he kisses me, meaning it.

I FINALLY RETURN TO THE ROAD FOR A DAY TRIP TO MEXICO ON FEBRUary 19, but by midmorning I'm struggling with this stupid, clunky boot and wondering if I've returned too soon. It's hot in Toluca, and we keep having to walk back and forth between two buildings that are a quarter mile apart. My foot is throbbing and it's not even noon yet. Everyone is miserable because there's no food and it's going to be an eighteen-hour day. The advance team has been puking all week, so no one is risking the buffet, and senior staff is annoyed with Teddy for not arranging bagged lunches from the Air Force One crew. *I should have let Lisa take this trip,* I lament as I limp back to the palace.

As POTUS shakes hands with Prime Minister Harper of Canada and President Peña Nieto of Mexico during a pool spray, I feel eyes on me. I turn around and there he is, smiling and waving. Jason. I haven't spoken to him since Hawaii. I glare at him as I walk by, but he follows me outside.

"What's wrong?" he asks. His upbeat friendliness makes me want to feed him to a tank full of starved piranhas.

"You knew I did this," I hiss, pointing at my heavy black boot as the press pool scurry by. They're being rushed out to sit in a window-less room in the basement of the palace for more than an hour as the North American leaders hold a trilateral meeting in a botanical garden. That's one thing I didn't miss about traveling—the constant hurry up and wait.

Jason shrugs, amused by my anger. "I figured you'd have reached out to me if you'd wanted to." Ignoring my palpable rage, he bends down and gives me a hug. I stand stiff, hating him, but also smelling his mint gum. "You look good," he whispers in my ear. He leans into me farther, squeezes me tighter.

Over Jason's shoulder, I watch a Mexican guard look away. "I've missed you, Beck," he says, his breath hot on my cheek. It feels like a kiss. He takes a step back to look at me, but I stare down at the tiled palace floor. If I fall into those blue eyes, he'll have me. I'll forgive him.

I don't look up until I hear him several feet away, slapping backs with his Canadian counterpart under an archway. We ignore each other when I hobble by in search of the press pool.

IF PRAYER
WERE MADE
OF SOUND

March–June

AS THE WEEKS PASS, THE PRESS BRIEFINGS COVER THE MALAYSIAN AIR-
lines flight that's disappeared, Ebola in Africa, Russia annexing
Crimea, a mudslide in Oso, Washington, and on and on. Either the
world was always a depressing place and I was just blissfully unaware, or we are dealing with a tremendous amount of shit.

As summer begins, Sam's campaign is heating up, which means
that when he does have a free weekend, he just sits and stares at his
phone. We go to my parents' beach house as a special getaway retreat, and even my parents, who adore Sam, are annoyed with how
he sits there, iPhone in hand. "One more sec," he says when I ask
when he'll be ready to walk to the beach, and then an hour will pass,
and I'll go to the beach by myself.

One Sunday afternoon while I'm reading just a few feet from the
ocean's edge, I hear Sam's phone ring. "It's a reporter," he says, and

picks it up before I can say "So what?" When he hangs up, I ask if he likes talking to reporters on Sunday while he's sitting on the beach with his girlfriend, and he says yes.

I roll my eyes behind my sunglasses. We could not be more different. I let my phone die as soon as we left D.C. Friday night. Ever since Mexico, Jason has consistently sent out feelers, especially on the weekends when Brooke is away. I've ignored them all, which only makes his texts multiply in number and sweetness, but I see through them. Jason doesn't want me—he just wants what he can't have. And while Sam may be a campaign junkie who likes talking to reporters on a Sunday at the beach, at least he's honest about how much he loves his work. At least he's honest about everything.

"Cookie," Sam asks, reaching for my hand, "want to go to Louisa's tonight before we head back?" Despite all the scar tissue we're trying to work through, Sam still gets me in a way no one else does. He is still my best friend, my confidant, my personal Pollyanna, my football coach, my puppy. He calms me down and lifts me up better than anyone else, and he reminds me to see the best in people, not the worst, especially when it comes to myself.

That night at Louisa's, my favorite restaurant, I can't decide which dessert to get—I love the chocolate bread pudding with caramel and sea salt, but the raspberry cobbler looks amazing. Sam wants the bourbon vanilla bread pudding.

"Let's just order all three," Sam says.

"Sam! We can't do that!"

"Yes, we can, Cookie," he says, his green eyes sparkling.

"They're eight dollars each! That's twenty-four dollars on dessert!"

"Listen, I'm paying for dinner," Sam says, his smile warm, familiar. "You can start picking up the bill when you sell your first book."

This guy. He believes in me so much—he always has. Even if he can't help but check his phone a couple of times throughout dinner, he's the only one who knows that my dream is to write and, more important, he thinks I'm good enough to pull it off.

Sam and I get back from the beach just in time for me to pack my bags again: POTUS is going to Poland, Belgium, and France. Lisa is doing pool duty for the first half of the trip while Peggy and I travel with the press charter; I'll swap in for Lisa when we land in Paris. In Brussels, Peggy and I go for a walk, which is when I notice her heavy breathing. "I'm just out of shape," she tells me.

"That makes two of us," I sympathize, since I'm still not allowed to run.

We shop for Peggy's granddaughters before Peggy asks if we can take a break on a park bench. As we watch tourists swarm around us toting sturdy bags filled with chocolates and waffles and Delirium Tremens Pale Ale, Peggy tells me story after story of life on the road as a stenographer during Reagan, Clinton, Bush 41, and Bush 43. "George H. W. Bush had the kindest staff, so respectful, so polite," Peggy reminisces. "And W. was a real jokester with a big heart. I didn't agree with his policies, but he's a good man. He used to yell out, 'We love the stenos!' at the end of every pool spray." I could sit and listen to Peggy talk about life in those previous administrations for the rest of the afternoon, but we haul ourselves back to the press hotel for a full day of typing.

After we land in Paris, I swap with Lisa and walk over to the staff hotel. When I arrive, Teddy and Noah are outside smoking.

"Bilat Becky!" Noah announces, proud of his new nickname for me. The boys call their smoking breaks bilats because they usually take place during the president's official bilateral meetings. I don't smoke, but I love attending these unofficial bilats in back alleys and on private balconies and by loading docks behind backstage. It's the best place to hear the boys tell POTUS stories and the only opportunity to get outside.

"Just in time!" Teddy says.

"For what?"

"We're going to that bar," Teddy says, pointing to a bistro on the corner.

"It's almost midnight!" I scold them. I'm exhausted after four days on the road.

"Suit yourself," Noah says, walking past me.

"Have fun," I tell them. Tomorrow is a big day—we're flying to Normandy to honor the seventieth anniversary of D-Day. I want to be sharp and well rested so I can write about it.

And then I hear his voice behind me.

"You're not coming?" Jason asks.

For months, I have ignored Jason's texts. For months, whenever I've thought of him, I've called Sam instead. I've sworn to myself that I'll be a good girlfriend. Now, standing outside the hotel with the boys, I remember what Hope had said last week, almost sheepishly, after I saw her beaming at Jason, who was charming her father in a photoline: *I hate him for you, but it's impossible not to love him for everyone else.* Maybe, just for tonight, I can be everyone else, and revel in the glow of his attention without knowing where it leads.

Before I know it, it's 2 A.M., last call, and everyone is heading back to the hotel. But Jason is beside me, and Noah is wide awake with jet lag, and Teddy wants to find a discotheque. We say good night to our colleagues, tell them we're right behind them. We don't want them to come. Tonight, it's just our gang. Jason's bill arrives, outrageous because he insists on treating everyone, so I lean over and he lets me sign for him, lets out a laugh when I leave a tip twice as large as the very large sum of our decisions tonight.

Stumbling to the curb, I lean into Jason and breathe in his mint gum as Teddy hails a cab and Noah responds to emails on his work phone. It is the four of us now, cramming into a car that reeks of cigarette smoke and a desperate desire to escape. Teddy sits shotgun. He asks where we might find a dance hall at this late hour, and the cabbie, charmed by Teddy's sweet face as much as his flawless French, promises to take us to the best place in Paris. I sit behind Teddy and focus on the orange tip of his lit American Spirit, dangling loosely from his fingers outside the window.

We pull up to a side street and the cabbie points out the disco at the end of the block. The music calls to us, and so does a man selling roses, and now Jason is putting a rose in my hand and taking me by the other, pulling me through the fog of Paris at 3 A.M.

We never make it past the bouncer—the club is closing—so we are back in a cab. Teddy is playing Clash of Clans on his phone, and Noah is asleep next to me, his forehead smushed against the window glass. Jason finds my hand in the dark and kisses my neck. Paris passes by in a blur.

Back at the hotel, the boys smoke one last round of cigarettes.

"Becky," Teddy mumbles, "make sure I'm awake and alive in the morning, okay?"

"In that order?"

"Don't get fresh with me, kiddo," Teddy says. "Come check on me at seven."

I look at my phone. It's past three. We're screwed.

Since it's so late and we're so drunk, Jason and I walk to his room together—a first. He pulls my suitcase along—I'd never even checked in to my room, just gone with the boys over to the bistro. POTUS is staying at the ambassador's residence, so there are no Secret Service agents lining the hallways. It's just him and me, the repeat offenders. I wish I never had to see Jason, because I'm not strong enough to overcome what I want. He slides his key card and we hear the familiar click.

"Beck?" he says, sliding open the glass door to his balcony. I'm still standing in the hallway. From the darkness, he calls for me.

The view from Jason's balcony is better than anything I've seen in a movie. We are across the street from the Eiffel Tower, somewhere between dusk and dawn. It's drizzling but it doesn't matter. It's perfect. While everyone else is dreaming, we are awake on a balcony in Paris, living a life better than any fantasy. We're so close I climb over the railing and stretch out my hands, expecting to touch the moon, the Eiffel Tower, the stars. They're within reach, I swear it. I hear him laugh behind me, feel his arms around me. Under that wet, inky sky, Jason pulls me back to him, back to the bottom of the Pacific Ocean. "Let me wash your hair," he whispers. What did Virginia Woolf write? *I am drowning, my dear, in seas of fire.*

THE NEXT MORNING, I UNZIP MY SUITCASE, PULL OUT A FRESH DRESS, and bury last night in a separate compartment I've designated for dirty laundry. At 6:59 A.M. I walk down the hallway to Teddy's room. I knock on the door. Once. Twice. Three times. I don't hear a sound from the other side and start to panic. I start banging on the door and finally, thank God, I hear Teddy go, "Hello?" like it's the middle of the afternoon and I'm some telemarketer harassing him.

"Teddy! You awake and alive?"

"Who is that?"

"Who do you think?"

"Just a second."

"No, it's okay, I just wanted to make sure you got—" And there is Teddy, every fleshy pound of him, plus a tiny washcloth he's holding up so I can distinguish between him and Michelangelo's *David*.

"Thanks, kiddo, I've got it from here," Teddy says, turning around, back into his room.

"Cute tush," I tell him.

"Dream on," Teddy says, giving himself a giddyup smack.

We go to the ambassador's residence to pick up POTUS, and then we helicopter to Normandy for the seventieth anniversary of D-Day. The crowd is huge and onstage are the survivors, the heroes, ancient and well wrinkled. My exhaustion takes a backseat to the emotional scene as I scribble notes into my phone.

POTUS walks onto the stage, and every man even slightly capable of standing attempts to rise. It's beautiful. Some are spry, others struggle to stand, and some remain seated in their wheelchairs. Each of us fights back tears. I want to hold the hand of every veteran on that stage and thank them. In their varying postures, the soldiers salute President Obama. They are proud. They are here, back here, remembering. Whose faces do they see as we applaud their valor?

"If prayer were made of sound, the skies over England that night would have deafened the world," the president says.

After the speech, POTUS does an interview with Brian Williams, and I'm right there, crouching in the bushes recording, when I look over to where the helicopters are staged and see Jason and Skye standing together, talking, leaning in to each other and laughing. I should have known. Skye is no longer a full-time White House staffer, but she's still doing advance work on the side. I wonder what else she's doing on the side.

I'm drowning in my own thoughts when Jason looks up and sees me. In one smooth move, he plants one foot, pivots, and turns so that his back is to me, his full attention on Skye. I'm sure he's telling her he just wanted to get the sun out of her eyes, and she's swooning, just as I would. As I squat in the bushes, Brian Williams in my ear asking POTUS about Bowe Bergdahl, I realize that I must be even dumber than Skye, which is distressing, because Skye is really dumb.

At the next site, I find Noah and Teddy off to the side, smoking. "Can I have one?" I ask Noah, nodding at his cigarettes.

"A cancer stick?" Teddy asks, his eyebrows raised with alarm as he lights up.

My fingers itch. I feel like a toaster in a bathtub, all live wires and sparks. I'm not a smoker, but I'm desperate.

"I don't think so, Becky," Noah says. "What's wrong?"

"Nothing, I just want one."

"What's wrong? Seriously," he asks again.

Without meaning to, my eyes flick over to Jason, a couple of yards away. Noah pretends not to notice, but his face hardens as he offers me his pack of American Spirits.

"Careful, kiddo," Teddy says, taking a drag. "One puff on a cig, and next thing you know, it's noon on a Tuesday and you're snorting angel dust off a donkey's you-know-what."

As Noah and Teddy talk golf, I sink into myself. Why did I believe anything he said last night? Don't I know better by now?

Jason avoids me on the flight home. Hope isn't on the trip, so I put on headphones and play "Fireproof" from the National's *Trouble Will Find Me* album on repeat.

When we land back in D.C., Lisa tells me that Peggy, our beloved, stoic boss, passed out on the press charter before takeoff. She wasn't out of shape, as she'd told me in Brussels; she was suffering from a massive blood clot in her leg. Thanks to a heroic Secret Service agent who stopped the plane, Peggy is alive and recovering in a hospital in Paris.

"If it had reached her heart, she would have died," Lisa says. "That agent saved her life." Thank goodness Lisa was there and able to help Peggy get to the hospital. She and I could not be more different, but we both love our boss.

THE GIRL WHO HAS EVERYTHING

Mid-June

NOT EVEN A WEEK AFTER PARIS, WE'RE MILLING AROUND IN THE UN-derbelly of a high school athletic center in Worcester, Massachusetts. The president is delivering the commencement address to the graduating seniors in the gym, and every few minutes I hear a stadium's worth of screams and cheers as the president moves through his speech.

Teddy is explaining Clash of Clans to me when Jason comes over and asks, "Is it true today is your birthday?"

We haven't spoken since I saw him with Skye at Normandy, but my knees go weak when I smell his stupid mint gum.

I nod, yes, today is my birthday.

"Have you ever been on Marine One?" he asks.

"No—and no," I tell him, so that he understands to wipe that idea straight out of his brain. I have no right getting on Marine One. On a staffer's last day at the White House, they may get to fly on the president's helicopter as the ultimate parting gift, but no one in my office has ever flown on Marine One.

"What do you get for the girl who has everything?" Jason asks.

"New shoes," I tell him, and show him the hole in the bottom of my flats.

"I can't believe it's your birthday," he says half to me, half to himself. It's been quite a week—just six days since Paris, five days since Normandy, four days of being back on American soil, not speaking.

"Do you have a first edition for me in there?" I ask, pointing to his black shoulder bag. Jason picks out thoughtful first edition books for his friends, and I want one. I want proof that I'm not just a dumb, easy, occasional mistress, that I'm also his friend.

Jason laughs. "No, no priceless book in here, sadly," he says. "You know what I do keep in here, though?"

"What?"

"That letter you wrote me last year."

"Why?"

"Because it's the best thing I've ever gotten."

"But parts of it were really mean," I say, confused. Sure, it was a love letter, but I'd done a good job eviscerating him for his shitty, shady ways, too.

"Yeah, but it's all true," Jason says with uncharacteristic seriousness. "I love that letter."

At the next site, Teddy pulls me aside. "Hey, kiddo," he says. "We're going to put you on Marine One for the next leg."

"H-how'd you do this?" I stammer.

"Not me," Teddy says. "Jason."

When I get out at the athletic field turned landing zone, I carefully step out of the Press 1 van—I'm finally out of the boot, but I've never been less sure of my footing or more wary of my every move. Despite how many times I've ridden in the presidential motorcade in the last two and a half years, I suddenly feel like a lost duckling trying to cross an intersection. Jason swings his bag over his shoulder and says, "Come on! Just follow me."

I watch as the president, surrounded by his Secret Service detail, traverses the field like a pitcher after a shutout. As I draw close to the stairs, Jason slows and then stops. So I stop. "Go ahead," he says. I climb the stairs onto Marine One.

Josh Earnest, the press secretary, pats the empty seat next to him, and my heart stops as I see I'll be sitting across from POTUS, who is looking out the window. As the helicopter lifts off I notice how quiet Marine One is compared with the Nighthawks, and how if I straightened my arm, I could touch the sleeve of the leader of the free world. Jason leans forward from his seat in the back, past Marvin and Dr. Jackson, and tells POTUS, "Sir, we've got a birthday girl with us today. It's Beck's birthday."

POTUS turns to me and cocks his head. "Is that so? Well, happy birthday! This isn't too bad, right?"

"No, sir, this is pretty magical." I'm aware of Pete Souza taking photos from the back of the helicopter, next to Jason, who also takes photos with his iPhone. I must look like a cartoon character that's just been run over or fallen in love: my eyes popping out several feet from my head, my mouth halfway to the ground. I sit on my shaking hands to conceal how nervous I am. My insides are tangled as the president asks me how old I am.

"I think twenty-eight is a good age," he says when I tell him. "Do you have someone taking you out to dinner when we get back?" Noah had told me POTUS likes to know the marital status of his staffers, but I can barely string an answer together, especially since Jason is sitting a few seats behind him.

"Yes, sir, I do," I tell him, folding my hands together as if I'm back in Sunday school.

"I'm happy to hear that," POTUS says. I smile and try my hardest not to stare at him the way reporters do, as though he's living history, but it's difficult to strike the right balance between rapt attention and stalker-crazy. "And if it doesn't work out," POTUS continues, "just let me know, and we'll find someone great for you." He winks and smiles, and for a second, I wonder if he knows I'm in love with Jason. But he can't, can he?

"Thank you, sir. Thank you for having me on your helicopter."

The president gazes out of Marine One's large square window

that is probably six inches thick, bombproof and bulletproof. I assume we won't speak for the rest of the flight.

But just a few seconds later, POTUS is thinking aloud. "Twenty-eight, twenty-eight . . . I was just starting law school in the fall," he says, "which means it was this summer that I met Michelle." He nods to himself. "It might have been this week, or even today, that we met for the first time twenty-four years ago."

He looks at me, and I feel compelled to say something. "Twenty-four years ago! We should have champagne!" I venture my first glance around after having sat down. It's a very nice helicopter, but it's small. There's no cart service, that's for certain.

"Well, you sure got comfortable quick," POTUS teases, his eyes glimmering with mischief. "You sit down all nervous and now you're already trying to drink champagne on Marine One!"

"Just to toast to twenty-four years!" I say. My voice sounds like a mouse who's just inhaled twenty balloons' worth of helium.

"Oh, I'll toast to that." POTUS then goes on to tell me the story of the day he met Michelle, how he didn't own a suit but had an internship at a corporate law firm, and how the day before he'd gone out and bought two suits feeling like a complete sellout. It was raining on his first day, and en route to the office building his umbrella broke, and he had already gotten mixed up on the subway so he was running behind schedule. When he walked in the door, the receptionist scowled at him, displeased with his disheveled appearance, and sent him back to the office of Michelle Robinson, who was going to be his supervisor for the summer.

"She was taller than I expected, long legs, and I thought—" He says nothing here, but instead shrugs and gives a sly grin. "The first thing she said to me was, 'You're late.' I responded with 'And wet.'"

POTUS continues, telling us about how he asked her out multiple times before she finally said yes. After Michelle tried to pawn him off on her friends, he finally got her to just go get ice cream with him. "Very low-key, very casual—she didn't even see it coming," he says, grinning like a proud hunter. "Like shooting fish in a barrel."

POTUS sighs and takes a sip of tea out of a white to-go cup stamped with the gold presidential seal. And then he looks over at me. "And you were only four when all of that happened twenty-four years ago, when that whole story started with Michelle," POTUS says, and it feels a bit like an accusation. I nod respectfully. I can only wonder at the speed of time passing, at the happenstance that dictates the direction of our lives.

"Yes, sir, and twenty-four years from now, I'll be able to tell my kids that twenty-four years ago I got to fly on Marine One."

He looks over at me. "You will," he says. "That's a pretty good story, too. Oh, hey, how's your foot doing? Because mine keeps bugging me. I'm still on the elliptical."

I found out the president had plantar fasciitis two months ago in Malaysia, in the gym in our hotel. Ambassador Susan Rice and I were on the only two elliptical machines. POTUS started to run on the treadmill but then stepped off just a few minutes after he'd started. In the glare of the television screen, I watched him walk behind me, over to Susan Rice, and ask her how much longer she was going to be on her elliptical, the way you have to in the gym when it's cardio rush hour. Susan offered to wrap up and he waved off that idea. I offered him my machine.

"You sure?" he'd asked.

"Yes!" I told him, fully aware that most presidents would have shut down the gym to work out in private, with full access to all machines.

"Were you finished?" he'd asked, still tentative.

"Yes," I lied.

And suddenly his concerned-dad look melted into the trash-talking competitor-in-chief smirk I'd grown accustomed to seeing above the whir of stationary bikes and the clank of the bench press.

"You should be running, anyway," he'd said, his eyes twinkling, feisty.

"I can't!" I'd bitten back, forgetting to say "sir." I'd yelled loudly enough for Susan Rice to hear me through her headphones and look over with an eyebrow raised. POTUS laughed, amused.

"Why not?" he'd asked. And as he started warming up on the elliptical, we talked about plantar fasciitis.

Now, on Marine One, I try to focus on everything and nothing:

the reading light that catches the shine from his shoes; the Kind bar and bottles of water that are set aside for him against the window. Having watched so many reporters interact with him, I'm acutely aware of how they always stare at him, unblinking, trying to drink in his face, as though interacting with a famous painting at a museum in a foreign country they'll probably never have the opportunity to visit again. I don't want to stare at him as though he's a painting. I want to remember everything, but also to show the utmost respect to the man who has taught me to look up.

"Twenty-eight," POTUS says as we touch down. "Well, enjoy it. Your body doesn't really start to break down until forty-five."

I don't remember the flight to Andrews or the motorcade from Andrews to the White House. I remember Sam picking me up in his car outside the EEOB and telling him that I flew on Marine One, but then when he asks me about it, I'm already half asleep. We drive to Sam's and I immediately pass out, but Sam wakes me up when he leans over to set his alarm. "It's three minutes past twelve, Cookie," he says. "Your birthday is over." I nod, accepting this truth. But when I wake up and it's no longer my birthday, it's still very much the morning after I flew on Marine One.

TRIPLE BOGEY

August

AS EXPECTED, SAM'S SENATE RACE GAINS MOMENTUM OVER THE SUMMER. After his political stints in Ohio, New Jersey, and now Virginia, I'm finally starting to understand how a campaign devours your life. When Sam isn't on the road traveling with Senator Warner around Virginia, or at campaign headquarters, he's on his phone, or writing memos, or drafting talking points, or reading through an upcoming speech. There's no such thing as a day off.

Weeks before the president's annual Martha's Vineyard trip in August, I begin my own campaign—to get Sam to come up with me. "Mark Warner himself is going up!" I yell at him in his kitchen on H Street.

"Just because my boss is going on vacation doesn't mean that I can!" Sam yells back, frustrated. "That's not how campaigns are won, Cookie."

I come up with new arguments for Sam to visit Martha's Vineyard because I'm desperate to have him with me; if he's there, I won't cheat. It's pathetic, I know, but I don't trust myself. I need my boyfriend to chaperone me.

"Warner is taking his own plane up there!" I say. "Just ask for a lift!"

Sam rolls his eyes. "I can't go. Period." As he picks up his phone and starts typing, Sam adds, "You'll just have to go up there and have a fun time without me."

After eight months, I'm finally able to start running again, and the timing couldn't be better: I'm on an island for two weeks with Jason.

The first night on Martha's Vineyard, all the staffers converge at the Seafood Shanty, and it feels like déjà vu as I find myself dancing with Jason, surrounded by couples decked out in Vineyard Vines. While Jason is getting Teddy, Noah, Cole, and me another round, we tease Teddy for his knee sweats—when he's hot, the front of his knees dampen before the back. Even POTUS joked about this uniquely Teddy phenomenon on the golf course after he noticed the dark patches on the front of his khakis. And then a young advance associate, Kendall, approaches me.

"Beck," she says. "What would Jason do if I grabbed his ass?" It feels like a test—or maybe she's just young and brazen—but I can't risk seeming jealous, so I tell her my honest answer.

"He'd probably grab yours back."

I feel my body tense up as I watch Kendall walk over to Jason and grab him. Jason whips around, bends down, and says something obviously charming and hilarious. I'm about to take myself home to Kelley House when I get body-bumped by Teddy, Cole, and Noah, who have suddenly surrounded me and are hip-checking me to each other as if I'm a beach ball, jostling me until I laugh. "Show us your moves, kiddo!" Teddy yells over the thumping bass. I rally, and try to ignore Jason and Kendall in the corner.

When I go back to the bar for a drink, a man with a sexy five o'clock shadow smiles at me from across the crowd and makes his way over. Next thing I know, I'm flirting with Jake, an attractive hedge fund manager whose shoes, even I can tell, cost more than my rent. "Are any of those guys your boyfriend?" he asks, nodding at

Cole, Teddy, and Noah, who have taken a dance break to check their work phones. I laugh and tell him no. Over Jake's shoulder, Cole gives me two thumbs up.

When Jake goes to the bathroom, I look at my phone and there's a text from Sam. "Having fun?" he asks.

I need to tell this guy I have a boyfriend. But before Jake returns from the bathroom, Jason's voice is in my ear.

"Do you like him?" he growls. I turn and there he is, wild-eyed.

"What?"

"Do you like that rich guy who's all over you?"

"Where's Kendall?" I ask.

"Let's go," he says.

The next morning, when I ask Jason if he wants to get breakfast together, he mumbles something about already having a girlfriend. A few hours after he leaves my room, he texts me that we need to talk. We stand outside Kelley House, across from the Quarter Deck and the Seafood Shanty, and as the sky spits down on us, he reminds me that he's impulsive and that I need to be better about telling him no when he gets drunk. "I'm seriously trying to make things work with Brooke," Jason says, looking me in the eye. "You and I—we're not dating. I'm just attracted to you."

"Okay," I muster, fighting back tears as I stare at the ground, embarrassed.

"I'm trying to be a good boyfriend, Beck," Jason says, holding my chin up so I look at him. "Help me be good, okay?"

I nod slowly. "How?"

"Let's try to steer clear of each other for the rest of the trip."

It's a punch in the stomach, but it always is.

THE DAYS CRAWL BY AND SO I SPEED THEM UP BY RUNNING, AND RUN-ning, and running. I run away from Jason—and straight into Skye.

I see her, but it can't be. She's wearing big sunglasses and an Orioles baseball hat. It could be anyone. I look again, longer. *Okay*, I tell myself, *you've actually lost it this time.* Jason is redoubling his efforts with Brooke. There's no way Skye would be here on Martha's Vineyard—it would be much too risky. There's no way to justify her presence here, since she's not on the travel team, and no one called in additional part-time staffers. I tell myself that I'm going crazy, and that I should get coffee and finish the book in my hand, Zadie Smith's *Changing My Mind*.

I look over one more time at the girl window-shopping on Main Street in Edgartown, and in the storefront glass she sees my reflection. Her whole body twitches, but she doesn't turn around. She freezes. Caught. A staffer with no reason to be here, sneaking around town in big sunglasses, not turning around to acknowledge a co-worker. And that's when I know it's her. Two ancient women walk by in a thick shroud of Chanel No. 5, but I can smell it all the same: Something is rotten in the state of Chilmark.

The other woman, who doesn't realize I'm the *other* other woman. I step closer to her, and I watch her in slow motion, her silky black hair catching the sunlight. Skye weighs twenty pounds less than I do. She has the IQ of a malnourished parakeet. She is, by all accounts, a more qualified adulteress—the Myrtle Wilson to Brooke's Daisy Buchanan. Unsuspecting roadkill.

I do the math in my head: Jason must have flown her up here, which explains why, two days ago, he reprimanded me outside the Quarter Deck, reminding me that he already has a girlfriend. He'd measured out his callousness—just enough to keep me away while his not-girlfriend unpacked her things and asked where he wanted to go for dinner.

It's a daring move. Edgartown is a tiny, crowded town, and we're here in high season. White House staffers all pack into Kelley House, a three-story inn by the water, and practically trip over each other on our morning stumble for coffee. We meet in the lobby before heading over to the Seafood Shanty. Everybody sees everybody. The walls are way too thin.

A humane person would have let Skye slip by; a confident woman would have shrugged it off with a "good riddance." But I am neither of those things, so I go, "Skye!" like she's my long-lost friend. Does she know? Impossible to tell. Talking to Skye is like reading the palm of a porcelain doll.

Skye does know, however, that she has no business being on the Vineyard. "What are you doing here?" I ask, my voice saccharine, high-pitched. She stumbles through an overacted, "Oh, hi! Just visiting!" with the authenticity of a Real Housewife.

Labrador retrievers learn to catch with a soft mouth. I am not a retriever. I am a wolf. I bite through bone and swallow without chewing. And so instead of saying "Great to see you," I ask whom she's visiting.

Another long, pathetic pause.

Skye has not thought this through. Foresight was never her strong suit—but clearly, the same could be said about me. Finally, Skye says she's visiting her cousins.

"Oh, nice," I say. "Which street do they live on?" I smile as I ask, just making casual chitchat with a colleague. She shifts her weight from left foot to right, readjusts her bag. I feel her eyes even though I can't see them through the incognito-celebrity sunglasses. Maybe she does know how much we have in common. Maybe she resents me as much as I resent her.

"Somewhere down there," she says, pointing toward the dock. Her inability to tell a good story infuriates me. I am a wonderful liar. Suddenly, I don't want to play nice. I don't want to pretend we're friends.

"That's so fun," I say with the warmth of a Russian hitman.

And then, at the same time, without a lick of sincerity, we both say, "Great seeing you."

I wish I were what Daisy Buchanan had wished for her daughter— just a beautiful little fool. Instead, I'm just smart enough to know how foolish I am, acutely aware that I've jeopardized everything for someone who doesn't give a damn about me, or that pretty piece of driftwood floating away from me.

I get to the end of Main Street and turn left, onto North Water. And suddenly my body collapses. My knees give out and I drop on the curb as my hands and legs tremble uncontrollably. I can't breathe, can't stand, can't get my heartbeat to slow down. An older couple in matching madras shorts asks if I'm okay and I nod, unable to speak.

I talk to myself the way I do at the end of long runs: "Okay, here we go, let's do this, let's get where we're going." I hoist myself up and take out my phone, but there's no one to call. No one can fix this. There's no one to blame but myself. What did I expect? This is what I deserve. And so I head back to Kelley House, my body now calm—

too calm—because I've decided I'm going to set Jason's room on fire. I just need to get the key.

Venom pulses white through my veins as I ask the receptionist about her kids, laugh about those silly boys getting too drunk last night. I'm grooming my prey. *Who knew?* I think, *I've been a sociopath this whole time.*

But then my phone rings.

It's Hope. I'd called her ten minutes ago from the sidewalk, or at least this is what she tells me. I have no recollection of doing it. But somewhere within the splattered madness of my mind, I'd called a friend. And now that friend is calling me back, asking where I am.

"Can you see water?" Hope asks, hearing the panic in my voice.

"Yes."

"Okay, that's good, that's a start," Hope says.

I take that as an invitation to begin. As I walk to the ocean, I tell Hope everything I'm going to do—sick, violent things Quentin Tarantino would have pumped the brakes on. But Hope lets me rant. She doesn't laugh, or gasp, or sigh. She listens. I end my monologue of insane but creative homicidal visions with "So now I'm going to set his room on fire."

Hope tells me it's okay to feel all these feelings. She's just calling to make sure I don't hurt myself. "Name a woman you deeply admire," she says.

"You," I say without having to think about it.

"Thank you," she says. "Now think of another."

"My mom."

"Nice. Another."

"Zadie Smith." Her book is still in my hand from a lifetime ago. "Another."

I list Amelia and Tess, Charlotte and Shilpa.

"Another."

"Susan Rice," I say more slowly, as I watch Susan walk into Menemsha Blues across the street, her agent behind her.

"Okay, wow, what a great list," Hope says gently, like a whisper. "Now, would any of those women end up in jail for setting a guy's room on fire?"

I watch the Chappaquiddick ferry cross the bay. Finally, I say no.

"I don't think they would, either," Hope says lightly, as if we're discussing whether strawberry cream cheese on an everything bagel is a good idea. "And you know what, Beck?" Her voice narrows, focuses, sharpens with its oncoming point. "Neither would you, because you are strong and smart and someone I admire very much."

Tears stream down my cheeks as her kindness gets my chest to soften, my whole body to unclench. "You are loved and you deserve much more than what he can give you," Hope says, sensing my quiet as a good sign.

I sit down on a big rock behind Kelley House. A family with three little boys walks by with ice-cream cones, talking about *Star Wars*. "Beck," Hope says after a good while, "you are someone to admire. You are a cool girl. And what do cool girls not do?"

I take a deep breath, a greedy gulp of the salt air, and then exhale all the venom, all the vitriol. "Cool girls don't set rooms on fire," I say, staring at the dark water, the pink sky, and the horizon line that divides them.

Hope bursts out laughing, a deep belly guffaw of surprise and amusement. "I was going to say cool girls don't give up," she says, joy glittering in her voice. "But yeah, you're right. Cool girls don't set rooms on fire."

THE NEXT DAY, POTUS AND THE REST OF THE TRAVELING STAFF FLY BACK to D.C. for two days of meetings with Vice President Biden and other senior advisers about the U.S. military presence in Iraq and the escalating tensions in Ferguson. The deputy press secretary tells me I can stay on the Vineyard because there won't be any press gaggles during the short flights to and from Washington. I'm relieved I don't have to travel back and forth with Jason. As the rest of the staff head back to the helicopter landing zone, I write by the pool. There are perks to being unimportant.

My first morning without the bubble on the Vineyard, I head out for a run and wonder how the president and his team even begin to address so many domestic and international crises simultaneously.

How can you prioritize when each situation is amorphous, but also life or death? I listen to "We Didn't Start the Fire" as I hit my stride, and the chorus seems apt as I head out of town: *It was always burning, since the world's been turning.* Abroad, the president is dealing with ISIS on the rise in the Middle East, Putin testing his power in Eastern Europe, and the Ebola outbreak in Africa. The United States is still in Iraq and Afghanistan, North Korea keeps testing missiles, and climate change is the silent existential threat no one can wrap their head around. *No, we didn't light it, but we tried to fight it.*

Domestically, the violence of a historical racial divide is as clear as the red, white, and blue of our flag. Ferguson, Missouri, is teetering on the brink while the public waits to learn the fate of the police officer who killed Michael Brown. He and Eric Garner are the most recent high-profile victims of police brutality, but there have been too many and there will be more. What hope, what sense of progress, have we given the next generation if young men of color grow up knowing the odds are they'll end up in jail or dead before thirty? It's as though we all need to go back to third grade and remember that poster of Dr. Martin Luther King, Jr., who said, "A threat to justice anywhere is a threat to justice everywhere."

Whom are we protecting if not the children of Newtown, brutalized beyond recognition by an assault rifle, whose parents could not convince an NRA-fearing Republican Congress to pass a single piece of gun reform legislation? Whom are we protecting if not fifteen-year-old Hadiya Pendleton, shot and killed after taking her final exams? What the hell are we doing? And was it always this bad? Was the world always on fire and I hadn't been looking up?

On my last free morning before the bubble returns to the Vineyard, Major Garrett, a White House correspondent for CBS, stops at my table outside Behind the Bookstore, my favorite coffee shop in Edgartown. "What are you typing?" he asks. Before I can answer, he gets the panicked look of any newsperson thinking a story has broken while he was waiting in line for a muffin.

"Did something happen? Was there a gaggle? What transcript is that?"

"It's not a transcript," I tell him. "I just like to write."

Major laughs and waits for me to elaborate but I don't, embarrassed.

"Oh," he says, blushing. "I'm sorry—I didn't mean—that's great. I've never met a stenographer who likes to write. I thought you were joking, because, you know, you already have to spend so much time typing."

Now we're both red. I should have just said I was working on a transcript.

"Really, Beck," Major says soberly. "That's wonderful."

THE PRESIDENT IS ON MARINE ONE, FLYING BACK TO THE VINEYARD from D.C., when he first hears the devastating news that ISIS has beheaded photojournalist Jim Foley. Zoe, a trip coordinator, calls to tell me there will be an emergency statement. So does Noah, just to make sure I don't miss it. All hands are on deck. At dusk, the bubble converges on the White House medical team's house, next to the First Family's rental in Chilmark, so that POTUS can deliver a statement.

Amelia has swapped in for Pete Souza as the White House photographer for the second week, so she fills me in on everything she knows as we watch WHCA set up lights and run mic check. "ISIL posted a video of it on YouTube," she tells me. "The video starts with 'A Message to America' and shows POTUS declaring air strikes in Iraq."

The press pool is holding in vans as the advance team coordinates between senior advisers, television networks, military aides, and valets. Everyone is shaken, faces drained. The brutality of Foley's murder, the fear it meant to inspire, the threat it poses to our country and also to our president, whom the executioner names . . . I haven't felt this since Newtown, this proximity to evil. I watch Amelia adjust the settings on her camera as darkness settles into the trees.

After several hours of hurry-up-and-wait, Kristie, a new deputy chief of staff, tells us to pack up. The president won't make a statement until he's spoken with the Foley family, and they've asked for a night to grieve. They will speak with the president in the morning. As we unhook, unplug, and load up the cables, mult box, and microphones from the backyard of the medical house, we think of the victim's parents, his brothers and sisters. Their pain fills the silence as we drive back to Edgartown.

In the morning, we return to the Edgartown School cafeteria for the president to deliver a televised statement, his third since we arrived on the Vineyard last week. Instead of focusing on fear, or hatred, or violence, the president condemns ISIL and explains why the terrorist group will ultimately fail, why good will prevail. "The future is won by those who build and not destroy," POTUS says. In the cafeteria turned press file, the president reminds the world, "ISIL has no place in the twenty-first century."

No one in that room can deny the power and sincerity of the president's address. But even more remarkable than the president's palpable anger is the sound that follows his words: POTUS walks away from the lectern in unprecedented silence. Only the clicks of a dozen camera shutters break through the thick, deliberate quiet. Perhaps it's out of respect for Foley, one of their own, or perhaps they're so shocked by the president's fury, but it's the one time the press choose not to chase the president with a frantic barrage of questions.

And then the president goes golfing.

The press immediately replace stories of Foley's murder with pieces condemning the president for golfing in the wake of such a horrific tragedy. It's not just Fox News, either. Congressional Democrats speak out; *The New York Times* runs a story; and even Ezra Klein of Vox tweets, "golfing today is in bad taste." A White House correspondent asks the press secretary, "He made the statement . . . and within minutes was on the golf course—is he detached?"

After I release the transcript of the president's remarks, I go back to my room in Kelley House and draft my own response to the negative press coverage. I write with the protective sensibility of a younger sister, as someone somewhat privy to the universe of pain and responsibility that the president carries with him every single day.

As I head out for a run, I ask myself why people can't understand that exercise is how POTUS copes with stress and grief. Golf doesn't provide the president an escape; it allows him the only breathing room he's afforded. Unlike the rest of us, the president can't go for a walk without inconveniencing everyone else within a six-block radius. He hasn't been allowed to run outside since 2007. His influence circles the globe, but his physical freedom is limited to eighteen holes.

I rant to Amelia as we drive six miles to explore Oak Bluffs. I wouldn't make the "Let POTUS golf" argument to just anyone, but I can certainly run my mouth at Amelia as we pass the *Jaws* bridge. It's not until we're sitting on a bench overlooking the ocean that I notice the tattoo of a sun on her ankle.

"It's a dumb thing I did when I was seventeen and angry and stupid," she says as we watch the rain clouds dissipate. The Amelia I know would not get a tattoo of a sun. But the Amelia I know isn't angry or stupid, either. It's crazy to think that two years ago we were strangers—Amelia feels like family now.

"The funny thing is that when my stepdad saw it, he said, 'What happens if you get invited to the White House someday and you've got that thing on your foot?'" We smile at each other because we know those former selves well—the ones who could never imagine we'd ever be where we are.

We sit in silence, alone with our thoughts but sharing this blanket of gray clouds, inhaling the salt air. Then Amelia tells me that she and her husband are separating. Seagulls caw overhead. Time slows down for me to process this. "It's for the best," she says, so it must be true. Amelia doesn't make big decisions lightly, or hold grudges, or withhold forgiveness. She is generous with her love, a steady force, but also fierce in depth and complexity. She has a beautiful toughness to her, like the sea at midnight.

"Want to keep walking?" she asks.

When we pass the Flying Horses Carousel, the oldest carousel in the country, I think of Jason. We've been on this idiotic loop for years now. Next thing I know, I'm crying as I stare at the little kids going up and down on their ponies, trying to grab the brass ring.

"What's wrong?" Amelia asks, touching my arm.

"Everything," I say, shaking my head.

I spend the rest of the day dumping my secrets into Amelia's lap. She listens closely and patiently, nodding with sympathy. It isn't until that night at dinner back in Edgartown that Amelia tells me what she thinks—that Jason is a happiness vampire, that he has no true joy of his own, no sparkle, and so he's attracted to mine. "Protect yourself," Amelia says over our pile of fries. "Protect your sparkle."

The last night on the Vineyard, Amelia and I go dancing. Good-looking guys in khakis and button-downs try to buy us drinks. Sometimes we let them, sometimes we don't. It's beside the point. We don't take breaks between songs. We don't dance with anyone but each other. We laugh more than anyone else in the bar. This bar is not our kind of bar. These people are not our people. This island is not our birthright. These rules are not our rules, and we flout them with the Rolling Stones and thumping bass. We don't wear heels or Jack Rogers sandals; we kicked off our flip-flops halfway through the first song. We don't belong here. The bottoms of our feet match What's-his-name-the-third's Visa Black Card.

The Amelia I know is the older sister I never had, the one who says it's important to learn the rules so you know which ones you can eventually break. We are the riffraff outside your window. We are the wild ones, ungroomed, uninvited to garden parties and galas.

What if you end up at the White House someday? What if you end up dancing in a crowded bar on Martha's Vineyard, turning down men with long names and deep pockets? There will still be a sun on your ankle and the people who matter will know why. If we are lucky, we turn out to be nothing but wiser, happier versions of our younger, stupider selves. If we are lucky, we wind up with jobs we could never have imagined and friends who run right beside us, down the stairs and out the door and onto the empty beach. Lifting knees, pumping arms, kicking up sand with our dirty feet, Amelia and I sprint as we chase the stars, the Seafood Shanty's techno music fading behind us along with the strobe lights and Vineyard Vines and boat shoes. Now it's just the salt air and inky sky and damp sand from high tide, the twinkling stars and sparkling souls of everyone who came before us. We are not where we expected, and we're exactly where we're supposed to be: the sea at midnight.

"That was just what I needed," I tell Amelia, still catching my breath, as we walk back to Kelley House. Under the yellow streetlamp, Amelia lets out a gasp. I look up and see Jason and Kendall, holding hands, sneaking around the back of the inn.

DO THE MATH

Late August–September

"EVEN THE POPE LIKES TO HEAR HE'S LOST WEIGHT," COLE SAYS OVER iced coffees from Swing's, the Thursday before Labor Day weekend. We've been talking about the day before, when Cole complimented the president's new suit and the president was clearly pleased that someone had noticed; he'd been feeling self-conscious because it was a narrower cut. "He doesn't get fed in that way, in that basic human way," Cole continues. "He just gets fed as Barack Obama the deity, not Barack Obama the guy."

Later that same day, the president goes before cameras in the briefing room to update the country on current events before the long weekend. I'm sitting in front of the front row of reporters when the blue pocket doors slide open and the president strides across the room to the lectern. We all do double takes; it's impossible not to. Photographers slide up next to my chair and take dozens of photos.

I wonder if they've had to adjust their camera settings for this sudden change.

You know when your mom is telling you something really important over dinner, but she has a piece of spinach in her teeth, and that's all you can think about? The president's update on ISIL in Iraq, and Russia in Crimea, is lost on us not because of what's in his teeth but what's on his body—a tan suit. Not black. Not navy. Not gray.

Tan.

Reporters sneak glances at each other when they're not typing frantically on their phones, texting with their editors. By the end of the press conference, Twitter has exploded with clever puns over the "Audacity of Taupe" scandal. According to the most recent polls, the president has hit a new all-time low. He's not the only one. As summer turns into fall, the administration is drowning in numbers:

6.5 million Syrians displaced within Syria

3 million Syrian refugees in neighboring countries, with millions more trapped in the civil war

63,000 unaccompanied minors fleeing violence in Central and South America cross the U.S. border only to be sent home

50,000 jihadists identify as members of the Islamic State

40,000 Yazidis trapped on Sinjar Mountain, facing imminent death by hunger or ISIS slaughter

20,000 men, women, and children killed in the Syrian civil war

7,000 Iraqi civilians killed by ISIS

3,000 people die in the Ebola epidemic sweeping across West Africa

2,718 killed in Russia's invasion of Crimea

2,200 lives taken in the seven weeks of bombardment and rocket fire between Israel and Palestine

300 women enslaved by ISIS (and we know this number is an
    underestimation . . . like all these numbers)

298 people die after Russian troops shoot down Malaysia Air-
    lines Flight 17

100 cities hold vigils for Michael Brown, an 18-year-old shot 7
    times by a police officer

2 American journalists and 1 French adventurer beheaded by
    ISIS

And so, naturally, while in the throes of these countless crises,
the president must go to Wales.

Summits are boring, and NATO in Cardiff is no exception—
security is strict, food is scarce, and the site is remote. While POTUS
is forced to sit in hours of meetings, chaos continues to swirl in the
media about how he's handling terrorism and Congress and Ferguson and Ebola and the millions of displaced Syrian refugees.

I devour newspaper after newspaper in the press hold—not only
because the wifi is spotty but also because I'm trying my best to
avoid Jason and to ignore my heart, which feels like a beating eleven-
ounce bruise inside my chest. I can't wait to go home, and when the
last day arrives, I finally feel safe.

As we load into the helicopters for the first leg of our trip back to
D.C. after an uneventful summit, the press wranglers let us in on
the big secret—we're going to Stonehenge. The photographers and
reporters jump up and down, the noise from the Nighthawk engine
drowning out their whoops and cheers.

When we land, we drive through empty fields, giggling with anticipation, and when we arrive, a family who lives nearby waves from
afar. POTUS walks over and takes photos with them in a scene off a
postcard. It's a day outside time, like a holiday, made all the more
special given the dreary context of this summer's domestic and international catastrophes.

As we clamber out onto the grass, I see Jason get out of the staff
van. He looks back at me before turning to help the Rattler, who is,

of course, wearing heels and complains loudly to Jason about the mud as the rest of us race toward history.

POTUS is as happy as a schoolboy as he tours the ancient stones and peppers his guide with questions. "How cool is this?" he asks the press during the pool spray. The photographers are equally excited and shove their heavy cameras into my hands so I can take photos of them as a group. Some of these guys have been traveling with the sitting president since Reagan, so you know it's a special day when even they say, "This is a first."

Despite everyone else's enthusiasm, and the fact that we're at Stonehenge, I sink as I think about Jason, and remember Petra—the last time we were at one of the Seven Wonders of the World. It seems like several lifetimes ago—Jason barely more than an acquaintance. How did I let a stranger ruin my life?

"You hide yourself away in more horcruxes than Voldemort," I'd told him once. But Jason had never read *Harry Potter* and didn't get the reference, which, let's be honest, should have been the first sign.

"You okay?" Hope asks as she jogs past me to catch up to POTUS.

"Snap out of it," Amelia says, punching me in the arm. "Don't let him ruin this for you." Holding up her Nikon, she ruffles my hair. "Now smile, we're at Stonehenge and we're taking a picture."

I smile into Amelia's lens, but in my head I'm doing the math. In a summer of numbers, I'm one more problem in desperate need of a solution. As Vice President Biden would say, I've got to know what I don't know, and I know I'll never know Jason, because the only honest thing about him is his dishonesty. If x is the constant, y is the variable and determines the outcome. So I guess I'm y.

I BELIEVE
IN HOPE

September

EVERY SEPTEMBER, THE BUBBLE TRAVELS UP TO MANHATTAN FOR THREE days to attend the United Nations General Assembly (UNGA). I've taken to calling it Hope's cowabUNGA birthday party, because my soul Sherpa always celebrates her birthday with all of her New York friends during this trip. This year, she's turning forty-five, and so, as a surprise, I've been in touch with her hundreds of cool, sophisticated New York friends because I have decided to honor Hope the best way I know how: by making T-shirts.

For the better part of the summer and fall, POTUS has been railing against the obstructionism in Washington by going out on the road and telling the rest of America there's still reason to have faith in him and in their government. He's stumping for Democrats across the country in hopes of winning back congressional seats. In California, POTUS riffs:

Cynicism is fashionable these days. But I got to tell you, cynicism didn't put a man on the moon. Cynicism did not create the opportunity for all our citizens to vote. Cynicism has never won a war, or cured a disease, or started a business, or fed young minds. I believe in optimism. I believe in hope . . . Don't let the cynics get you down. Cynicism is a choice—and hope is a better choice.

"I believe in Hope!" I say as I raise my glass to Hope on the plane as we go wheels up.

"You're so cheesy sometimes," she says, our seltzers with lime clinking, but I know she loves it. When POTUS met Hope during the campaign in 2007, the first thing they bonded over was her name. He'd say, "I've been telling everyone about you," or "I tell ya, we've got to take you to Washington with us." If it's good enough for POTUS, it's good enough for me.

I order a hundred T-shirts that read CYNICISM DIDN'T PUT A MAN ON THE MOON, and on the back, underneath a sketch of Hope on top of a mountain, the words HOPE DID.

The surprise goes perfectly, in large part because Hope has a gazillion friends, and they're all eager to put on their T-shirts, even though it means concealing their sartorial nuance. Hope is surprised, teary-eyed, and the night is beyond fun as Shilpa, Tess, and I order round after round of drinks at the bar.

"Well, here's to you, Tess," I say, raising my glass. In my best Harry Caray impression, I joke, "If you ask me, you're less staff sec, and more staff sexy!" I'm not in the same zip code as sober, and Tess cracks up.

"What's so funny?" Shilpa asks, returning from the bathroom.

"Beck is just out of her mind!" Tess cackles, wiping tears from her eyes.

"Shilpa, you have a smile so bright it could light up a whole Christmas tree!" I shout, quoting Joe Biden from his annual holiday photoline. They laugh and shake their heads, and Shilpa asks the bartender for three waters.

Turning to me, Tess leans in as if she has something juicy to tell me. Shilpa and I lean in, too, eyes wide.

"Okay, so I know you have a boyfriend," Tess says slowly, her cheeks rosy, "but have you ever considered Jason?"

I look at Shilpa as I feel my intestines quadruple-knot themselves, but Shilpa just looks away.

"I know he's older," Tess continues, oblivious, "but you two are so similar—like, you guys have the exact same sense of humor, and almost, I don't know, the same approach to life."

I shrug. I don't trust myself to say anything and if I've learned anything from my friendship with Shilpa, it's that I don't want to implicate any more of my friends. I don't want to compromise Tess's professional relationship with Jason just because I happen to be in love with a philandering narcissist.

"Just think about it!" Tess says, grabbing my wrist. "You two would make such a fun couple!"

I smile and promise Tess I'll think about it before turning to the bartender and ordering a double.

Lawrence and Chuck the photographers show up, along with a bunch of advance people and speechwriters. Noah and Teddy and Cole huddle together downing Scotch, and even the doctor, nurses, and military aides make an appearance. They all wear the shirt I made. I'm so proud of myself. I feel my confidence returning when Terry the speechwriter tells me I'm an undercover sniper of potential. Bobbing from group to group, I dance my way around the bar as Hope introduces me to her former colleagues and mentors and college friends, and I see a universe bloom before me. Maybe after this is all over I'll move to New York and work for one of Hope's friends.

The world buzzes with possibility as I down Cape Codder after Cape Codder with my road family. Shilpa and I accidentally wore the same gray Nike high-tops again. Tess is cackling. Hope is beaming. The bartender lets me blast my music over the killer sound system. It's turning into one of the best nights of my life.

And then Jason shows up.

There's no way the music actually stops, but it does in my head when I see him bending down to give Hope a birthday hug and present her with a bottle of her favorite gin. She and I lock eyes over his shoulder, and she gives me a wink. *I can do this. I can be cool.* He's a sad, limited human being I haven't spoken to since the Vineyard. Hope told me once that people make sense to themselves—that he isn't evil, but he's not good for me. Jason and I are professionals; we can coexist.

I watch Jason migrate to the boy group, watch as Noah hands him a Scotch, watch as he takes in the room, the crowd, watch as he scans the bar, watch as his eyes find mine through all the other people living all their other-people lives. I wish it didn't feel like that moment in *West Side Story* when Tony and Maria spot each other at the dance, but that's what it feels like. Everything stops and speeds up at the same time. He walks over and gives me a hug, whispers in my ear that the T-shirts came out great, and any chance there's one he can wear?

I look up before I can catch myself. His eyes twinkle. Our mouths are mirrors as we smile at each other through a kaleidoscope of time, where we are strangers and kindred spirits who have never screamed at each other in the Wagoneer, our voices giving out at the same time as he reached for my hand and unfurled my fists, kissed my fingertips. No, we have never fought like feral cats on a dark side street in Georgetown, or compared our kindergarten teachers, our grandmothers. I have never punched him in a Miami hotel stairwell and he has never flown Skye up to the Vineyard. Nothing and everything has happened between us. Now, tonight, we glisten with familiar charm and infinite potential.

"Tess says we'd make a fun couple," I tell him as he hands me a fresh Cape Codder I hadn't asked for.

Flirting with Jason is like playing chicken with the ocean. You should know you will never win, no matter how fast or how clever you think you are.

"Is that right?" he asks, clinking my glass with his, locking eyes with me to avoid bad luck. Jason flashes me his secret half smile, the sexy one I usually only see when we're alone.

The ocean always wins, because the ocean never cares. But you, my dear, can drown in six inches of anything.

Seconds or minutes or hours later, all of the White House staffers walk home together in a big group wearing our matching gray HOPE

T-shirts. Noah and I dare each other to balance on the curb; then to balance on the curb with our eyes closed. We lumber into the hotel lobby and pile into the hotel elevators. We say good night as the numbers light up on our floors. I get out at 7, but before I do, I watch Jason look to see which number lights up for me. We never say a word about it. Our dance is so well rehearsed, I remember the steps with my eyes closed, balancing on a curb into oncoming traffic.

Propped door.

Triangle of light.

"Hello?"

SINKING

October–December

WE FLY TO CALIFORNIA FOR SEVERAL DNC FUNDRAISERS BEFORE THE
midterm elections, including one garden party at Gwyneth Paltrow's
house. After the president delivers his remarks in the backyard,
there is a star-studded photoline in the living room. I am trying not
to stare at Gwyneth's flawless face when Julia Roberts walks by with
her mother. Nothing will make you feel more like a bedraggled pigeon than standing between Gwyneth Paltrow and Julia Roberts.

As I stand in the kitchen, out of sight next to the rotisserie spit,
the advance lead explains to me they'd had to swap out the painting
that usually hangs above the mantel.

"It was a painting of a large ship that was sinking," he says.

"Oh, dear."

"Yeah. It was also on fire."

The advance team might as well have left Gwyneth's sinking ship hanging right where it was. Because on election night, the Republicans keep the House and gain the Senate, and the mood goes from dark to darker. Cole and Noah had told me that Mark Warner, Sam's candidate, would win by a landslide. Instead, the vote margin is so narrow there's a recount. What should have been a resounding victory feels more like a disappointing tie.

At the election party, Sam works the room by thanking his volunteers, his interns, his young staff. I love the way they look at him, and I know he's proud of the work he's doing. He started off as a volunteer, then an intern, then a young staffer; now he's a senior adviser. And yet, while Sam is inspiring the next generation of career campaigners, I find myself detached and tired.

"I'm going home," I tell Sam as he stands at the bar, ordering a round of Scotch for a bunch of boys who are trying to grow beards like his.

"I'll see you there," he says.

It's only after I get in the cab and give the driver instructions to Swann Street that I realize Sam assumed I meant we'd meet at his place on H Street. I try not to read anything into the miscommunication. I try not to think about how my home is on Swann, with or without Sam.

THE BIG END-OF-THE-YEAR NEWS COMES WHEN THE PRESIDENT ANnounces plans to normalize relations with Cuba. "We are making these changes," POTUS says in his reveal, "because it's the right thing to do."

Meanwhile, I get news of my own. David Remnick has asked me to interview for an editorial position at *The New Yorker*. I'm beyond excited as I imagine everyone at the White House going, "Wow, I never knew she was smart." In the days between Remnick's note and the interview itself, I float through the air, feeling valued and wanted. But when I go up to New York, and I get to the office of the most esteemed magazine in America, everyone asks me why I'd leave Obama and how I could ever give up the travel and the stories.

Thankfully, I don't have to make a choice. David doesn't offer me the job, because I have zero editorial experience. We figure out it's a mismatch as soon as I sit down in his office, and we both burst out laughing.

Even though it doesn't work out, my brush with *The New Yorker* makes me think more seriously about leaving the White House. Sam is even more excited than I am that I'm ready to move forward. He looks at my résumé, helps me with cover letters. He's thrilled that I've decided I want to move to California, where he's from, and also 2,668 miles away from the bubble—I googled it because the more distance from the White House, the better. Sam starts looking at campaigns on the West Coast so that we can get new jobs together, and when we go to the dog park on Saturday afternoons, the possibility of having a dog suddenly seems much more realistic.

When *The Colbert Report* comes to D.C. to interview POTUS for one of its final shows, Stephen Colbert runs by me and gives me a double high five. I take it as a sign. Everything has an expiration date, including *The Colbert Report*. It's time for me to do something new, too.

I apply to teach at a school in California that didn't offer me an interview in 2011 but now immediately flies me out. But as soon as I get there, everyone I speak with says the same thing, "Why would you ever leave the White House?" "What's Air Force One like?" "Won't you miss traveling with the president?"

It's a real mind trap. I get the job and turn it down.

A friend at the White House tells me that the new deputy chief of staff needs an assistant; am I interested? Sam thinks it's a no-brainer—becoming someone's assistant pays off down the road. In the meantime, though, it will take me off the road and strap me to a desk. I don't want to be someone's assistant. But what other options do I have?

I'm on a morning run when I realize the velvet handcuffs of my reality: This administration has an expiration date. It is drawing close, too close, and we have too much left to do. Like any relationship with a known ending, those of us who have invested time and energy in cultivating a more perfect union are living under the stress of a very heavy, very loud clock with a face that says we haven't done enough, personally or collectively. This, I imagine, is how Captain Hook must feel, eternally hunted by Tick Tock Croc.

Despite Jason, despite Sam, despite Lisa and Margie's melodramatic antics in our office, I don't want to leave. I can't run away. Maybe, instead of letting luck and love, disappointment and failure find me, I can confront them, own them, manipulate them to my benefit, like a clown turning balloons into animals.

It's early on a frigid December morning when I decide to tell Sam that my new plan is to stay in my old job. As I walk him out to his car, Swann Street is empty. It smells like imminent snow.

"You're kidding," he says flatly, unlocking the car as we stand in the middle of the street.

I shake my head and feel my chest tighten.

"But you're miserable!" Sam yells. "That's the worst thing you could do!" I blink back tears. I knew he'd be mad—we've had so many fights about how my self-confidence has plummeted. He's tolerated so much of my glamorous gutter-ball life, and he doesn't even know the half of it.

"But if I'm actively deciding to do this for two more years, I won't feel trapped. You could plan around my being here, and get a job in D.C."

Now Sam is the one shaking his head.

"I can't," he says finally.

"Yes, you can—there are campaigns—"

"No, Beck, I can't, because I have a new job already."

Time chokes. Everything freezes.

"No, you don't." He can't. He wouldn't. He would have told me.

It starts to snow.

Sam looks at me, his green eyes wet, guilty.

"It just happened. I was trying to figure out a good time to tell you," he says.

"Where."

"St. Louis," he says, barely looking at me. "I thought you could come with me."

"So eight months."

Sam shakes his head again. "No," he says. "November 2016."

"Two years?"

"Come with me."

Act IV
2015

Leading always with the example of our values—that's what makes us exceptional. That's what keeps us strong. And that's why we must keep striving to hold ourselves to the highest of standards—our own.

PRESIDENT BARACK OBAMA,
STATE OF THE UNION ADDRESS, 2015

LONELY
AT THE
TOP

January

AFTER NEARLY FOUR YEARS OF LOVE AND TUMULT, BETRAYAL AND TRUST,
Sam and I are done. He's in St. Louis and I'm in D.C., so sick from
the breakup that I can't think straight. I have chills. I feel feverish.
My whole body aches like one big dislocated shoulder.

And yet.

And yet, for the first time, I've purposefully decided my path. As
painful as the breakup is, it is the necessary choice, the right decision. There's no way I was moving to Missouri for two years while
Sam worked fifteen-hour campaign days, not when I'm still drawn
to the nonstop swirl of the White House. If I'd moved to St. Louis, I
would have developed acute and potentially fatal FOMO.

The motley crew of colleagues I've found between the wings of Air
Force One have become my advocates, confidants, siblings, and best
friends. How could I leave our secret club, complete with helicopters,

special phones, and far-off places? The future is hovering, Tick Tock Croc is coming for us. I've got only two more years to run on a treadmill next to Barack Obama, or sit at a hotel bar in Kansas City with the boys until two in the morning, or stand on West Exec, midstory with Shilpa, and say, "I'll just tell you the rest on the plane." After January 20, 2017, I won't find myself looking up the definition of a big word POTUS used in an interview in the Oval Office. I won't sit in my assigned seat in the staff cabin laughing at Amelia's jokes as we go wheels up from Tokyo. I know you're supposed to leave the dance before the lights come on, but there's no way I am skipping out now. The lights are going to come on all too soon, long before I'm ready.

Sam's dream required him to pack up a U-Haul and hit the road. He cried, and I cried, and we cried, but I knew I needed to stay here. I don't know what my dream is yet, but it's definitely not sending out cover letters from a kitchen table in Missouri.

So here I am, walking to work and pretending there's not a hole in my chest the size of a 12-inch LP. "If you're going to do it, just do it," Sam had said on that awful Sunday night. And I had done it, surprising us both. "This is the biggest mistake of your life!" he'd yelled, and it took my breath away. But I hadn't called Sam and taken it back, and I haven't regretted the decision to stay.

I know in my heart I need to be here, in this swamp of a city, among the D.C. creatures and happy-hour suits. I'll endure the bruises my heart and ego will inevitably incur for the sake of seeing what this president can do in his two remaining years. I will keep my head down for the sake of looking up. "My presidency is entering the fourth quarter," POTUS had said in December. "Interesting stuff happens in the fourth quarter."

There is no time to be sluggish in the finals. So here I am, ready to take outside shots, go in for rebounds, intercept, block, take the fouls to earn the free throws, play my heart out through the buzzer.

As Michael Jordan said: "Some people want it to happen, some wish it would happen, others make it happen."

Here we go.

IT'S 2015. REPUBLICANS ARE IN CONTROL OF THE HOUSE AND SENATE. As I cross Pennsylvania Avenue on my way in to work, I wonder how many unforeseen crises will delay or displace the president's agenda. For starters, there's immigration reform, criminal justice reform, gun reform, closing the prison at Guantánamo Bay, and getting out of Iraq and Afghanistan. There doesn't seem to be enough time left to get it all done.

President Obama addresses the country in his second-to-last State of the Union address: "I have no more campaigns to run," he says, and some conservative congressmen clap. And then, like a boss, he says, "I know, 'cause I won both of 'em."

Game on.

THE FIRST OVERSEAS TRIP OF THE YEAR IS TO INDIA. ON THE FLIGHT TO Delhi, we watch movie after movie: *Guardians of the Galaxy* and *Birdman* and *Unbroken* and *The Theory of Everything*. It's a fourteen-hour flight, and for some reason, each hour seems to crawl by.

When *Planet of the Apes* ends, Teddy stands up just as I do. We both need a bathroom break, and we both know there's only one bathroom. I get the first step on him but he pulls me back by yanking the collar of my sweatshirt. The hallway is narrow on Air Force One, and we lean into each other like hockey players, trying to edge ahead, only to be stopped abruptly by an adult.

"He's back there," the agent says, nodding in the direction of the guest cabin behind him. Several congressional leaders are traveling with us, so it makes sense that he would go back to say hi. The agent is on post, standing straight as a telephone pole, not smiling, feet hip-distance apart, hands clutching suit jacket lapels. The agent means the president, obviously—that's what we all mean when we say "he"—so we turn around and go back into the office of the staff cabin to wait.

"Let me go first," Teddy bargains. "I'll be faster than you." I shake my head, absolutely not. Enough years of traveling with the same core group of fifteen staffers, and you devolve into petulant siblings. A moment later, POTUS walks by and looks at us but doesn't say anything, just processes our presence as though we're two Ikea chairs, before continuing up to the conference room.

Teddy leans against the door, sensing my disappointment that he didn't say something funny or even hello. "His world is so strange," Teddy reminds me. "We all know so much about him, down to his every movement of every day, and he barely knows our names."

It's true. We are a team of professional stalkers, a congregation of believers who have followed this man around the world several times. I know this, and yet I can't help but wonder what he thought when he saw us. Maybe he was preoccupied by what the senators had said, or the phone call he was about to make. If that had been the case, we had done our jobs well. The goal when you are traveling with the president is to stay out of his way. If he needs something from you—the briefing book, the next set of remarks, a hot tea—you are to be as crafty and fluid as a magician, putting things in his hands without his knowing, a moment before he needs them.

"It's lonely at the top," Teddy says, gripping my shoulder like a coach motivating his player, before pushing off me, using my shoulder to launch himself through the guest cabin and into the bathroom. I catch up to him just as he winks at me and closes the door. Laughing in my defeat, I realize that the cabin is full of politicians, and they're staring at me.

WE SPEND TWO DAYS IN DELHI, A DIZZY BLUR OF BRIGHT COLORS AND gold tea services and labyrinthine gardens that go on forever as we sweat in the midday sun. The soundtrack for the trip is a song the Indians wrote specifically for the president's visit. From the moment we arrive and Prime Minister Modi greets POTUS on the tarmac with an impressive bear hug, the jubilant song "Obama, Obama, Oh!" seems to play on repeat, blasting through the streets and playing on television screens wherever we go.

Several friends who've spent significant time in India had warned me about the unimaginable destitution in Delhi—the starving children roaming the streets, the begging mothers with babies screaming on their backs, the toothless men with protruding ribs hunched over in pockets of shade, the dogs too sick and thin to do anything but wait for death, the piles of trash and their permeating stench everywhere. But I don't see any of these things during our time in India. We're protected from the poverty in the countries we visit, which present like the glossy, two-dimensional Disney World version of themselves as we motorcade through manicured streets from hotel to palace to memorial to cultural performance to palace and then back to the hotel. We do not see the slums or hear the screams. No matter where we are in the world, Dar es Salaam or Indianapolis, the field always looks the same: red carpet, white tent, blue velvet drape. From reports, we know about the human rights violations, the injustices and discrimination, but we are spared the emotional toll of bearing witness to the beaten boys, the dead-eyed girls.

We're scheduled to visit the Taj Mahal our last day in India, but the cultural trip is canceled because of King Abdullah's death in Saudi Arabia. After just two days in Delhi, we pack up to meet the new Saudi king.

"Good job, people," POTUS announces to the staff cabin as we take off from India. As the wings whoosh and we go wheels up, the president leans in as if to tell us a secret. "The Indians are very happy with us," he says, which is generous, because President Mukherjee and Prime Minister Modi weren't exactly charmed by *us*—the lowly staffers who kept their heads down in meetings while wearing wrinkled blazers to hide our sweat-stained shirts. During a working lunch, over lotus stem kebabs and figs, POTUS even tried to speak in Hindi—always a crowd pleaser. So yes, the Indians are satisfied, but only because of the president. He knows this, but he's throwing us a bone anyway. Humility is a privilege of the great.

POTUS starts to walk back up to the front of the plane when he pivots back with a mischievous smirk. He clacks away on his Nicorette, feeling out the tempo for his joke as if he's hopping between two jump ropes. "You know," he begins, "it's not every day you can make a *billion* people happy!"

He gives us that toothy grin you see in photos, the one where his whole face is a huge smile. The joke isn't even that funny, not even really a joke, and yet he's so pleased with his line, like a proud dad.

In these moments, it's easy to see his younger, lighter self. POTUS takes a couple of moments to enjoy the sound of our laughter before his National Security Advisor walks with him out of the staff cabin, past the conference room and senior staff cabin, and into his office to update him on the Japanese hostage situation.

"Death, chaos, and destruction is what I read with my tea every morning," the president proffered in an interview the day before we left for India. He knows all too well he can't save the world, or even those journalists held captive by ISIL, but there are other things he can prevent, or at least mitigate. We leave the billion Indians behind and prepare for the Saudis, which starts with changing our clothes.

The women on board have been advised to avoid bright colors, anything tight-fitting, low-cut, or "mini." As I dig in my bag for my Saudi ensemble, the First Lady's trifecta—her hair, makeup, and clothes people—march through the staff cabin and straight toward the front of the plane. They will spend the majority of this flight styling Mrs. Obama for her visit with King Salman, even though he may refuse to acknowledge her presence because she's a woman. "Can someone remind me again why we're doing this?" a senior staffer asks the group as she cocoons herself in a black silk scarf.

As usual, there's a line to use the bathroom in the guest cabin, which doubles as the only changing room. Senators traveling with us wait in line behind young staffers and follow their lead by taking off their shoes to shave thirty seconds from their time in the plane's most coveted space, which is no bigger than a closet. But the wait is long, at least fifteen minutes, so they strike up conversations while standing in their polka-dotted socks. On other trips, if I'm pressed for time and the line is deep, I sneak back and use the press cabin bathroom, or the Raven bathroom, but today I anticipated the rush and got in line early. When it's my turn, I put my pile of clothes on the bench covering the toilet because there are no hooks. I change into black pants and a long, shapeless dark blouse. I put on tall black boots and roll down the sleeves of my black blazer to avoid any flash of ankle or wrist. On the other side of the bathroom door, Lawrence the photographer and Terry the speechwriter debate the outcome of the upcoming Super Bowl. When I walk out, Terry compliments me: "I've never seen you look so oppressed."

We touch down at the Royal Airport where we find a huge welcome delegation of men wearing traditional thawbs and keffiyehs. It's game time. You can see it on everyone's faces. As we are corralled toward a big brass band that plays the visiting and then the home country's national anthem, it's as if we're two undefeated baseball teams, standing with hands over hearts, heading into the World Series.

On these trips, Barack Obama shows up to win. "I'm a competitive guy," he likes to say, which is an understatement. But we serve at the pleasure of the president, and even if most of us are young and unimportant, devoid of a fancy title or a famous face, it all counts. Someone is always watching, listening, waiting for a slip-up, especially the press. Don't be a story.

Most staffers get kicked around on the road. It's the nature of supporting the most powerful man in the world when he is abroad. The people who make the president look good on these trips often look terrible and feel even worse. It is degrading and embarrassing and awkward when a twenty-two-year-old advance person scolds you for disappearing to the bathroom, and when you're so hungry you eat three bags of stale cookies in front of a vanful of trigger-happy photographers. Civility takes a backseat to survival as you chug water, throw elbows, and down half a bottle of Advil. You work through the pain to keep up with the action. Ballets are full of bloody slippers.

Prior to the president's arrival his advance team and the host country have streamlined his schedule. The Secret Service has plotted his every step. Staffers focus on honoring local customs, respecting cultural norms, and being extremely polite. We abide by the State Department's protocol guidance and what our parents and kindergarten teachers taught us. In most places, this is easy enough to do—just smiling and saying thank you can get you pretty far—but in Saudi Arabia, every move needs to be thought through twice. Do not wave to the soldiers or talk to your motorcade driver. Don't make eye contact with men. Stay in a group and keep a low profile. Avoid an international incident.

"We crushed that!" one female senior staffer says to another back on Air Force One, collapsing into her seat and kicking off her shoes. Teddy high-fives Pete, the ambassador of protocol. We did well with the Saudis, and everyone seems happy with the dinner and discussions at the palace tonight. The last leg of the trip is finally over. It's time to celebrate.

The flight home is a trip within a trip, a little country in and of itself with its own cultural norms. We dance the midnight jig with jet lag as we cruise through time zones. Life takes on a heightened clarity as the stress and responsibilities of the road become tiny little specks going, going, gone as we climb into the sky. Goodbye, King Salman. Good night, Riyadh. Sweet dreams, Prime Minister Modi. Sleep well, you billion happy Indians.

The senior staff, usually treading in political and logistical sludge, enjoy a temporary reprieve from the stress awaiting them thirty-five thousand feet below. The communications director reads *People*. The deputy National Security Advisor tells us about the closed-door meeting with the new king, whose father had been obsessed with horses. Terry the speechwriter leafs through his *New Yorker* while enjoying his last Ziploc bag of jelly beans, and Hope sips a glass of red as she edits seventy-two hours' worth of footage. Internet is spotty. Phones are on airplane mode. The boss is sleeping. There is a buzz in the stale cabin air as we order second and third rounds of wine, beer, and whiskey. What's said on the plane stays on the plane. For once, almost no one is working.

As we fly over the Mediterranean, we're so tired that we're not tired at all. We'll be sick by the time we land, jet-lagged and moody for most of next week, but for now, we revel in the scenes we'd been too hungry or hot or afflicted by digestive issues to appreciate while they were happening. Crouching in the corner of a bilateral room in a palace, I hear POTUS greet the prime minister the way you would a college teammate: *"Modi!"* Sitting alone in a hallway in a different palace in New Delhi, typing up the president's remarks and suddenly feeling someone's gaze, I look up to see Prime Minister Modi waving to me as he enters the state dinner. The parade in the rain that draws hundreds of thousands of Indians. The First Lady's tight-lipped smile as she shakes the hands of Saudi men while Twitter explodes with criticism and commendation for her uncovered head. The three soldiers in Riyadh praying outside the Press 1 van as the sun sets on their backs, their shadows on the wall rising and falling with them. We shape these scenes as we relive them, the memories still malleable like melting candlewax.

Soon enough Air Force One lands in Germany to refuel. We stumble out into the cold night air at Ramstein Air Force Base and head toward the designated smoking area, a much-needed nicotine oasis for the boys after eight hours on the plane.

Crossing the tarmac, I can see my breath as I talk to one of the Ramstein Air Force guys. He asks specific questions like what we ate for dinner in Delhi, and he carries a huge black gun slung across his chest. I ask if his fingerless gloves are warm enough for such a cold night and he says no, but it's okay because he knows they look cool.

"Do we take Ambien on this leg?" Noah asks as everyone lights up, clustered under the streetlamp. Teddy recalls the doctor's strategy as though it's a football play: "Don't sleep to Saudi Arabia, don't sleep to Ramstein, sleep to Washington." It's 11 P.M. in Ramstein but 1 A.M. in Riyadh and 3:30 A.M. in India, where we were this morning, and in D.C., where we're headed, it's only 5 P.M. the night before. Traveling back in time makes everyone a little loopy. So do the drinks. A senator who's flying with us can barely keep his eyes open or his words coherent as he throws his arms around young staffers he's ignored the whole trip.

None of the smokers leave the picnic tables before dousing themselves in Purell, smearing it up past their wrists, and chewing several sticks of gum into a wad. This is the postsmoking ritual. I've watched it a hundred times in a hundred different back alleys around the world. These guys all started with POTUS in 2007, when Senator Obama still partook. But now, after years of immeasurable stress around a boss who quit years ago, these guys know better than to board the plane reeking of a bad habit. POTUS understands their desire to smoke, but that doesn't mean he wants to smell it on his staffers as he clacks away on his Nicorette. Noah comes up to me and puts his face in my face, asks if he smells okay.

"No worse than usual," I say.

"Back at ya, Becky," he says, pinching my cheek. We walk across the tarmac together and look up at the sky full of stars before traveling back to the future.

As we take off after the refuel and the group debates which movie to watch, I go to the cabinet and hand out sets of headphones to everyone. Senior staffers I've never formally met raise their hands like fifth graders when I ask who'd like a set. Everyone takes out their drug of choice—Sonata or Xanax or Ambien—and in that place between awake and unconscious, the forced, awkward intimacy with colleagues is suddenly just funny and bizarre. I mean, you're having a sleepover with your boss, your boss's boss, and a ton of other people you can't fathom seeing in their pajamas, even as they stand before you in their pajamas asking you to pass them a pillow. POTUS passes through wearing all black, and it's like being in third grade and seeing your teacher in the grocery store. Mrs. Brenner lives at school, and the president sleeps standing up in a suit, ready for anything, right? As we tuck ourselves in, turn our earphones on, and watch *Love Actually* over bowls of popcorn and raspberry tarts, I tell myself this is the best sleepover party ever.

Seven hours later, I wake up when the wings whoosh outside my window. All the lights are on in the staff cabin, and everyone is quietly eating their huevos rancheros in their business casual. Terry's empty jelly bean Ziploc is in the trash can along with someone's eye mask. A movie with Liam Neeson is playing, but no one watches as they organize stacks of papers, zip their bags, turn on their cell phones, and look around for their shoes. I return my pillow to the closet, fold up my blanket, and wait in line for the guest cabin bathroom so I can change out of my pajamas—the solemn postsleepover party rituals are just as depressing on Air Force One. Hearing the wheels groggily rotate out from the belly of the plane and into the wind, I don't feel the resistance so much as anticipate the drag of landing.

Soon enough, this flight will end, and this presidency will, too. Everything we worked for will be in the past tense, just part of the record, a paragraph in history. Barack Obama will be a predecessor. The forty-fifth president will run up the airstairs as staffers take selfies and photographers get their front-page clicks. We'll see the photos from our kitchen tables and office desks.

Soon enough, we will no longer be able to say, "I was there when . . ." Soon enough, these wings will find the ground. But staring out the window as the sun sets on an endless horizon, we fly in the eye of history. And for just a few moments longer, we are cruising at altitude.

THE
PATH
AHEAD

February

TESS, HOPE, AMELIA, AND I ARE SITTING IN FRONT OF A ROARING FIRE at the Tabard Inn, enjoying a round of drinks in the library while we wait for a table. Somehow, magically, we are all free tonight—a Friday night in February. Of course it was spontaneous. Whenever we actually try to put something on the books, at least two of us need to cancel because of work. But usually it's all four of us who need to ditch: a last-minute pool spray, a possible announcement, a meeting that's just been rescheduled for an hour from now. We've become friends on the road, but it's proven difficult to find time outside work to see each other.

But no one got stuck tonight, and so here we are, letting the alcohol slowly seep into our bloodstreams as we lean back into this plushy sofa and play with each other's hair like sleepy chimpanzees. I realize I know everyone's cocktail of choice: Hope opts for a martini, just like her dad, and Tess and Amelia go for glasses of Malbec. The Cape Codder in front of me reflects my kid-sister skipper standing.

We order a bottle of red after we're seated for dinner upstairs in a cozy side room. There's a large table of women behind us, all over the age of seventy, and there are two men beside us who I guess are journalists based on their wire-rimmed glasses, their oversized blazers with stretched-out pockets, and the fact that they're having a dialogue rather than a series of monologues. If they're not reporters, they're certainly not politicians.

After two rounds of drinks downstairs by the fire, I'm at the far edge of tipsy. As we study the menu, Tess sighs and says she wants to get back in shape with a daily exercise routine.

"Just do it in the morning!" I tell her for the millionth time.

Tess rolls her eyes. "You," she says, pointing an accusing finger at me, "are the most annoying morning person in the history of the world."

I balk just as Hope says, "It's a little true," which makes everyone laugh.

"Hey, at least I *have* a daily exercise routine," I say, and Tess reaches over and pinches my arm. I realize we're causing enough of a scene that the large table of women and two reporters are glancing over at us—concerned or curious, I can't tell.

"Guys, what's our toast?" Amelia asks, eyeing her wine like Gollum eyeing the ring.

Tess raises her glass. "To Pathahad," she says. Hope and Amelia nod.

A bolt of anxiety cuts through my boozy head. How do they all know this word? Is it a person? A place? Did I miss something?

"What's wrong?" Amelia asks. I haven't lifted my glass to toast with them.

"I—I don't know what that means," I confess, my face getting hot.

"What what means, honey?" Tess asks, sensing my spiraling concern.

"Pathahad."

"Pathahad?" Hope repeats, confused.

Before anyone can say anything, there's a sharp screech as Tess pushes back her chair against the hardwood floor. At first I think she's sobbing into her lap, her whole body shaking violently, her napkin to her mouth. I reach over to touch her, and when I do, she spits her mouthful of wine into her napkin and lets out a cackle. Amelia and Hope are laughing, too, as the other tables watch.

"What?" I ask, but everyone is too hysterical to answer me.

Amelia grabs my shoulder as if to ground herself and regains her breath just long enough to say, "Tess said, 'To the path ahead,'" before collapsing back into silent convulsions.

"So there's no such thing as Pathahad?" I ask, after taking several deep breaths.

"There is now," Amelia says.

"To Pathahad!" we all say together as our wineglasses do not so much clink as clash in the center of the table. The other two tables lift their glasses to us. They have no idea what we're toasting—neither do we—but I believe in Pathahad with my entire being.

GET UP, STAND UP

March–April

WE'RE IN NEW YORK FOR A SERIES OF FUNDRAISERS, AND IT'S THE LAST event of a long night on the Upper East Side. The president will be wrapping up the photoline soon, so I should get in position for his remarks in the living room. I put in my earbuds to do a mic check when I hear someone. My microphone picks up Jason's voice; he must be in the stairwell, up one flight. And then I hear another voice, a woman's. My chest clenches as though my ribs are biting down on my heart. How can his flirting still catch me off guard? This is who he is, this is what he does.

I take a deep breath and look up, and there he is, looking back at me from the top of the stairs, only this time Jason seems as caught off guard as I am.

"Hi!" the young woman next to Jason calls down to me. She's still giggling at the last thing he'd said as they walk down the stairs. Wearing a tight black strapless dress, she is my age, with cascading blond hair, a beautiful face, and a perfect tan even though it snowed earlier this evening. She is also unaware of the undertow as Jason and I try to read each other. I wonder if she's the hostess for this fundraiser, she seems so at home here among the wealthy and powerful, the penthouse peacocks of Park Avenue. I register her diamond necklace a moment before she tells me what my animal instincts already know.

"I'm Brooke," she says, her hand outstretched.

"Beck is a stenographer!" Jason jumps in, swaying between us with uncharacteristic restlessness. He fidgets with his tie. "She travels every once in a while," Jason says, suddenly interested in his watch.

"Wait," Brooke gasps. "Are you the—the thingy—with the microphone?" She points to the mic in my hand.

I nod, speechless. This is Brooke.

"Well, I am like, super impressed, because that seems like the hardest job in the world!" Brooke says.

"It's not hard," I say flatly.

"It must be! Like, what if you try to transcribe Jason—" and with that, Brooke grabs the mic out of my hand and puts it up to Jason's mouth. "He's so tall, it would be, like, really hard for you to reach up that high."

I hear myself gulp.

"Beck is really good at her job," Jason says, watching me watch his girlfriend. I've never seen him look like this. Tentative. Pale. Nervous.

"What are you doing here?" I ask her, forcing a smile as my stomach bottoms out. It comes out sharp, unpolished, the opposite of Brooke's wispy, blasé L.A. chatter. When she speaks, I'm reminded of what Nick Carraway had said of Daisy Buchanan: *Her voice is full of money.*

"Oh, my dad flew in from California for the fundraiser, so I came up to surprise him and Jason!" With that, Brooke leans back into her boyfriend. I feel horrible. She seems sweet. Blissfully naive, but sweet.

"Wait, do they feed you at these things?" Brooke asks me as she follows me into the foyer of the fundraiser.

If I were a dog, I would say no, they do not feed me, please feed me, I'm so hungry, the last thing I ate was half of Doug Mills's PowerBar in the Press 1 van four hours ago.

But I am not a dog; I am a cog. So I try to shrug casually. "Sometimes."

Jason is watching, his blue eyes burning a hole through me, telling me to behave.

"Well, they always give me way too much food," Brooke says, smiling and patting her concave middle. Her diamond earrings catch the light of the crystal chandelier overhead. She leans toward me and puts her hand next to her mouth as if to tell me a secret, which is exactly what she does. "If you can, sneak over and I'll give you whatever is left at our table."

My smile feels like a wince. Is she dancing circles around me? Is she drunk?

"Well, it was so nice to meet you—" Brooke begins, before realizing she doesn't remember my name.

"Beck."

"Beck! And good luck doing the thingy with the microphone!"

She threads her arm through Jason's, and I watch them go back to the cocktail party. I wait for him to turn and give me a grateful look. He doesn't. Why would he? I'm the antagonist in this story, not Brooke.

Even though I hate myself, I realize as I stand in another millionaire's foyer that I'm still right here. I didn't disassociate or disappear. I am here, and so I take several deep breaths, the way Amelia taught me, and I stand up straighter. Before I attempt to navigate the room full of East and West Egg residents, I look up. In a gold-framed mirror hanging over an imposing stone mantel I see myself. I am more than a thingy with a microphone.

WHEN WE GET BACK TO D.C., I FORCE MYSELF TO SEND HOPE, TESS, AND Amelia some of my writing. Ever since that night at the Tabard Inn, we refer to our group as Pathahad, and so I check my phone obses-sively to see if Pathahad has replied to my writing. POTUS an-nounces, "The bear is loose!" before going on a spontaneous walk, much to the chagrin of the Secret service, and I check my phone mid-walk. We fly to Jamaica, and I check my email again and again, but no response. I check my phone for Pathahad's reaction as we tour Bob Marley's house and hit Refresh as I brush my teeth with bottled water in my hotel room. I wait and I wait. I've become so good at waiting.

I remind myself that Tess, Hope, and Amelia are all extremely busy and probably haven't gotten around to reading my stuff yet. After all, they've been shuttling between New York and D.C. and Jamaica, too. But sharing my essays with Pathahad feels like volun-teering for open-heart surgery, and when days go by without a word, I feel as if I'm walking around with my skin inside out.

"Are you taking notes?" Amelia asks as we sit on the steps of the palace in Kingston. I nod as I hear her smiling next to me. I don't ask her if she's read my essays yet because she's busy changing camera lenses and I'm typing my observations from this morning. We sit silently, comfortable in each other's company as we focus on our separate jobs.

Instead of looking for the boys on their cigarette break, I'm doing what Pathahad does on work trips—working. Not for Peggy or the press office, but for me. I am finding the windows of freedom in a jam-packed schedule and remembering to look up and write it down. While I recall POTUS singing "Three Little Birds" in Bob Marley's bedroom from last night and the sweet smell of fried plantains from this morning, Amelia aims her camera at the crowds across the street, on the other side of the gates, who wait in the hope of seeing POTUS.

While everyone else fixates on the president, Amelia focuses on catching the crowd reactions—the looks of joy, awe, disbelief, pride, love. Hope does the same thing with her video camera—more often than not, she's zooming in on the people, not POTUS. I've learned from Pathahad that it's easy to get distracted. It's human to fall in love with the wrong guy. It's normal to see what everyone else is watching. The trick is to learn from your past and to go toward the good in your future. Pathahad's collective empathy and individual drive to grow is what draws me to them. And right now, it's Amelia's compassion for the little kids playing barefoot in the street and the old women waving their hankies at the motorcade from eighth-story tenement windows that makes me appreciate Amelia's awe-inspiring character as much as her award-winning eye.

Four hours later, there is a vibrant rainbow arcing over the plane on the tarmac. "Over here!" Amelia yells. I follow her lead and position myself under the wing. When the president jogs up the airstairs and waves to the crowd, I get photos of his hand touching the rainbow, and also of the rainbow landing on the tops of his shoulders, as if he were the pot of gold at the end of it. Is he reaching out to embrace progress, or is the ideal pushing him forward, like a Technicolor wind at his back? The story changes with the frame.

From Kingston, we fly to Panama for the seventh Summit of the Americas and stay in one of the nicest resorts I've ever seen, which by the spring of 2015 is saying something. From my balcony twelve stories up, I count seven swimming pools and three hot tubs. The ocean is just beyond the pools, and I wish we had gotten back to the hotel earlier—there's no swimming past ten, and it's close to midnight now.

Instead, Amelia and I meet for a walk on the beach. She says she wants to give me feedback on my writing in person. I'm nervous but beyond grateful that she's taken the time to read the essays, that she's willing to talk with me about my writing when she could be drinking a glass of wine while drawing herself a hot bath after a long day.

"You can tell the stuff you've written more recently," Amelia says, her shoes in her hand as we walk along the water's edge. "It's cool to see how you've matured in every way—I'm proud of you." My heart fills with helium as Amelia goes on about which essays were her favorites, the killer whale analogy she snorted over, the bravery it takes to write so honestly. I'm not only overjoyed that Amelia likes the essays—I'm also relieved. I guess part of me has always wondered whether my mom and Sam were just humoring me about my writing, or if I've actually got what it takes. And now here's Amelia, telling me under a bright sky of Panamanian stars that I've got it, and that she gets it.

"I think your writing has improved since you started taking better care of yourself," she says, and even though I know her eyes are on me, I look down at the moonlit sand.

I know Amelia means breaking up with Sam and avoiding Jason when she says I'm taking better care of myself. She'd been helpful in the months of hurt after ending it with Sam, everyone had. I'd been allowed to grieve over a loss I'd created. Pathahad knew about breakups, knew there was no way to expedite the super-shitty part. I'd be walking to work, enjoying a song or a text or a moment, and I'd suddenly remember that Sam and I weren't together anymore. Sometimes it hit me like a blindside tackle—all muscles and blood in free fall so it's impossible to breathe, everything hurting all at once and the world seeming upside down. Other times it settled into my bones, like winter in New England, and I couldn't shake the loneliness for weeks, the cold stones of Sam's words skipping across my brain. *You'll regret this the rest of your life.*

But what about the breakup that never was? Ever since Martha's Vineyard, ever since seeing Jason sneak off with Kendall on the last night, Amelia has been under the impression that I've washed my hands of him. I've allowed her to think so. But Jason is bigger than I am, and I'm tired of fighting whatever this is between us, so I've hidden the fact that ever since Hope's birthday party in September we've been on again, that he's wheedled his way back into my heart and into my bed. Seeing him with Brooke in New York hadn't altered our arrangement in the slightest. "Sorry that was so awkward," he'd texted the next day, and we'd moved forward—as much as you can move forward on the Flying Horses Carousel. It's shameful, and embarrassing, but the fastest way to drown in a riptide is to fight it, so I've surrendered. Secretly.

I don't tell anyone—not Hope, not Shilpa, and certainly not Amelia. I've set Sam free and I've put my friends through enough. I have learned to keep the secrets to myself.

. . .

THE FOLLOWING MORNING, THE PRESIDENT'S HELICOPTER KICKS UP A thick layer of dirt and dead grass right into my face. I spit gravel and pluck the grass out of my hair. The sunscreen I'd applied moments earlier serves as a nice adhesive for the dirt. I know right then it's going to be a long day. And it is—16 hours, 4 sites, 3 helicopter lifts, 2 summits, 1 castle ruin—all in 90-degree heat.

"Hon, do you have any swag?" Tess asks as we motorcade to the state dinner. "I should have grabbed M&M's from the plane—this one concierge at the hotel has been so helpful."

"I'll grab something from the guys," I tell her. Jason gives me two boxes of M&M's and an American flag pin during the next smoking bilat, which I hand over to Tess as we load back into the motorcade.

"This is going to make his week!" Tess squeals. I feel proud for a moment before realizing all I'd done was ask Jason for a few trinkets. I'm just a gofer. But what if I didn't have to go to Jason when I wanted to do something kind? What if I had the agency to be my own ambassador? Would Jason still radiate magic if I could make someone's week by myself?

We return to the hotel wrinkled, weary, and ready for bed. Music blasts from the bar we pass on the way to our rooms—a live band covers "Lady Marmalade" while a few middle-aged women dance with each other.

"That's a different kind of night," Mary from ABC says to me, shaking her head with tired envy as we get to the elevator bank. She says good night, but the music has revived me. *I can sleep eight hours a night when this is all over,* I tell myself as I head to the bar.

The air is perfect—not muggy like it was all day, but just warm enough that you feel nothing at all, as though you're floating through liquid equilibrium. A silky breeze skirts off the ocean. Glasses clink as toasts are made around the dark bar. I scan the room and see Noah and Jason, still in their work clothes, the dirt caked in or sweated off so you can't see it anymore. Jason orders Scotch for them and a Cape Codder for me. We walk out into the night where a group of exhausted colleagues has collapsed in high-backed chairs on a veranda overlooking the water.

At this point, I know who my friends are, and although everyone has pulled their chairs into one big circle, it is made up of invisible smaller ones. Ben Rhodes of the NSC is here; Terry of speechwriting and Kristen of research, too. Pete from the State Department makes a funny face at me from across the way while Gary, Greg, and Tim huddle together. Tess makes room on the couch and summons me over. In the corner, Marvin speaks quickly to Noah, Jason, and Chase, the director of scheduling. All of them took heat for the hard day. POTUS is a trouper on the road, but today he was furious.

While the rest of us could sit backstage in the air-conditioning, swigging Cokes and sharing snacks, the president was on for fifteen hours straight—shaking hands with heads of state, delivering remarks, answering questions that could easily lead to bad press or an international incident if he wasn't careful. The schedule ran him into the ground, which isn't easy to do.

Keeping the boss relatively happy and comfortable is essential for productive meetings with foreign leaders, and the last thing anyone wanted was for the president to be in a bad mood when he met with Raúl Castro for the first time. And so the fact is, the true hero of that historic U.S.-Cuba bilat at the Summit of the Americas was not the president or Ricardo Zuniga or Ben Rhodes or any of their Cuban counterparts—it was a tech guy named Steve who figured out how to stream the Masters in the president's hold while he waited for the first plenary session to wrap. Getting to watch golf with Marvin, Teddy, and Noah for half an hour before the briefing on the Cuba bilat allowed the boss to reset. Consequently—and unsurprisingly—POTUS crushed the meeting with Raúl Castro and made it memorable for all the right reasons.

The garble of different conversations washes over me and I sit there on the outer ring of several rippling discussions. I'm too tired to engage, mind, or move. "Wake up!" Tess says, elbowing me. As the person responsible for every piece of paper, every classified memo the president sees on a daily basis, Tess rarely gets to be this far from a printer or photocopier on a foreign trip. She is ecstatic about her current liberation and clinks my glass more than once. We talk about the day, about how beautiful the night is, and we mix a-fresh cold beer with her warm beer like mad scientists so that they're both lukewarm and barely drinkable, but that's what friends are for.

Tess leans across me to ask Jason about the boss's mood. I could tell her myself based on his eyes and his tendency to use names more when he's trying to check himself, but Jason can tell Tess straight up, and she shakes her head sympathetically.

It's a lonely world, this exciting one we orbit. No one will admit it, but it is. I fought Jason for so long and it didn't matter. He has his own gravitational pull, so fine, I'm here, I give in. Let's keep this exciting, let's make this about us and what we can get away with when everyone else is sleeping toward the alarm and following all the rules. And when we get back to D.C., whatever happened will stay out of the West Wing, stay out of everything, because these dreamless nights don't exist after sunrise—it's just the alcohol, the exhaustion, the taste of someone in the dark, the hunger to be touched after a week on the road. These hotel rooms are five-star, and you have a suite on the top floor. I'll listen to your stories if you stay longer than you did last time, the last time this never happened, and in the morning I won't call out to you as we sit at different tables, enjoying our complimentary breakfasts with our bright-eyed colleagues. We can do this and not look up, not look back.

As I head back to my room before dawn, passing the agents standing post in the hallways, I remind myself that I'm actively engaging in this not-relationship now. I am deciding to do what I'm doing. I am no longer a victim of Jason's charm. Never mind the shame—I push it to the back and pretend it isn't there. I'll deal with the sour stink of it later. Not now. Because I am here, and so is he, and we will never again have this view from his balcony. We will never again find ourselves in Panama together. Which is why I write it all down.

WHEN WE RETURN TO D.C., I FIND OUT THAT JENNIFER PALMIERI, THE White House communications director, is leaving to go work on the fledgling Hillary Clinton campaign. In direct contrast to the Vagiants, Jen has always gone out of her way to make me feel a part of the team—she says hi in the hallway, she initiates conversation if the two of us are stuck alone in a room waiting for POTUS, and her face always lights up when I ask about her dog. Maybe Jen is just a not-rude person, but by 2015, the bar is low. As Tess would say, "It's supposed to be human first, staffer second." Too often, that's not the case.

On Jen's final day in March, I print out a piece I'd written the year before about style in the White House to give to her. Jen is one of many West Wing women I admire for using her wardrobe to express her independence. And yes, there's something inherently appealing about cutting price tags off a dress, something intrinsically empowering about purchasing a jacket that was outside your price range a few years ago. I don't think Van Morrison was wrong when he noticed, "All the girls walk by, dressed up for each other." But it's more than that.

Style is so important to West Wing women because there is no mental escape at work, no world except this one. Most offices lack windows; the only art on the walls are candid photographs of the president and his team in action. And so women at 1600 Penn purchase dresses in bright colors, buttery Italian shoes, and new lipstick to provide an aesthetic distraction as much as a grounding in the moment, in the work. Days at the White House are long and tough, but a pair of joy comes in a size 8 heel and makes Susan Rice two inches taller when she enters the Situation Room. A pink blazer with black trim gives Secretary Clinton a pop of color when she arrives on West Exec or in West Africa. Samantha Power's sharp wardrobe complements her elevated thinking. Their sartorial splendor is not only impressive but, more important, reflective of their willingness to challenge the status quo.

I read over the piece one last time and hope Jen will understand I'm not giving her this letter so I can get in her good graces for a job down the line. I don't write to get something from someone; I write because they've already given something to me.

And then there is this image I still think of, years later: Jen Palmieri wears a navy panted jumper that ties at the neck in

Palm Springs. Female reporters rush to her side to clamor over the daring look, complete with wedges. They laugh together, and no one asks about embargoed conference calls or off-the-record briefings. I watch Jen toss back her hair and shower in their enthusiastic compliments as we all stand around sweating in the dry heat. The romper is cool, whatever, but her confidence makes her undeniably beautiful.

After leaving the envelope with Jen's assistant, I think about the last time I did this, with David Plouffe, more than two years ago. This time around, I look over my shoulder before I hit Print to make sure Lisa isn't behind me. I know better than to tell her I'm breaching the hierarchy again by giving a senior staffer a piece of writing. The whole administration is in its final sprint, so this is my outside shot at the buzzer.

When I return to my desk, there's an email from Jen waiting for me. What is it about these high-powered people with record response times? Jen has written such an effusive note I'm worried my heart will explode or, worse, Lisa will sense my happiness and come over to see what's wrong. Jen not only praises my writing but also tells me to please come to her going-away party that night. I guess Jen understood what I was trying to tell her through my writing: Thank you.

As I reply to her note, I feel something bright and warm blossom in my chest. I realize I'm smiling at my computer screen before knowing why.

Since I joined the bubble, POTUS has told me I'm fast, and Jason has told me he's attracted to me, and Nancy Pelosi has told me I have cute clothes. All of it has felt good, but none of it compares to what this feels like. I silently thank Jen, and Plouffe, and Sam, and Pathahad. When I put pen to paper, people listen. It's like I'm my own Pacific Ocean, only bigger.

IMITATIONS
OF INTIMACY

May

NOAH'S BIRTHDAY FALLS ON AN OVERNIGHT TRIP IN MIAMI. "DON'T turn this into a big deal," he tells me when we realize our good scheduling fortune. *Everyone* is going to be on this trip: Jason, Teddy, Cole, Noah, Pathahad. It's rare we have the full gang on the road for a domestic trip—usually office rotations leave one or two of us at home. "I just want to have a good time with my friends," he says. "A *low-key* good time, Becky. I mean it, no sparkles, no surprises." I promise I won't do anything wild, but that's because Cole says he's planning our big night out, and Cole always comes up with cool stuff to do.

After a couple of fundraisers in Coral Gables, we motorcade back to the hotel. There's another private cocktail reception POTUS needs to attend on the top floor, so while the boys go there to help staff him, I meet Amelia down at the bar for a drink. Hope and Tess are calling it a night—Tess is waiting on several memos for tomorrow's presidential briefing book, and Hope needs to edit the day's footage before a midnight deadline.

One drink turns to two, and by the time the boys arrive, Amelia and I are in love with the world.

"I hope you guys are ready for the best night of your lives," Cole says, grinning and rubbing his palms together like a chef preparing a feast.

We head to a fancy club in the basement of a top hotel. As the boys and Amelia sit around our fancy-pants bottle-service table, I do laps on the dance floor, loosely weaving between grinding couples to harass the DJ about which song to play next. I wait until Amelia is in the bathroom and Teddy is scoping out some girl with a high pony in a crop top to ask Jason if he'll come dance with me.

"In a bit," he says unconvincingly, over the booming bass. Just then Amelia returns, and I head back to the dance floor.

Noah agrees to do a lap with me, and then Teddy joins us on our little adventure. Soon girls on the dance floor are grabbing Noah, so Teddy and I dance together to a techno remix of Boyz II Men's "Motown Philly." Dancing with Jason is always electric, but dancing with Teddy is always the most fun. We compete for who does the better sprinkler, the better grocery store, before heading back to the table for another round of drinks.

"Cheers!" I toast, holding up my glass just as Noah returns. "Happy birthday, Noah! I love you all!"

Around two o'clock, the boys pay the tab—they make at least twice as much as I do, so I don't feel bad that they usually foot the bill when we go out—and we return to the hotel and pile into my room to give Noah our joint birthday present—a fluffy robe from The Beverly Hilton. I knew Noah had been eyeing it for years, so we all chipped in, and now here he is, in my room, modeling it for us and unabashedly delighted. We all hug and finally everyone leaves to pass out before motorcade departure at 9 A.M. We have just enough time to sleep that we may not be hungover.

Except that five minutes after everyone leaves, Jason is back in my room. He pins me against the wall just outside the bathroom, and I melt into him for the millionth time. How does this still feel so urgent, so necessary?

"Wait," I tell him as he starts to pick me up. "I really need to pee."

"Okay," he says, not moving.

I go into the bathroom and close the door, but I still get bathroom stage fright. I can't pee so close to the guy I'm in love with, even if there is a door separating us. But then Jason pushes open the door and comes into the bathroom.

"What are you doing?" I ask.

"What's more intimate than being able to pee in front of someone?" he says.

Intimate. Watching someone pee is definitely intimate. Washing someone's hair is intimate. Sleeping with someone, at least for me, is intimate. Sharing a secret, for years, is intimate. It's all devastatingly intimate. I sit down on the toilet, but instead of peeing, I start crying.

Jason, confused, kneels in front of me, asks what's wrong, but I can't speak.

"Beck, come on, talk to me."

I keep opening my mouth but I'm sobbing too hard, all the memories gushing back—of Sam, of the Wagoneer, of Skye on the Vineyard, of the months we don't talk and the nights we don't sleep. The way I've felt about this man for so long. What I have broken for him, given up for him, lost for him. Before I can tell myself not to say it, I say it.

"Please don't hurt me again."

And now he is on his feet, towering over me, yelling at me that he never wanted to hurt me, that this is all so royally fucked up, that I can't keep doing this to myself, that he isn't leaving Brooke and I need to get that through my head, that he doesn't like hurting me, that he doesn't like being the bad guy I make him out to be, that he has no self-control, and that he is going to leave because this is more than he wants and more than he asked for.

After he leaves, I look in the mirror, all black mascara and drunk zombie eyes. The girl looking back at me is a pathetic nobody who stands for nothing, who lies to cover the lies, who will never be as wealthy as Brooke, as skinny as Skye, as appealing as the next attractive stranger.

I want to call Shilpa or Hope but I know I can't. My friends' loyalty, their noble honesty, only highlights my own deception. How many times have I lied to them, have I avoided their texts and ignored their calls as I chased Jason down a dead-end hall. I deserve to be alone. I've botched this too often to keep track. This shit is on me. It isn't love when you have to lie to all your friends. It isn't love when you go through bottles of Visine on the road because every time he leaves angry you cry yourself to sleep and wake up bloodshot. It isn't love if he makes you hate yourself.

THE NEXT MORNING, I MEET UP WITH HOPE, TESS, AND AMELIA FOR breakfast. After a run and a shower, I almost seem like a normal person. I just need to get through two more events, one flight home, and then I'll have the weekend to recover. I can't think about last night without wincing.

"You guys missed a fun time!" Amelia tells Tess and Hope.

"Oh yeah?" Tess says. "A little too fun, Beck?"

I nod, chugging a paper carton of chocolate milk and envying my friends with their full nights of sleep, their unfractured hearts, their focus on what actually matters. "I've got to go find Advil," I tell the group, pushing back my chair and standing up. My eyelids sting—maybe from the crying, or the not sleeping. Probably both.

"I have some in my bag," Amelia offers. "Come with me up to my room."

When we're safely in her room and I'm chasing three Advil with the rest of my chocolate milk, Amelia sits me down on the bed.

"Jason hit on me last night," she says, staring at me. "I'm so glad you stopped messing around with him when you did. He's pathetic."

Antifreeze runs through my veins as I make myself nod. I am stunned. But why wouldn't Jason hit on Amelia? She's gorgeous and cool and smart and funny. She was also one of two women at the club last night, and I was a given. She was the challenge. I wonder if he only came back to my room after trying to walk Amelia to hers.

"While you were dancing, he kept asking me if I was serious about my boyfriend," Amelia says, disgusted. "And the worst part?"

I look at her.

"He was saying the cheesiest shit," she says, "like, lines that high schoolers would be embarrassed to use." Amelia is pissed, indignant. She's in full-blown big sister mode. I've let her down more than I can fathom. That shame I've hidden in the back, out of sight, is now curdling inside my chest, souring in my stomach. I'm going to puke.

"What did he say?" I muster.

"Get this," Amelia says, glaring at the memory. "He leaned in to me and whispered, 'I've had such a crush on you.'"

WHEN WE RETURN TO THE WHITE HOUSE, I CONFRONT JASON ON WEST Exec. If I had consulted anyone first, they would have asked what I hoped to achieve. But I've used up all my credit with my friends. I've maxed them all out. I could confide in Tess, but protecting her from all of this drama is the only shred of dignity I have left. I won't tell Tess.

But I'm not thinking of strategy or dignity when I see Jason unlocking the Wagoneer at the end of the day. Visceral pain leads me across West Exec to his side. I want him to know that I know. I want him to tell me it was all a gross miscommunication. I want him to tell me that he's sorry, that he loves me, and somehow make everything right, turn all the lies I've told my friends into truths, like a magician.

"She's a bad friend for telling you about that," he says.

The argument throws me on my heels. I touch my gold alligator necklace to ground me.

"You're a bad guy for hitting on my friend!" I bite back. Two young women from the press office walk by, but neither of us looks over. It's twilight on West Exec, and we are just friends catching up after yet another trip, never mind the intense eye contact, never mind the fact that people will talk. Jason makes my world small, my concerns narrow. Let them talk—I care only about what Jason has to say.

He shrugs. "I was drunk. And besides," he says, "I do like Amelia. Why wouldn't I?"

He stares at me intently, daring me to say what we both know—that he wouldn't like Amelia if he liked me.

"Why would she want to hurt your feelings like that?" Jason asks, his head cocked to the side. "Now I'm mad at her."

"You shouldn't be mad at her," I tell him, my chest tightening. *Fuck. How did he just flip this? I've just thrown her under the bus, and for what?*

"I'm actually really, *really* mad at her," Jason growls.

Up until now, I'd betrayed my friends by lying to them. But this is different. This is terrifying. "I never want to hurt you—I go out of my way not to hurt you," he says, opening the Wagoneer door and tossing his bag into the passenger seat. This strikes me as untrue, but I don't say anything. "I care about you, Beck, and it seems to me Amelia just made you feel like shit for no reason. I went to your room last night, not hers."

I wonder if he thinks this mental jujitsu is working on me. He's the one who hurts me, not Amelia. So why the hell am I standing here telling him? What did I expect? Crackheads have more self-control than I do.

Jason drives away. I felt like absolute garbage this morning, but now I feel exponentially worse. This will catch up with me. Jason is going to be mean to Amelia on the road. He's going to make her job difficult, only because she'd watched out for me the way a big sister would.

"What's up?" Shilpa asks when I get home.

But I don't tell her what I've done.

I don't tell anyone.

Lying in my bed that night, I look at the stacks of notebooks I've kept since starting this job and realize that my own life is in the margins. Sam and Jason take up most of the lines. Hope likes to say her work is only as good as she feels—when was the last time I felt sure of myself? Not high on Jason, but good about me? It's hard to recall.

AMAZING GRACE

June

THE DAY AFTER THE AFFORDABLE CARE ACT IS UPHELD, THE SAME DAY
that the Supreme Court rules in favor of marriage equality, we fly to
South Carolina so the president can deliver the eulogy for the Reverend Clementa Pinckney. The taste of this morning's Supreme Court
victory is mixed with the racially motivated terror that takes us to
Charleston. "It's like fifty steps forward, fifty steps back," Cole says
on the drive to Andrews.

We watch the president's Rose Garden remarks on Air Force
One. All eyes are on the television screen in the staff cabin. When
Congressman John Lewis boards the plane, his presence inspires an
immediate and palpable reverence. Senior staff approach him slowly,
this man who fought for so much, who famously said, "Get in trouble: good trouble, necessary trouble." Here is this man, continuing
to fight. More than fifty years after leading the March on Washing-

ton, John Lewis has boarded the first black president's plane as a United States congressman to attend the funeral of nine African Americans gunned down in their church.

Fifty steps forward, fifty steps back.

THE EVENT IS HELD AT THE COLLEGE OF CHARLESTON'S TD ARENA, SO IT doesn't immediately feel as though we're arriving at a sanctuary and entering a funeral. The floors are poured concrete, the cinder-block halls are painted a garish red and white. The staff hold is an athletic office. This is an especially sensitive site to navigate—not only are there four principals here, the president, vice president, and First and Second Ladies, but also the surviving victims and families of victims.

While most staffers sit in the athletic office during the service, I decide I need to see this. I don't want to sit in a room at a safe distance from the pain. Nine people were killed out of blind hatred. I need to be here, in church, honoring their lives, not backstage, unscathed by the tragedy that brought us here.

I walk halfway around the arena and then out of the secure area to the main entrance and up the stairs to the balcony. The stage is across from me, and the purple-robed gospel choir are up on their feet, about to sing. To the left of the choir is a white sign that says in bold black letters WRONG CHURCH! WRONG PEOPLE! WRONG DAY! Directly below the stage, below the lectern, is the Reverend Pinckney's dark wood casket. Several figures are acknowledged—the Reverend Al Sharpton, the Reverend Jesse Jackson, the King family. Each of them rises and waves to the crowd, and the applause is deafening, loving, reverberating off the arena walls. And then a man at the lectern begins to sing, and soon everyone is on their feet, and six thousand voices join in unison.

Halfway through the song, a woman enters the arena followed by two girls in white dresses with white ribbons in their hair. The smaller girl wears a light pink cardigan over her dress. Mrs. Pinckney and her daughters. I watch them as they walk, and despite all the singing—all the lights—all the energy—all I can think of is, *Who thought to pack that pink cardigan so that little girl wouldn't be cold at her father's funeral?*

Right behind the Pinckneys are the president of the United States, and the First Lady, and the vice president, and the Second Lady. The arena seems to see them all at once as they walk across the front row, and the place cracks open like a rain cloud. Thunderous applause rolls in and ricochets while the president joins in, swaying and clapping to the singing wholeheartedly, as though he is home. The crowd sees and feels his energy, which reinvigorates their own—the volume swells as the organ builds and the clapping crescendos, as old women and little boys smile and sway.

Remember this. The stadium alive, vibrant, beating. We're no longer in an arena. We're in a sanctuary. We're in church.

When the president stands up to deliver his remarks, he hugs the men and women in their purple robes sitting on the stage. It is no accident that his tie matches their robes. As he begins, I watch the backs of the heads of the little girls in the front row.

"What a good man. Sometimes I think that's the best thing to hope for when you're eulogized—after all the words and recitations and résumés are read, to just say someone was a good man." Just like Tom Sawyer listening from the rafters, I hope the Reverend Clementa Pinckney and the eight other victims can hear the president speak of them, of their grace, their "reservoir of love," their "open hearts."

It is not a sad service. There is strength and hope. There is community, forgiveness, and compassion. "Justice grows out of recognition of ourselves in each other," the president says, as applause and "Amens" punctuate the eulogy.

After speaking for more than thirty minutes, the president lowers his eyes. It seems at first as if he is just looking for his next line from his notebook, not summoning an E flat from his core. "Amazing grace," he begins to sing, and behind him, the robed men's and women's faces light up in shock and joy. From across the sanctuary, his voice stirs such a disorienting visceral reaction—chills and electricity all at once, a dizzying pride as I think, *That's our president.* As six thousand people stand and sing an old slave song with humility and pride. With sorrow and strength. With one voice. *And grace will lead us home.*

People leave immediately after the president's remarks, a clatter of shined shoes and kitten heels racing down the stairs to the parking lot. I join them but duck left at the bottom of the steps, where a man with a clerical collar holds the door open and tells me to have a blessed day. I head to the athletic office to talk to others about the speech, and through the window to the hallway we see blurs of people being escorted backstage, and the profile of the president and his entourage as he is ferried from one room to another. He meets with the family members of Walter Scott, shot in April by a North Charleston police officer during a routine traffic stop, before going into seven rooms of surviving Emanuel AME Church shooting victims and families of victims. Cole had brought White House yo-yos and M&M's with him for the kids. I think back to Newtown, when there were so many families that they were spread out throughout the school—in the band room, in the gym, in classrooms.

The snack on the flight back to Washington is baked macaroni and cheese—comfort food. POTUS walks through the cabin but doesn't look at anyone, doesn't pause to say hello. If we are emotionally exhausted, he is drained. I can't help but think he saw Sasha and Malia in those two little girls wearing white dresses.

When we land back at Andrews, I wait for Noah and Cole in the parking lot when a Nissan SUV stops to let me cross. In the passenger seat is Congressman Lewis. He rolls down his window and gives me a warm smile. As his driver releases the brake and the congressman heads home after a historic day, his eyes do not sparkle with pride or triumph, nor are they dulled by exhaustion or sorrow. John Lewis's eyes shine steadily at me. Good trouble and grace.

GO
TOWARD
THE GOOD

July

"SO, I DON'T WANT YOU TO FEEL LIKE I'M ABANDONING YOU," SHILPA begins slowly as we sit on the front stoop of our Swann Street house one Saturday morning, iced coffees in hand.

"This cannot possibly be good," I say, sucking in my breath.

"I'm moving out," Shilpa says evenly, "but only because I'm going back to law school in the fall."

"Everything is ending," I sigh, putting my arm around her.

We watch the beagle brother puppies across the street. They're actually not puppies anymore, but they were when we first moved in together. They're still excitable, all floppy ears and happy tails.

Shilpa's departure announcement starts the slow roll of such announcements throughout the White House, and it signals a shift in priorities. It's hard not to feel that people are jumping ship, but the sad fact is that senior year will end, and life will go on. We'll have to figure out our futures, so better to do it sooner rather than later. We've got only eighteen months left to ride the president's coattails before we get kicked out of "the rental," as POTUS jokingly calls the White House during backyard DNC fundraisers.

Meanwhile, the president plows ahead with his agenda as June melts into July. And in the wee hours of the morning of July 14, the United States finally brokers a nuclear deal with Iran. Ernie Moniz, a nuclear physicist and the current secretary of energy, whom POTUS regularly calls a genius, has led the negotiations. As a thank-you to Secretary Moniz, POTUS invites him to fly on Air Force One.

The next morning, July 15, we fly to Oklahoma City. I see Secretary Moniz in the guest cabin before takeoff and realize I'm star-struck. When did this happen? When did I become such a Washington nerd that the secretary of energy has my heart all aflutter?

"Do you realize," I whisper to Shilpa, who is printing out the president's memos in the staff cabin, "that Secretary Moniz had to broker a nuclear deal with Iran before flying on Air Force One, and we get to come on here all the time, even though, between the two of us, we probably have half as many brain cells as he does?"

"Half?" Shilpa says. "That's far too generous. I'd say a third at best. But yeah, B, news flash, we're really, really lucky." And with that, she slams the senile printer with her fist. Tess has a line about technology on the plane: "Air Force One, where the flight is fast, the food is great, and the Internet is so goddamn fucking slow."

It's Shilpa's last trip before she leaves the White House. She'll drive away from D.C. in a couple of weeks, and I will be a mess. I'll send her pictures of potential outfits and ask if they're okay. When Shilpa says she misses traveling with POTUS, I'll write up horror stories about the Rattler, just so she remembers how lousy work can be. But this is all in the future. For now, I still have Shilpa by my side as we fly on Air Force One together one last time.

We land in Oklahoma for the president to deliver remarks about the ConnectHome Initiative to tribal leaders of Indian Country in the Durant High School gym, which is on a Choctaw reservation. During a conference call I covered yesterday to preview this trip, I learned about the president's plan to make sure everyone has access to high-speed broadband Internet. A reporter from the Choctaw Nation called in and asked what the feeling was in the administration, because the reservation was buzzing with excitement and pride— "so I'm just wondering about the energy within the administration— this incredible, incredible administration," he had said, with a reverence and gratitude not often heard on press calls.

These kids live out past the electric lines. High-speed Internet is one more luxury I've taken for granted—the president isn't talking about free wifi in airports; he's shining a spotlight on the fact that way too many students in rural America do not have access to the Internet from their home. How can you be expected to apply for scholarships for college, if you can't even go online to download the application?

Before he takes the stage in the auditorium, POTUS meets with Native American teenagers to hear about their struggles and dreams. The press never has access to such closed-door meetings, because the president wants them to be a true conversation, not a photo op. But POTUS is the best in these situations. His humanity, his core decency, burns brightest when he is sitting in a circle of metal folding chairs, surrounded by nervous kids wearing beat-up sneakers. I wish everyone could see it.

The president is slated to spend thirty minutes with the high school students, but I know he'll spend closer to an hour with them. So I head to the gym, where I find a basketball and shoot around to pass the time. Teddy and Noah walk through on their way to smoke, and we play a few rounds of Pig before their nicotine cravings get the best of them. Shilpa and Eliza, a senior staffer, cut through and stop when they see me.

"I didn't know you were a basketball player," Eliza says. Despite having a thankless, stressful job in National Security and being a wife and mother of three, Eliza always makes time to say hello. I'm about to answer when Eliza's phone rings. Her phone rings a lot.

"Hi, honey," she answers. I assume it's not the Joint Chiefs.

"Oh, I'm in Oklahoma, in a gym, hanging out with my two friends Shilpa and Beck."

I grin as I watch Shilpa's eyes grow big. We're thinking the same thing. When Eliza walks out of the gym on the phone, Shilpa blurts out, "Did you hear that?!"

"She called us her friends!"

"I can't believe it!"

"Friends! Like, we're cool enough to be friends with Eliza!"

There are the Vagiants, and then there are the Elizas, who are in the government for the right reasons and who are confident enough in their own abilities to want to mentor the next generation. The beautiful thing about the Obama administration is that the longer I'm here, the more female mentors I discover, and the Vagiants seem to matter less and less.

When I see the Rattler these days, I remind myself to feel sorry for her. It must be hard to be so angry all the time, and probably not that awesome. But Pathahad is awesome, and so are Shilpa and Eliza. You will not find a warmer, funnier person who loves her children more than Susan Rice. That's the thing about Eliza and Susan Rice, and several other women involved in National Security: They don't mind being the unsung heroes, because this isn't about ego or personal perks for them. They joined the bubble to protect and fight for a better world for their kids.

That night, Shilpa and I head out to an empty bar in Oklahoma City to commemorate her last trip before law school. We toast to the best adventures, to the dance parties we threw on Swann Street, to the times we accidentally wore the exact same outfit. We laugh as we do impressions of Teddy at our Valentine's Day party, when we'd run out of wood and convinced him to break my bed slats over his knee so we could keep the fire pit going. The bed slats had won, but not before Teddy had let out an impressive coyote howl of pain.

When we walk back to the hotel and say good night, I ignore a message from Jason, who continues to send out feelers whenever we're on the road. I set my alarm and put my phone on airplane mode. I've stayed away from him since Miami, because I've finally realized the bottom of the Pacific Ocean is just a romantic euphemism for drowning.

In the same week that the president commutes forty-six nonviolent drug offenders, we motorcade to El Reno Federal Correctional

Institution. POTUS is the first sitting president to visit a prison. We are instructed to leave our personal phones in the vans; no photographs while we're here. It's a beautiful, cloudless day as we walk through gates topped with huge silver spirals of barbed wire.

The first event is a roundtable discussion with six inmates. Shane Smith and a crew from *Vice* meet us at the prison; they're doing a special on the criminal justice system that coincides with the president's commutations. As I set up my equipment behind the *Vice* camera monitors, I look at the prisoners: five relatively young men of color and one older white man. They wear tan jumpsuits and sit in a semicircle. The president opens up the discussion with the question, "What can we do to help the next generation not end up here?" Each inmate started doing drugs before age thirteen, but every man in a tan jumpsuit takes responsibility for his conviction— selling drugs, conspiracy to sell drugs.

POTUS talks about the mistakes he made as a younger man, and how he was lucky enough to grow up in an environment where he could afford to mess up without suffering life-altering consequences. The men lean in, watching him carefully, this fifty-four-year-old black man, free man, most powerful man, sitting on a chair in the middle of their prison block, Secret Service agents eyeing them from every corner.

When the roundtable wraps, senior staff who had been told to wait outside suddenly flood the room, and I realize that only a handful of people got to see what I just witnessed. As I collect my gear, POTUS offers to take a photo with the inmates. I wonder whether and how these men will get these photos—mailed to them? Immediately? Upon their release?

After a tour of an empty prison block, POTUS addresses the press pool. He sticks to the talking points that the speechwriting team sent out this morning, but as he wraps, reporters yell out questions as they often do.

"What's been most striking to you?" a journalist asks.

"These are young people who made mistakes that aren't that different than the mistakes that I made and the mistakes that a lot of you guys made," POTUS says. "That's what strikes me. 'There but for the grace of God.'"

We follow POTUS out of the prison building and across the green to the idling motorcade. We don't see the cafeteria, the gym, the men in their cells, or the huge building for solitary confinement. We leave nothing behind but echoes and stories that will get passed around like a well-worn basketball. Stories that will circulate for days, months, years: The president was here. He sat right over there, in a chair, in the middle of the hallway, in cell block 8. He shook my hand and said, "Good to meet you." His shoes were black and well shined. He looked me in the eye and listened to my story, my ideas for change, about protecting the next generation. He was kind. He was sympathetic. His suit fit him perfectly. His hands were smooth but his handshake was firm. I could see us getting along at a backyard cookout, you know? He made a joke and we all laughed together, like we were all just hanging out, like what we were doing was the most normal thing in the world.

Before I get into the Press 1 van, I look up at the cloudless sky. Today, forgotten voices spoke truth to power. Today, power heard what victims of a broken system had to say. Today, I witnessed a world leader take a backseat to other people's stories. Today, we saw ourselves in the faces of strangers. Today, "Only by the grace of God go I." Today, we got the paragraph right.

Driving away from the prison, I watch a blur of green fields whiz before and behind me. I embrace the silence, and then the voices around me, then the whir of the air conditioner, the soft click of BlackBerry buttons. I have a text sitting in my phone from Jason. I ignore it. My work is only as good as I feel.

SWANN
SONG

August–September

I'VE NEVER BEEN GOOD AT GOODBYES, AND I'VE BEEN ON SWANN STREET, in the same bedroom, for four years. I know which creaky floorboards to avoid in the morning, the best burner on the stove top, and that Nell next door will always let me borrow her snow shovel. My D.C. life is in that Swann Street house; it's where everything important has happened.

Shilpa and I take several coffee breaks to reminisce as we pack. Megan Rooney, a White House speechwriter I don't know very well, has offered her apartment because she is part of the mass exodus leaving D.C. at the end of the summer. When Megan moves to Brooklyn for the Hillary campaign, and Shilpa moves to North Carolina for law school, I'll move to Megan's condo in Adams Morgan. It's not even a half mile from Swann Street, but it feels a world away.

Megan's apartment is devoid of the Swann Street memories and ghosts. It's a fifth-floor two-bedroom that's much nicer than anything I'm used to, with killer sunset views and a basketball court across the street. I wish everything could stay the same, but Hope reminds me, as she drops off more boxes, that change is the only constant. Megan will be my roommate over the summer—she won't move to Brooklyn until August—and I'm nervous to live with her. We don't know each other that well, and I'll be living on her turf. I'm nervous like Grover in *Grover Sleeps Over*—what if Megan tells scary ghost stories or doesn't like Monsterberry Crunch? What if we don't get along? What if she hates me?

"You and Megan will get along great," Shilpa says, reading my thoughts as we sort through piles of clothes in the living room. She's bought into Marie Kondo's *The Life-Changing Magic of Tidying Up* and is determined to get rid of everything she doesn't wear before moving to North Carolina. As part of the process of decluttering, we touch every item that we own, and if it doesn't "spark joy," we chuck it. I'm trying to follow Shilpa's lead, but I'm struggling to toss anything away.

"I'm such a hoarder," I whine. Shilpa's giveaway pile is three feet high. I sacrificed one soccer jersey and then took it back. I played some good games in that shirt.

"I can't say I'm surprised," Shilpa teases. "You get attached so easily, like everything has a story."

"But everything *does* have a story."

"Right, and you lived it already, and now you're supposed to move on from the story if it's not adding to your life anymore."

Jesus—are we talking about my four Dr. Dog T-shirts or my love life? We fall silent. We haven't talked about Jason in a long time, our own version of Don't Ask, Don't Tell, even though POTUS repealed that shit because it's a dumb rule.

Since Shilpa is leaving, maybe I can confide in her again, the way I did in the beginning. But maybe her whole point is that Jason was a story, and now he shouldn't be. Shilpa is trying to simplify and streamline her life, so I'm not going to bother her with my mess. Instead, I think about the life-changing magic of tidying up. If Jason were hanging in my closet right now and I touched him, could I honestly say he brings me joy?

"I know you're nervous about moving to Megan's, but it's going to be great, B," Shilpa says, chucking a black sweater into the give-away pile. "It's different, but I think you need different," Shilpa adds. "I think we're all in desperate need of a fresh start, a new story."

Shilpa is right—Megan and I bond as soon as I walk in the door. She's funny and compassionate and so entirely different from the D.C. creatures. We talk and laugh, and she sprinkles words of wisdom wherever she goes. "Just because I work in the bubble doesn't make me cool," she says one evening after cocktails. "The president makes it cool. The whole operation makes it cool. But you and me"—she looks at me—"we're cogs. And we're easily replaceable."

"Fine," I tell Megan, "we're replaceable cogs."

She nods victoriously.

"But we're *cool* replaceable cogs!"

It's so much fun living with Megan that when she leaves to work on the Hillary campaign, I hit a new low.

Her absence hits me like a punch. Sam is gone, Shilpa is gone, all my college friends have moved on, and now Megan. Even Jon Stewart has abandoned me—he leaves *The Daily Show* in August. In the few short months we lived together, Megan and I bonded over so many things—*Freaks and Geeks*, Joe Biden jokes, $10.99 Malbec, our favorite POTUS moments, and boys who broke our hearts. Megan encouraged me to send her my writing, and I forced her to get a new pair of sneakers. Megan made fun of my junk cereal collection until I caught her pouring herself French Toast Crunch and forced her to admit it's bliss in a bowl.

I don't want a boyfriend, but I need a companion—someone who will listen to me, or at least sound the alarm if I slip in the tub and break my neck. The lightbulb finally goes off one morning when I walk by the S Street dog park.

"No," my mom says on the phone. "You can't afford a dog walker every day, let alone with all the travel." I look up prices in D.C., and yep, not for the first time, my mom is one hundred percent right. No way can I afford a dog. So . . . a cat?

I get the dog of cats, a fourteen-pound Maine Coon I name Bodhi after the Patrick Swayze character in *Point Break*. Bodhi is such a dog-cat that he cries when I leave in the morning and runs to the front door when I get home. My misery doubles as I realize my cat is miserable. He's so lonely. So then I get my cat a kitten, Mary Jane.

"Wow, you have two cats," Cole says over dinner. "You just increased your feline assets by two hundred percent and decreased your desirability as a single female by two million percent."

I learn from Facebook that Sam gets a dog the same week I get Mary Jane. We've replaced each other with quadrupeds. And then I freak out because now I have *cats* and I'm *single* and turning thirty in nine months and *Holy hell, what will become of me?*

My sister comes down to visit and forces me to join Bumble. I go on a date, ever so reluctantly, with a guy who has a severe Napoleon complex and, I assume, undiagnosed dyslexia, since his profile said six foot four and he comes up to my chin. Mostly I just swipe left, eat Cookie Crisp for dinner, get depressed, open another can of cat food, clean the litterboxes. My sister texts to ask if I'm Bumbling, so I force myself to do ten swipes at a time, the way other people force themselves to do ten push-ups.

Jason finds me on West Exec a few weeks after the leaves start turning, and I tell him I figured out that the secret to happiness is not to have any expectations, and that way I won't be disappointed. He gets cutesy and says, "Right?" like I've cracked the code to a successful relationship. But instead I explain that since I can't have expectations, I can't mess around with him anymore. Seriously. I'd rather just hang out with my cats. Bodhi and Mary Jane may be apathetic, but at least they're consistent. And they spark joy, which is more than I can say about Jason these days. I must be getting older.

Jason bends down and gives me a rib-clunking hug. He picks me up so my feet leave the ground, but I keep my head level. Thanks to Marie Kondo, I realize Jason brings me about as much joy as that expensive but ugly jacket that Shilpa helped me finally get rid of. At some point, it doesn't matter what you paid or how much you invested if it makes you look and feel like the last bag of potatoes at the county fair. As Jason holds me, I let him go.

SINGLES, DOUBLES, AND STRIKEOUTS

November

"WHAT'S UP WITH HIM?" AMELIA WHISPERS TO ME AFTER WE PASS Jason in the hotel lobby. We're in Manila, speedwalking to the president's press conference with President Aquino. Amelia had greeted Jason, and he'd given her a blank stare.

"No idea," I say, feeling sick to my stomach. Jason has been cold to Amelia ever since Noah's birthday in Miami. I don't have the guts to tell her I confronted him about hitting on her, because that would mean admitting not only that I gave in to the sparkle vampire but also that I betrayed her trust. The sour stink grows more potent with every little lie I tell.

Before Amelia says anything else, we push through the double doors into the press conference, where the air is buzzing. Last night, GOP presidential candidate Donald Trump had tweeted, "Refugees from Syria are now pouring into our great country. Who knows who they are—some could be ISIS. Is our president insane?" This comes on the heels of GOP pushback about President Obama's plan to allow ten thousand Syrian refugees into the United States.

When Ed Henry of Fox News questions the president about looking "strong" in his foreign policy strategy, the president's eyes darken, his jaw tightens, and he calls Ed by his name. These are the telltale signs that POTUS is quietly enraged and disgusted.

He explains that looking strong interests him less than protecting the American people as their commander in chief. POTUS won't say his name, but he is responding to Donald Trump's tweet. "And that may not always be sexy," POTUS continues, clearly revved up. "But it avoids errors. You hit singles, you hit doubles; every once in a while we may be able to hit a home run. But we steadily advance the interests of the American people and our partnership with folks around the world."

It's November 2015. Fuck Trump—this time next year, he will have lost the election and ridden back up his stupid gold escalator, gripping the sides with his tiny white-knuckled hands because he's terrified of stairs. He will never be heard from again except when he tweets about Kristen Stewart's love life. He will disappear, and the world will be better for it.

WEEKS LATER, I AM WALKING OUT OF THE CVS ACROSS FROM THE EEOB when I get a text from Amelia, who is with POTUS in Louisiana for a day trip. "I figured out why Jason has been so cold to me . . ." is all it says.

I stop in my tracks. I wait for those three dots to give way to more information. And then, like a levee breaking, Amelia unleashes a flood of anger. She writes full paragraphs, documenting what happened back on the Vineyard, and in Miami, and what must have taken place between Jason and me. Line after line, her words burn my hands and make my eyes well. I am frozen. I just watch the messages pour in. I type, "I'm sorry" and "Let me explain," but Amelia doesn't want to hear it and tells me as much. I'm too late. She knows exactly who I am. A sneak. A liar. A weakling. A D.C. creature.

Amelia goes on and on, and I stand there in the middle of the G Street sidewalk letting the tears fall. I imagine her typing as she rides in the motorcade, surrounded by people who have no idea that pain and hot fury are pulsing through her. And finally the messages stop, and I am left with the very last one staring me down like a bull provoked. I cannot look away, I cannot unsee the words. Even when I'm up in my office, back at my desk, typing up the president's remarks, I see only Amelia's final truth: "You betrayed me."

She's right about everything. I'm exactly what she says I am.

Before the sun comes up the next morning, I sit down at my computer and write her an email. I apologize profusely and I don't try to make excuses. I messed up. There are consequences to bad behavior. Amelia doesn't write back that day, or the next day, or the day after that.

This is what I deserve, I think. *This is all my doing.* As the first snowfall descends upon D.C., I feel winter settle into my bones.

WE
WILL
NOT BE
TERRORIZED

December

I'M IN MY OFFICE WHEN I HEAR, AND IT'S A BIT LIKE DÉJÀ VU FROM Newtown, and from the Boston bombing, and from Charleston. Lisa gets a news alert on her phone and we turn on the TV to see a flood of images coming in from San Bernardino. With fourteen victims, this is the deadliest attack since Newtown, and the worst terrorist attack on American soil since 9/11. But now I'm colder, more jaded. "Will it ever stop?" Peggy asks. I want to tell her no, it won't, but I keep my mouth shut.

In the silo of the stenographers' office, not much changes. I keep an eye on my White House email, knowing the press office will send out an updated guidance, maybe an announcement about the president delivering a statement. It's still too early to tell.

In the West Wing, however, staffers try to keep the swirl at a minimum. There is protocol, there is order, there are procedural steps.

Phone calls are made, memos are sent, remarks are drafted. In the Oval Office, the president receives a briefing on the ongoing investigation from FBI Director Comey, Attorney General Lynch, Homeland Security Secretary Johnson, and his intelligence leadership. The homegrown terrorists, a couple who left their six-month-old daughter with her grandparents, will be dead in a few hours, following a shootout with police. But that's not yet. Right now, we wait.

In the days to come, the schedule and advance teams scramble so the president can visit San Bernardino and meet with survivors of the shooting and the families of the victims. This has happened too many times before. The frenzy is organized, eerily familiar. There is protocol.

And once again, before traveling across the country to console victims of gun violence, the president asks Congress for their help. In his weekly address, POTUS calls on Congress to close a loophole that allows people on the no-fly list to purchase a gun. As it stands, you can be on the FBI's terrorist watch list and still legally buy an AR-15. The San Bernardino killer used military-style assault rifles to murder as many innocents as possible. "If you're too dangerous to board a plane," POTUS says in the video, "you're too dangerous, by definition, to buy a gun."

The president's anger treads just below the surface, as if he already knows Congress will reject this effort. Protecting American lives should be a bipartisan issue, but the Republicans in Congress refuse to support the president on any measure, regardless of how many children are killed, parents murdered, families destroyed. "We are strong and we are resilient," POTUS says, "and we will not be terrorized."

At the end of the day, as I walk through Lafayette Park on my way home, I pass a dozen preschoolers on a walk with their daycare teachers, each tiny kid holding on to a communal rope as a way of sticking together. They are three and four years old. They totter as they walk, their eyes big and bright, their limbs soft, their baby teeth still years away from growing loose. It's been three years since Newtown. Nothing has changed.

While POTUS and the team fly to Hawaii, I go home to Philadelphia to lick my wounds. I'm lonely. I miss talking to Sam. I miss my friends. Amelia isn't speaking to me. How did I screw everything up so badly?

The night before Christmas Eve, my brother and sister and I pile into our ancient Wagoneer to pick up a pizza while my mom makes a salad and my dad builds a fire. Zach blasts the Staple Singers and Caroline adjusts the bass levels accordingly.

The three of us sing along with the windows down and the volume up: "If you don't respect yourself, ain't nobody gonna give a good cahoot, na na na na." Driving through the familiar streets of my hometown with my siblings, I dance in my seat to make my sister laugh, and I sing a little louder.

Before we'd parted ways for the holidays, Hope had pulled me aside and said, "You deserve the best; you deserve love." I'd shrugged her off. *Anyone at the White House will tell you Jason is the best,* I'd thought. But now, far from D.C., in the family Wagoneer, with a piping hot extra-large pizza on my lap, surrounded by my siblings and the Staple Singers, Jason doesn't matter. He wouldn't fit in here, and his power doesn't exist here.

David Foster Wallace wrote that freedom means "being able truly to care about other people and to sacrifice for them, over and over, in myriad petty little unsexy ways, every day." I may have betrayed Sam, and Amelia, and fallen for a false idol, but I am still good at caring about other people and sacrificing for them. How many times have I helped out Zach and Caroline? How often have I come through for my friends? I show up. I listen. I sacrifice in unsexy ways.

I am good at love. *Actually,* I realize as we pull back into the driveway, *I am* great *at love.* I have been a shitbag, but I can be better. I *will* be better. And even right now, when everything is so screwed up, I am still worthy of happiness.

Hope is right: I deserve the best.

And so is Mavis: If you want anybody to give a good cahoot, respect yourself.

Act V
2016–
2017

Clear-eyed. Big-hearted. Optimistic that unarmed truth and unconditional love will have the final word. That's what makes me so hopeful about our future. Because of you. I believe in you.

PRESIDENT BARACK OBAMA,
STATE OF THE UNION ADDRESS, 2016

DON'T BLOW IT

January

IF INTERESTING STUFF HAPPENS IN THE FOURTH QUARTER, STRAIGHT-UP crazy shit is bound to occur in the final minutes of the game. We're running a full-court press with a mix of seasoned starters and fresh legs, determined to run up the score while we still have time on the clock.

It's easy to get caught up in the game—until one cold morning in January when I see Amelia walking on West Exec. Perhaps the only thing more painful than seeing an ex-boyfriend at work is seeing a friend you betrayed. Amelia sees me, but she doesn't wave.

When I get to my desk, I do a double take. Amelia has sent me a text: "Can we talk?"

That evening, we meet across from the North Gates in Lafayette Park on the winding brick path. "Amelia, I'm so sorry," I blurt out as I walk toward her. I try to slow down, try not to sound so desperate.

"I know that you need more than an apology, but I'm really, really sorry."

"I know you're sorry. I read your email more than once," Amelia says. "I need to know that I can trust you. If we're going to be friends, I need to know you will never do that ever again."

"He and I are over," I tell her.

"That's not what I'm asking," Amelia says, stopping in her tracks to look at me. The thin winter sunlight catches Amelia's shiny brown hair, her almond eyes. Anger doesn't make her any less striking, although it does make her appear taller—I feel like she's towering over me. "I need to know from you, Beck, that no matter what happens with Jason or anyone else, you will not betray me again. I need to know that you have my back, that you will not throw me under the bus professionally or personally ever again."

Her words hurt, but they're not untrue. In my attempt to show Jason what real friendship looked like, I'd sacrificed it. In my effort to highlight how spineless he was, I'd handed him my own backbone. I want to tell Amelia that it's hard to have her back when I don't even have my own, but I catch myself. I need to be tougher, better, stronger—if not for myself, then for Amelia.

"You can trust me," I tell her.

"Promise?" She stares at me fiercely, as if she can see through to the back of my skull.

"Yes." No one has called me out like this before. My eyes feel like pinpricks. The truth hurts.

"Okay, good," Amelia says definitively. "Now come here, I've missed you," she says, hugging me. "Tell me how you've been."

THE WEEK FOLLOWING THE STATE OF THE UNION, WE FLY TO NEBRASKA and then Louisiana. The president is doubling down on his vision for economic progress and curbing climate change. When we arrive at the hotel in Baton Rouge, I run into the boys in the lobby.

"We're buying Powerball tickets," Teddy says gleefully. "It's over a billion, kiddo. I hope after I win we can still be friends."

"Why wouldn't we be friends?"

Teddy runs to catch up with Jason, Noah, and Cole, who are already out the doors of the hotel. Over his shoulder he yells, "Mo' money, mo' problems!"

Pathahad is also on this trip, but they all have work to do. Not every overnight trip can be exciting. Besides, I'm exhausted. It looks like a tub/read/tuck-in-early kind of night.

I'm just getting out of the bath when there's a knock on the door. It's Hope and Layla, one of the new speechwriters.

"Want to go get a quick nightcap down at the bar?" Hope asks. Her long brown hair is down, waving its way past her shoulders—the ultimate sign that the workday is done.

The three of us find an empty green booth in the hotel bar, and soon Tess and Amelia join us. "I guess these magical get-togethers can only happen when we have absolutely no expectations," Tess says, shaking her head as she peels off her blazer and collapses next to me. Her hair still smells like the gardenia shampoo she uses. I put my arm around her, my bossy big sister.

"How you doin', hon?" she asks, leaning into me.

"Living the dream, Tess, just living the dream."

We've all changed into comfy clothes—jeans, loose-fitting shirts, and zip-up hoodies—except for Tess, who's still in her black suit, waiting for some memos from National Security, which means she might need to deliver more stuff to the president's suite before the night is over.

And even though Tess is the only one still expecting emails, we all have our work phones faceup on the table, just in case. It's not rude. It's work.

When Layla stops mid-sentence to see why her phone just lit up, Amelia effortlessly scoops up the conversation like a loose ball. These days we don't even notice the starts and stops, the "just one sec," the hurry-up-and-wait. Layla probably just got edits back for the remarks tomorrow and needs to respond immediately. We're here to serve POTUS, which means checking our phones religiously.

Tess and Amelia order red wine; Layla gets a Jameson neat; Hope orders her dirty martini with a twist; and I ask for a White Russian. I'm tired and want to stay for only one drink, but these are some seriously smart women squished into this booth, and one White Russian turns into two turns into three.

Layla asks us about other trips we've been on; this is her first overnighter. I'm appreciative she's here, because fresh blood always breathes new life into these late-night conversations, particularly when Pathahad is tired and stressed and a little grouchy. Plus, Amelia and I are still feeling each other out; only time will mend the wound I've inflicted. And opportunities to earn her trust. And nights like this—we need many more nights like this.

After the server delivers our third round, Layla asks, "So what's next for you guys?" We all groan but laugh and sigh and take big gulps from our glasses. It's a horrible question to ask—not unlike when you're a college senior and every man, woman, and child wants to know if you have a job yet. But this green booth is a safe space, even if the endless abyss of the rest of our lives is scary. It's no accident that Layla doesn't bring up "the afterlife" until our third cocktail. After all, she's in the same boat.

We talk about our fantasy lives after January 20, 2017—inauguration day—when the forty-fifth president will take the oath of office and POTUS, our POTUS, will take his final flight on Air Force One. It's hard to fathom. Tick Tock Croc is gaining on us.

Amelia talks about opening a B&B in Asheville. Hope wants to go on an international walkabout and take her time digesting the last eight years. Tess can't wait to get back into rock climbing and hiking and return to a career in sustainable agriculture.

When it's my turn to speak, I don't know what to say. I shrug and say, "I'll probably stay and see what it's like to work for the first female president." Unlike everyone else, the stenographers are not political appointees; my job carries over into the new administration. But everyone at this table knows I've grown antsy in my post as a stenographer, so I add, "I used to teach—I'll probably go back to that," and am ready to listen to Layla's big plans when Hope interrupts.

"Our dear friend Beck," Hope says, looking at Layla, "is a writer, but she has a hard time saying it."

"You write?" Layla's eyes grow large and she leans forward, across the table and over the graveyard of glasses. She is, after all, a speech-writer.

"Not really," I tell her. I barely know Layla and now she thinks I'm some dummy who thinks writing is easy and not a big deal.

"She writes," Hope says sturdily, now turning to look at me, "and it's a gift." I stare at my White Russian.

"So you write," Layla says definitively. I can't tell whether she's judging me or telling me.

"Kind of," I feel obligated to say, since everyone is waiting for my response.

"Listen," Layla says, "I swim in a shark tank of dicks all day, and if you were a guy, you'd say you were a writer, and that you were writing the next great American novel. If you write, you're a writer, and you should be proud of yourself."

I feel the pinpricks of tears behind my eyes. Here's a real writer, a professional who currently writes speeches for the president of the United States, telling me I'm good enough to do this thing, too, and that she supports me. It knocks the wind right out of me, like when you catch a basketball with your face and you can't help but cry.

Amelia can't stop laughing—"'A shark tank of dicks' is an amazing phrase," she says. Like Layla, Amelia is the only female in her office.

"We work in a crazy world," Tess says with a big smile, lifting her glass.

"And we're lucky to be part of it," Amelia says as we clink drinks.

BACK IN THE GAME

February–March

A BLIZZARD BLANKETS D.C., AND AFTER THREE DAYS ALONE WITH MY cats and many cups of coffee, I reactivate my Bumble account. Nothing like a little cabin fever to remind you how much more fun it would be to share the cabin. Soon enough I schedule a brunch date with a guy named Charlie who is tall and played water polo at the same college that Sam attended and graduated the same year as Sam. I think I have a type. I'm excited to meet Charlie but nervous to go to Pearl's Oyster Dive on Fourteenth Street; the last time I was there was with Sam.

I get to Pearl's first and a couple sits down at the next table—a real couple. You can tell they're rock solid: The man orders for both of them. There are no nerves between them, only understanding. I text Charlie, "We're next to a real couple—don't blow it!" Sam and I used to sit at bars and point out who was on dating-app dates, like the smug spoken-fors we were.

When Charlie shows up, I can't believe it: He actually looks like his profile picture, and he is as tall as he said he was, six foot six. I prefer my men somewhere between Shaq and Sasquatch size. After two hours and two rounds, we go back to his place, which is just down the street. On the walk there, Charlie puts his arm around me and makes sure he's walking on the outside, closer to the road. He takes my hand to cross Fourteenth Street.

We make out on his couch, and I leave midafternoon, still pretty drunk. On my walk home I text Pathahad. They want to meet him, want to know if he's a good kisser, if he's as tall and bearded as Sam; the answer is yes to all of the above. Then I text the guys to let them know that Becky is back in the game! Teddy wants details on this guy, Noah says phew, and Cole asks if I left room for Jesus. I giggle as I walk through the snowbanks left over from last week's blizzard.

I get home, drunkenly sing to my cats as I feed them, and feel better. As I chug a glass of water and reread Charlie's newest text about seeing me again, I think, *Oh, maybe this is why all this shitty stuff has happened. Now I get the good guy.*

Jason, of course, hears about Charlie through Teddy and starts texting. Suddenly he wants to drive me home, wants to take me to the movies, wants to go out to dinner—all the things I've been begging for, for years.

But I like Charlie. We work well together. He sneaks me notes, texts to ask how my day is going, sends me articles about rescued puppies living millionaire lifestyles. As in the beginning weeks of my relationship with Sam, Charlie is easy to be around. He feels as at home in a relationship as I do, and we quickly fall into the patterns of a well-worn couple.

On weekends, I wake up and go for runs while Charlie makes waffle batter. He heats up the waffle iron while I shower, so the smell of waffles wafts through the apartment as I get dressed and wonder how I got so lucky. I find I'm singing to myself again. On weekdays, I walk to work imagining flash mobs dancing on Pennsylvania Avenue again, just the way I did when I first started at the White House.

I barely see Jason, and when I do, he tries too hard. One time he tells me he loves me. Another time, he grabs my hand when we're sitting in the carpet vans, and I yank it away. I'm done with him.

The world is slowly righting itself, and I'm pleased to be living proof that being a cat lady and a desirable woman are, contrary to popular belief, not mutually exclusive.

I bump into Noah on West Exec and he's grinning.

"You ready for this?" he asks, teasing me.

"What!"

"Never mind. You'll get too excited."

"Just tell me!"

"We're going to Cuba," he says coolly, checking his BlackBerry.

Cuba! Cuba! Cuba! Cuba! Cuba!

Lisa did the last international trip, so I know this one will be mine. This is going to be amazing! And historic! And totally badass! Noah says they're putting a baseball game together between the Tampa Bay Rays and the Cuban National Team. I'm in the middle of a victory dance when my heart sinks: *Jason.*

Overseas trips are exciting but also exhausting, and I know Jason will try something. I don't want to screw this up with Charlie. I don't want to be worried about Jason when we're walking through the streets of Old Havana, so I do what I never thought I could do after years of telling lies. I tell Charlie the truth.

As we're lying in the dark one night, his arms draped around me—*God, he's such a good spooner*—I confess to Charlie about the past three years, how racked with guilt I've been, how excited I am about him, and how nervous I am to be around Jason for a week on the road, exploring Cuba and stressing out about the lack of Internet reception that renders my easy job suddenly impossible, while staying in the same hotel as the man whose spell I've fallen under too many times to count.

Charlie says he understands, he's been hung up on another girl (*um, what?*) he met on a surfing retreat in Costa Rica and dated for a while. I try not to get bothered about the surfer girl and remind myself that most people our age have baggage. We can use it to bond rather than let it pull us apart. Charlie holds me closer, kisses the top of my head, my cheeks, my neck. He does what Jason has never, ever done: He stays all night.

Telling Charlie the whole truth feels good. It's liberating. I'm not sticky with secrets. Mark Twain said, "If you tell the truth, you don't have to remember anything." Suddenly, without having to navigate the labyrinth of lies, I have space in my brain to write. I have more energy. I'm reading more and reaching out to old friends I've neglected. I tell my parents that I've officially kicked my Jason addiction once and for all, and I hear them breathe a sigh of relief from two hundred miles away. This relationship is nothing like the one with Jason. This is real. This is healthy.

THE DAY WE BOARD AIR FORCE ONE EN ROUTE TO CUBA, MY NAME CARD isn't in the window cup holder of my usual seat. Amelia and Tess are in their normal seats—Hope isn't on this trip because of a wedding—so they help me look.

"Don't worry, hon," Tess says, reading my face.

"Yeah," Amelia says, giving me a warm smile. "You're coming with us no matter what—you can share my seat if you have to!"

I laugh nervously.

"Hey, why don't you check the guest cabin?" Amelia suggests. "They've put me back there on occasion."

I tentatively enter the guest cabin, where Nancy Pelosi, Patrick Leahy, Jeff Flake, and Dick Durbin are getting situated at the nearest four-top. At the other four-top table are two name cards that both say Mrs. Robinson. I start to make my way back to the staff cabin when Matt the attendant, who knows my name and face, directs me back to the guest cabin and shows me that I'm sitting at the table with the two Robinson women, who've just arrived. I sit across from them and explain I'm the president's stenographer. As I'm shaking their hands I realize that I've seen the older woman before, and then I connect the dots: Rachel Robinson, the widow of Jackie Robinson. Her daughter, Sharon, is the other Robinson, and she immediately asks with genuine interest what a stenographer does. I like them right away.

We're on our way to Cuba with the first sitting U.S. president to visit the island in more than half a century. "This is pretty neat," Sharon says as we hear the wings whoosh. When the plane levels out, POTUS and FLOTUS come back to say hi, which they usually do when there are members of Congress on board. They greet the four of them, but FLOTUS just waves and then goes directly to Rachel and Sharon Robinson.

After POTUS and FLOTUS return to the front of the plane, I ask Mrs. Robinson if she's been to Cuba before. She nods and says '47. I ask her if she remembers anything about the trip and she shakes her head, says, "It was just a ball game back then."

The water below is turquoise as we begin our descent. We're all lined up at the windows, taking pictures with our phones. When I look up the aisle, to the front of the plane, I see POTUS and FLOTUS are watching out the windows, too, and farther up, Malia and Sasha are on the bench where the agents usually sit, taking photos with their phones.

We head off the plane, and the Robinsons head in a different direction. The MLB has arranged for a tour guide to take the Robinsons sightseeing—we won't meet up with them again until the baseball game.

It's pouring rain when we step out of the motorcade and into Old Havana, where the First Family is on a walking tour and the rest of the staffers trail behind them. My pink flats are so stretched out from the downpour that I can barely stay in them. We're all so excited to be here that nobody minds getting soaked as we make our way, but my shoes are done. It's like trying to keep soggy paper bags on my feet, so I take them off. I keep a safe distance behind the Rattler and the rest of the group so they don't see me, but of course the locals are watching this parade of government officials dressed in black pursued by a barefoot blonde holding hot-pink shoes in her hand, and they yell things in Spanish at me from their windows. I smile up at them with my mouth open and taste the rain. I'm in Cuba, walking barefoot through the streets of Old Havana, looking up.

THAT NIGHT, THE BOYS AND I MEET IN THE LOBBY TO GO OUT ON THE town.

"Teddy! Cuba looks good on you!"

"Cuba looks good on everyone!" he says, strutting toward me in a seersucker suit, ready to party, Havana-style. The only thing he's missing is a cigar, but not for long.

Jason and Noah join us in the lobby a few minutes later. I ignore the twitch in my heart. I can do this. I can have a fun time out in Cuba with the guys and not end up in Jason's room. I have a boyfriend. Jason is better as a friend, anyway. We look at each other and smile, give each other a nod of acknowledgment. Maybe we're on the same page?

The hotel calls a cab for Teddy, Jason, Noah, and me; Tess and Amelia are still working. We squish into a blue Chrysler from the fifties, as though we're in a movie.

We bounce from bar to bar all night, never settling into one place, just ordering rounds of Cuba Libres, asking each other if we should have let them put ice in them (no), and then drinking the cocktails really fast to avoid ice cube meltwater.

When we return to the hotel, Jason asks me to take a picture of the boys in front of a vintage car. As I crouch low to get the full body of the Chrysler in the shot, I wonder if they're going to show this to POTUS tomorrow, and as on so many other nights, it's like I was never there.

In the elevator up to our rooms, Teddy gets out on three, Noah on four. As luck would have it, I'm drunk and alone in an elevator with Jason, who's also drunk. Once the doors close on Noah, Jason scoops me up and asks if he can tuck me in. And even though I want him to, even though I can feel his breath on me as he whispers in my ear, "Just one more time," I say no. I've got Charlie at home and I'm not cheating anymore. The doors open on five, but I'm still in his arms, telling him no, when a girl from the advance staff walks by and sees us. "Great," I tell him, "now she's going to think this is happening."

"Might as well let me sleep over as long as everyone thinks it already," Jason says.

"No."

Jason sighs, kisses me on the cheek, and presses the Door Open button. I pat his head as I get down from his arms and scoot out of the elevator.

"Have a good sleep," he tells me as the door closes between us.

I see the advance girl down the hall, and I'm tempted to yell, "I'm going to my room now! By myself!" but she pretends she doesn't hear my footsteps behind her, doesn't turn around, which makes it so much worse: She doesn't think Jason is coming over—she *knows* it.

IN GENERAL, PRESS CONFERENCES ARE SO STIFF AND COOKIE-CUTTER that I find them boring—the president weighs his words carefully to avoid international incidents. I usually just hit Record and leave my recorder running on the press riser before going outside to stand with the boys while they smoke. But not here, not today, because everything in Cuba has the potential to break news, so here I am, riveted with everyone else, wondering whether Raúl Castro will answer Andrea Mitchell's question at the end of the press briefing.

POTUS prods him. "Okay, now I'm done, but Señor Presidente, I think Andrea had a question for you just about your vision. It's up to you. He did say he was only going to take one question and I was going to take two. But I leave it up to you if you want to address that question." He's gentle with Castro, respectful but also trying to ease a tense moment that could fall apart at any second.

"Por favor?" Andrea Mitchell asks into her microphone, and the tension breaks as everyone laughs.

Castro answers her question. As the two leaders shake hands and then exit the stage, I think, *Way to go, sir. Way to go.* If something doesn't work, change it. POTUS is getting his paragraph *muy correcto.*

THE SECOND NIGHT IN HAVANA, MAJOR LEAGUE BASEBALL THROWS A party in celebration of tomorrow's game—the Tampa Bay Rays against the Cuban National Team. Noah and Teddy are still working, and so are Tess and Amelia, so I meet up with Cole's assistant, Ingrid, and we ride to the party in a powder-pink 1956 Ford Sunliner convertible.

When we arrive at the MLB soiree, it's a whole different level of insane. Ingrid and I go to the bar, order Cuba Libres from attractive bartenders wearing white shirts and black bow ties, and then head out back, where three hundred people are milling around an empty stage. "You know Jimmy Buffett is playing," she tells me. We sip our drinks and ask ourselves how on earth we got here. While Ingrid does a lap looking for baseball players, I go in search of Amelia and Tess, who have texted to let us know they've arrived. "Did you see those cars?" Tess asks, elated. There are two mint-condition vintage cars on display, and you can go in and sit behind the wheel, kind of like the ultimate photo booth.

"Let's get in!" Amelia says. We hop in the car—Amelia behind the steering wheel, Tess shotgun, me in the back.

"Take us somewhere amazing!" I yell.

"You mean better than an MLB party in Havana?" Amelia hollers over her shoulder. The air is sweet and sultry, but also electric.

Jimmy Buffett takes the stage just as the Cuba Libres kick in. Ingrid comes over to tell us that Derek Jeter is here and she's going to go say hi with some folks from the press office, but I tell her I'm happy where I am. I spend the rest of the night in a Havana Club haze with Tess and Amelia, and without a care in the world.

When it's time to leave, I walk out to the White House staff bus with Terry, the kind, dadlike speechwriter. As the bus headlights hit me in the face, I'm struck with a moment's sobriety and realize I'm still holding my drink. I start to put the drink down in the grass, out of the way, but Terry goes, "Beck! You're going to give up that glass?" I look down and see it's a Havana Club glass, complete with the little signature logo, and I realize he's right, it would be crazy to give up this glass. It will bring me joy, Marie Kondo, I promise.

I hold on to my glass and thank Terry for looking out for me. As I find a seat on the bus, I hear the warning bangles jangle behind me. Eyeing my glass, she glares at me and hisses, "Are you fucking serious right now?"

"Don't mind her," Terry says from the seat behind me, and gives me a pat on the head.

I take a deep breath in and tell myself not to mind the Rattler;

that if I were a guy, she'd have made a fuss over the cool glass and asked coyly why I didn't get one for her. It's not my fault she's an angry person. It's not my fault she can't find happiness on a school bus driving through Old Havana. The world is what you make of it.

THE UPSIDE DOWN

April

FOR THE FIRST TIME IN A LONG TIME, SOMEONE PULLS ME BACK TO D.C. I loved the trip to Cuba, and after that to Argentina, but I'm most excited to go home and see Charlie. Maybe because he's a lawyer and outside the White House bubble, Charlie doesn't get caught up in the hierarchy or power players or name-dropping that's polluted my head for years now. Charlie is the opposite of a D.C. creature.

Because of him, I'm a better coworker these days. I remember to communicate with Lisa whenever I leave the office. I tell her how long I'll be gone, even if it makes me feel as if I'm in third grade and asking for a hall pass. I'm a better friend, and I make the effort to call my old housemates just to ask how they are, not to complain about Jason.

Charlie shrugs off the circus, and I'm slowly learning to follow his lead, which gives my head and my heart more space to be productive. I'm a better listener. I'm learning to forgive myself for Sam and Jason, and I'm putting both of them in my rearview mirror.

The weekly therapy sessions I began in January are helping, as are the support of my friends and the growing span of time since my last Jason relapse. Tick Tock Croc is helping, too—the countdown is so loud, the end so close. It's hard to think about anything besides all of this becoming the past tense.

CHARLIE DUMPS ME IN FRONT OF THE WHITE HOUSE MY THIRD DAY back in D.C. It turns out he's still infatuated with Surfer Girl. He confesses that they started seeing each other again while I was in Cuba.

"It's kind of funny, isn't it?" I ask him as we stand on Pennsylvania Avenue.

"What is?" Charlie asks. He can barely look at me. I wonder if she's waiting for him back at his apartment as I fight back tears.

"You made me confident that I'd never cheat on anyone again, and then you go and cheat on me," I tell him.

Charlie winces. He says he's worried I'm going to relapse into Jason and he doesn't want that. "I'm really sorry," he says.

Yeah, me too.

BLACK-TIE DISGUISE

April–May

CHARLIE DUMPS ME ON THURSDAY, AND FRIDAY IS THE START OF THE White House Correspondents' Dinner weekend. All my high-minded outside-the-bubble thinking gets torched when I realize I wasn't invited to more parties—and by "more parties," I mean *any* parties. I email David Remnick, and he puts me on the *New Yorker* guest list, but I'm a little embarrassed to have to ask to be invited.

You're not supposed to run in the West Wing, but no one really cares what you do in the EEOB, the Hoboken of the White House complex—cheaper real estate, better views, lower status—so I am sprinting down the black-and-white-tiled floor because I'm late to cover a POTUS interview. When I get to West Exec I stop running and start walking like a calm, poised person who is on time and not like the recently dumped, sad and tardy train wreck that I am.

The interview is with the actor Bryan Cranston, and it's moderated by Philip Galanes from the *New York Times* Style section. When

I enter the West Wing lobby, I see a group of people clustered on one of the sofas, including the photographer Damon Winter, who traveled with us on the campaign trail in 2012 and who won a Pulitzer for his photograph of POTUS in the rain during the 2008 campaign. We hug and grab each other by the shoulders, it's been so long since we've seen each other.

Bryan Cranston stands up when Damon introduces us. He could be a friend's gentle father, the way he takes an interest in me without any sort of agenda but just because I'm a human being and here we are, being humans together in the West Wing lobby. A few minutes later, I overhear Cranston, in his theater-ready baritone, say, "What's happening with this generation is a false sense of intimacy," and even though I don't know the context, I nod in agreement from across the room. After Jason and Charlie, I'm beginning to think I'll live the rest of my life with a false sense of intimacy.

Ferial, the president's assistant, gives the green light that POTUS is ready, so I trail the group as the president proudly gives a tour of the Oval before leading them back to his private dining room. On the back wall is a large, familiar painting of Lincoln, with a rainbow overhead. In a glass case are signed boxing gloves that belonged to Muhammad Ali. A whole set of ancient-looking Lincoln volumes rests on an antique desk. For a moment I forget about Charlie as I hit Record and absorb the scene.

THAT EVENING, WHILE THE REST OF THE PRESS OFFICE TEAM PRIMPS and pregames for Correspondents' Weekend parties, I sit in the bird's nest typing up the Cranston interview. Even though we travel with the press, and we cover every press-related event at the White House, the press office does not include the stenographers in Nerd Prom weekend. We're on the team, but we're not part of the team.

But this year, the final Obama year, is different: Tomorrow night, Saturday night, I get to attend the dinner as a guest because Carol Lee and Jeff Mason, two journalists on the White House Correspondents' Association board, have personally invited our office after realizing the press office never shared their pile of tickets with us.

"You guys work your butts off," Carol had written to me in an email, "of course you should be at the dinner."

After releasing the transcript of the interview, I head over to the *New Yorker* party on the roof of the W Hotel to meet Ingrid, Noah, and Cole. I step out of the elevator and onto the roof, and the air is chilly but buzzing with low frequencies of possibility. It's not as busy as I anticipated. There tend to be migration routes to this Friday night, so I guess the *People* magazine party must be packed, and then the general stampede will soon make its way over here.

None of this, I remind myself, will ever be real, will ever amount to anything—not for me, anyway, because to make a cocktail party in D.C. count, you must have something to trade, and I have no currency. It's a weekend of transactions cloaked in floor-length, black-tie seduction. The famous and the powerful blend together better than the vodka, soda, and cranberry juice in this Cape Codder I'm holding as I watch the D.C. creatures around me swap assets. Everyone is smiling, but no one seems particularly happy. I drink half my Cape Codder and tell the group I'm taking myself home. I'm not in the right mental state to be at a party.

"I'm leaving, too," Noah says. "We can ride the elevator down together."

As we wait by the elevators, a short man with Coke-bottle glasses appears out of thin air, like some B-side character from *Alice in Wonderland*. He says hello and thrusts his hand into each of ours before we can adjust our eyes to his neon paisley suit. The man asks Noah and me where we're from, and what do we do, and oh, my, it doesn't get much better than personal aide to the president, he hiss-whispers at Noah, and something about his steady eye contact makes me think he already knows exactly who Noah is, and that this whole interaction was premeditated, and now I am the B-side character who is not supposed to have any lines. Noah asks him what he does.

"I'm in the art business, selling art."

"It would be weird if you sold something else," I chirp.

"Excuse me?" he says, his beady eyes twitching in my direction.

"Since you work in the art business, it would be weird if you were selling something other than art."

Noah laughs. When the elevator door opens, the little man asks if we're getting in, but we shake our heads and wave goodbye. He disappears, paisley suit and all, the Rumpelstiltskin of Washington.

"I need to go home," I tell Noah. "I'm just going to swat at people all night."

Noah shakes his head. "No, that was funny, and you were right, and he deserved it."

He says it in that cool, distant tone I love or hate, depending on whether he's being cool toward me or for me. In this case, I swim in Noah's nonchalance—he seems impartial, like a referee of social interactions. We stand there, leaning our backs against the wall, watching the elevators open and close. People coming up and going down. The ebb and flow of who's who.

"Want to go to another party?" Noah asks after checking his phone while I stand next to him, missing Charlie and his lack of interest in this world.

"I wasn't invited to another party," I remind Noah with the tone of a petulant teenager.

"No, you'll come with me, I'll get you in." Noah explains he's going to the HBO-Google party at the Renwick Gallery, which is right across from the White House.

"Well, it's on my way home," I say slowly, as though I'm doing Noah a favor. We both know I'm grateful, even if I can't say it.

The inclusion and rejection and satisfaction of being where everybody else is or isn't is the whole point of this weekend. You're in or you're out. Almost everybody feels out even when they're in.

At the whiskey bar, I order bourbons for the boys since Cole is meeting us any minute, and a flute of champagne for me. The bartender scowls as he tells me there's a two-drink maximum and that he's making an exception. It's not flirtatious, there's no wink, it's a real admonishment. I explain that these bourbons are for my friends who have had very long days. I hope that from the deft way I carry three big drinks in two hands, he can tell that I, too, was once a server, that I have spent long, thankless shifts on my feet.

The boys are congregated at the bottom of the steps in the front of the Renwick. It seems as if they were waiting for me, but I'll never know. Let them keep their veneer of cool as long as it means I don't have to balance these three drinks up the flight of steps. I make them clink glasses with me, and then we head up the red-carpeted stairs, passing women bedecked in diamonds walking carefully down in breakneck stilettos, thousand-dollar scarves draped over their bird-bone shoulders.

Entering the crowd at the top of the stairs feels like walking into the ocean, toward the point break, where you know the wave is going to crash down on you unless you either dive under or ride it in. If you stand still, the impact will crush you. The boys dive in, and I follow their lead.

A hazy amount of time later, Noah, Cole, Ingrid, Teddy, and I find ourselves huddled together near the back of the venue, and after too many hours of open bars, we form a circle around a six-foot speaker and dance to Prince's "Let's Go Crazy."

"Let's get out of here," Noah says at the end of the song, so we hop into a cab and head to Noah's apartment. Back at his place, I open the refrigerator door and, finding nothing except a half bottle of Chardonnay and two hard ciders, start searching the cabinets for snacks. Noah's apartment is every bachelor pad cliché—no food, no toilet paper, no clean water glasses, but a bunch of gorgeous furniture facing a huge TV with a killer sound system.

Ingrid finds a bag of wasabi peas, and she holds them up like a proud kid holding up a bass on her first fishing trip. We applaud her discovery, dive into the peas, and sit up talking until five in the morning. Cole does hilarious impressions of everyone we know, from POTUS to Teddy to Noah's mom to Ingrid when she's drunk. We laugh so hard we beg him to stop.

When I can no longer keep my eyes open, I decide to walk home. The sunrise is a good one—fat splotches of pink and orange stretch across the sky as I climb the hill to my place. The parties were okay, but hanging out at Noah's was by far my favorite part. Those boys used to seem like such grown-ups to me—now I troll them if they don't respond to my texts fast enough. I guess the best things happen when you least expect them.

SATURDAY NIGHT IS LESS SUCCESSFUL, AND I WAKE UP ON SUNDAY morning with memories flooding my head. After the Correspondents' Dinner where POTUS literally dropped the mic, I'd been rejected from the MSNBC party. All my friends got in, and I was left standing on the sidewalk feeling like a dummy while the two nineteen-year-old interns who'd turned me away reveled in their first taste of power.

I face-plant into my pillow. I miss Charlie. I wish he was here so he could tell me what he always told me—that my D.C. was a skewed, especially messed-up and crooked D.C. I could go for a run while he made waffle batter, and then maybe we could drive to Hains Point and read while the afternoon drifted away from us like a cumulus cloud. But I can't do any of that, because Charlie dumped me last week.

I call Lucas, my old friend who used to work in the stenographers' office before he pursued his music full-time. We meet for coffee and he tells me he's proud of me, that I seem stronger than I was when he first met me four years ago—more clear-eyed.

"When are you going to quit that dead-end job and start writing, girl?" Lucas asks. He's chasing his dream every day. I can't say the same.

I go home, and even though it's early, I get into bed, thinking about what Lucas said. When am I going to move forward?

Just before I fall asleep, my phone lights up: My old roommate Megan Rooney texts me from Hillary headquarters and says, "Isn't this weekend in DC the worst?" I laugh out loud in the dark. Megan gets it—even from New York, she gets it. You can cover insecurities with eyeliner and douse self-doubt in champagne, but getting past the velvet rope at exclusive parties is never going to feel as good as real friends you can putter around with on a Sunday night. Everything from this weekend—from the lists of names to the over-the-top centerpieces—are all gone, chucked in some back-alley dumpster. But Megan is real. And Lucas is real. And they are working toward a better future. What am I working toward?

In the morning, my eyes burn and the sky outside is gray, but I force myself to go on a run. As I push myself down the street, the old familiar feet-on-pavement sensation jolts me into the present, far away from the weekend. I don't feel better, but I feel cleaner.

ALL
IS
FAIR

April–May

AS I WALLOW IN CHARLIE'S BLINDSIDE BREAKUP, THE BUBBLE FLIES TO
Illinois where the president will speak to the University of Chicago
Law School about the judicial process. In the wake of Judge Scalia's
death, POTUS has nominated Merrick Garland to the Supreme
Court. And when I pull back a curtain backstage, there he is—Jason,
his left hand in his pocket, leaning in to a little man, saying, "Is that
right?" They look up at me and smile before returning to their conversation. The little man proudly tells Jason about his brand-new
Tesla parked out front and suggests they go for a quick spin.

Jason's eyes sparkle as he sees through me, down to my marrow,
and asks, "Do you feel up for a quick spin?" I work through my options, taking long, deep breaths. Is saying yes an active step toward
the bad, or is it the first step toward a healthy platonic friendship?

Jason turns around as I buckle up in the backseat, asks if I'm
okay. He's heard through the boys I've been sad about Charlie, and

he hopes I've been feeling better as he reaches back to pat my knee. As the little man presses the pedal and we speed past the agents and the red tape, the police and the Beast, I realize this was a mistake. I cannot be trusted around Jason. He is not just the magician who turns handshakes into hugs—he is the magic. He has the power to turn this regular afternoon into an adventure.

Off we zoom in a car designed to go from 0 to 100 in 4.2 seconds. We're on a blink-fast tour of Chicago—that's Oprah's house, that was Muhammad Ali's mansion. As we roll through a drive-thru window, we grab milkshakes. And now we speed up to a breakneck stop outside the president's home in Hyde Park, agents glaring through their black sunglasses as we nearly crash into the concrete barricade.

Jason opens my door back in the UChicago parking lot: "Did you have a nice time?" He takes the milkshake I haven't quite finished and throws it in the trash, destroying the evidence, but I remember what Ken Kesey wrote: *It's the truth even if it didn't happen.*

He touches the small of my back and lets his hand linger there as we cross the parking lot. The agents murmur into their wrists, and we hear "Renegade depart" over the advance team radio. This is the circus I signed up for, so I smile and take a bow. It's all part of the show.

SPRING ENDS ON THE OTHER SIDE OF THE WORLD. IN VIETNAM, AS WE motorcade through the streets crowded with smiling locals who are holding signs of welcome, I'm suddenly overwhelmed as I wave back to the throngs from the passenger seat of the Press 1 van. I'm so proud that President Obama is our ambassador, that he wants to go to these places where we have complicated histories and address it all head-on, openly and honestly, like a good professor.

Early the next morning, we arrive at the bright yellow President's Palace in Hanoi. We stand outside while the boys smoke, talking about the Vietnam War, how impossibly awful just existing in this damp heat must have been even before you add in guerrilla tactics, tunnels, bombs, death, corpses—war. It's too hot, but I'm excited to be here.

"Good morning, Vietnam!" I say, my arms outstretched. The boys groan. I look down at my pink flats against the lush grass, and then up at the Vietnam sky, where birds I've never seen before make journeys of their own. I'm happy to be looking up, remembering why I'm here.

"Beck, seriously, enough with the photos," Teddy tells me. The yellow palace makes an excellent backdrop.

"We'll never be here again, all together, like this," I say, and all of them look at the ground. They let me take as many photos as I want.

The next night, I step into a black dress and zip up my angst. Noah, Jason, Teddy, and I are going out in Ho Chi Minh City. Teddy's friends who live here take us to a local bar and then to a dance club. Jason flirts with a girl as soon as we get to the club, so I'm posted up against the wall, staring at him. We've become friends—as good a friend as I can be with a guy who has routinely broken my heart for years—but it's still hard to be around him.

While Teddy takes a call outside, I pout in the corner with my arms crossed. Noah grabs me and pulls me onto the dance floor. I don't want to go, but he won't let go of my arm, so I acquiesce. The DJ is playing *terrible* techno, and I don't even know how to dance to this, but Noah is right in front of me, and it's so weird because we're the same height, which makes us good matchups in basketball but awkward dance partners. It's uncomfortable being eye level with him, and his hand is on my waist, and this is just too weird for me, even after sitting at that dinner table an hour ago staring at a bowl of pig knuckles. Why is Noah doing this? Why is his face so close to mine? I feel claustrophobic and self-conscious and my skin is tingling where Noah is touching me and I can't take this anymore so I lean in and kiss him because that feels less intimate than how close he is to me right now.

Ha! His lips are a brick wall.

"Whoa, Becky," he says, stepping back from me, his face blank.

"Forget it!" I say, blushing in the strobe lights.

I'm still trying to read Noah's expression when Jason emerges and signals it's time to go home. The boys always follow Jason's lead, so off we go. As we leave, I can sense Jason behind me. He touches me on my lower back, and Noah's rejection of a minute ago becomes a faint, peripheral memory. I turn around to grab Jason's hand, and he scoops me up into his arms. Feet off the ground, I breathe in his mint gum—an addict's indulgence against her better judgment. Before Jason puts me down, we look at each other without speaking, which says everything we need to know about the rest of the night.

When we get back to the hotel, I want to get a revised final schedule from the senior staff office, and Teddy and Jason say they'll go with me. Noah says he's going to bed. When the three of us walk back down the hall with freshly printed schedules in hand, we see that Noah's door is propped open. I throw myself through it, Teddy and Jason laughing behind me, and ask Noah who he's waiting for. It's funny, we're all drunk, Noah doesn't have a shirt on, and he tells us to scram.

And then, for the first time in such a good, long, healthy time, I leave my door propped open and invite Jason in.

"You sure?" Jason texts from his room down the hall.

"Yes," I respond, because I've never been more sure of everything: More sure that I'd mistaken Charlie for a Darcy when the world is made of Wickhams. More sure that Charlie cheated because everyone cheats and no one cares. More sure that tonight I can be as reckless and impulsive as the best of them and beat them at their own game. I can be just like Jason and take what I can get with zero expectations beyond tonight. This is just a little familiar fun, nothing I can't handle. We're overseas, so it doesn't count, and we're drunk, so it doesn't matter. I watch the triangle of light grow across my ceiling.

THE NEXT MORNING WE FLY TO JAPAN AND TAKE HELICOPTERS FOR THE president's historic visit to Hiroshima. On the way to the memorial, a reporter points out a river that people jumped into trying to save themselves, and my stomach turns. I think of the Iran deal. I think of North Korea. I think of the mushroom cloud, and the hundred thousand people who died, and the deformed generations that followed.

When we arrive at the Hiroshima memorial and I listen to the president's remarks, I'm so glad POTUS is POTUS. I'm so proud he wants to make amends rather than escalate. He wants to do the right thing for future generations.

After POTUS speaks, Prime Minister Abe gives his address, and then they abandon their lecterns and approach the seated audience before them. POTUS bends down and hugs a survivor of the Hiroshima bombing seventy-one years ago. I watch from the press riser, fighting back tears. The president holds on to the man in a quiet, prolonged moment. And in their embrace, I witness grace after unspeakable pain.

WELCOME TO THIRTY

June

I GUESS I THOUGHT IF I PLANNED A FUN PARTY, MAYBE I WOULDN'T turn thirty. If I made a big enough deal over my birthday, maybe I'd like myself. Holy shit, what a disaster.

On Tuesday, Noah, Teddy, Cole, Ingrid, and I go to see the band Lord Huron at Wolf Trap. Cole has joined the ongoing exodus and has a week left of work at the White House. Everyone's emotional. Everything is ending.

Ingrid will assume Cole's role at work. Part of me is jealous—Ingrid is, after all, two years younger than I am, and she has nimbly climbed the rungs of a ladder that I can barely keep a grip on, let alone ascend. But Ingrid is talented and a hard worker, and she has become a friend. Cole's position comes with some power, which I trust Ingrid to use wisely. Perhaps the most promising sign that she won't turn into a junior Rattler is that she's concerned about it.

"You'll be fine," I reassure her as we toast each other on the Wolf Trap lawn, our drinks sloshing in the plastic cups we packed. "You can bear the ring without losing your shit. You're like Frodo."

"But way cuter," Ingrid says, her freckled nose scrunching up as she smiles at her joke.

"A blessing and a curse," I tell her. Because she is a young, attractive female, navigating the corridors of power will be more complicated for Ingrid than it was for Cole.

Lord Huron takes the stage, the crowd cheers, Teddy stops playing Clash of Clans on his phone, and we let our bodies swim in the sound, in this short passage of time we still have together. When I ask to take a group photo, the boys don't complain.

The night turns into one of the best kinds of blurs—all F sharps and second frets. We put our arms around each other during "The Night We Met," and the lyrics nearly knock me out: *I had all of you, most of you, some and now none of you.* I think of Sam and Charlie and Jason—it's hard not to want to go back to the beginning and do everything better. But what would that even look like?

On the night before my birthday, I host a dance party in D.C., which begins with a pregame at Noah's house. The week before, Jason had asked me what I'd wanted and I told him that I wanted the same thing I asked him for every year—a first-edition book.

At the pregame, I am presented with a bounty of gifts—a presidential pen POTUS had used, a Shinola journal with my name engraved in gold, a pink-and-blue L.L.Bean tote bag. They know me. They get me.

And then Jason goes inside, and I feel something open up, my heart, blossoming like the first spring day at the promise of what is to come. This is it. He's going to show Noah, Cole, Teddy, and Ingrid that he cares about me, and it will be okay, it will be proof that I mean something to him. This is what joy feels like. Jason comes back into view with a small package behind his back.

"That's just from Jason," Noah says, not smiling as I take the wrapped gift.

The package is too bulky to be a book, and too round. Through the paper I feel plastic. *Maybe it's even better than a first edition,* I tell myself. But the first day of spring has disappeared and in its place is leaden dread. Something tells me not to open it. Maybe it's Noah, who is staring at me as though I'm the hardest problem on a math test.

I open it.

I stare into my lap.

I can't look up. I can never look up.

I need to disappear.

No.

He wouldn't do this to me.

"You got me a vibrator?" I whisper. My lips are trembling as my face reddens.

"Not just any vibrator!" Jason grins, ignoring the tears welling in my eyes. "It's the best one on the market, babe!"

"You got me a vibrator."

"A really expensive one!"

Jason cocks his head to the side, slowly realizing I'm not going to play along. This hurts too much.

He thinks of what to do, what to say. For once, he seems stumped, speechless.

"Who needs another drink?" Ingrid asks into the wall of silence.

"I'll help you," Cole says.

"Yeah, I need another brewski," Teddy adds.

Noah goes inside with them.

"It really is a nice vibrator," Jason says, his eyes softening. The tears are flowing freely down my face. "It was over three hundred dollars. You can return it and get the cash."

My phone rings. Shilpa, Charlotte, Emma, my brother, my sister, Hope, Amelia, and Tess are all at the bar already, telling me to come join the fun and put on the playlist I've been curating all week. "I'm going to go," Jason says. "I didn't mean to upset you. Happy birthday."

I do more tequila shots at the bar that night than I did in all of college. Cole corners my sister and asks if there's something going on with Jason and me. She freaks out, and I freak out, and I do more shots at the bar long after the boys retreat back to Noah's.

At two in the morning I storm over to Noah's to yell at Cole for asking my dopey-drunk baby sister about Jason and me. Did Cole know this whole time? Did Noah? Have they just been watching me get skewered over and over again and not saying anything, or are they in some kind of bro club with Jason, and they all think it's some kind of entertaining sport? Was I that delusional to think they didn't know? I'm humiliated and hurt—TSA is right, *If you see something, say something*—but it's so late and I'm too wasted to argue. The next thing I know everyone else is leaving Noah's except for me because I'm on the couch, nearly passed out. Noah comes over and tells me there's no point in being upset, who cares?

"I care!" I slur, my eyes half closed on his couch.

"My point is you shouldn't. You're caring about the wrong thing. None of this matters. Friendship matters. The people who take care of you matter. The people who love you matter."

"What are you talking about?" I ask, even though I know exactly what he's talking about. I've jeopardized my most important relationships for a guy who doesn't care.

"I watched my best friend die, Beck," Noah says. He's talking about the beloved Obama staffer who died in October from leukemia. "Life is too short to allow yourself to be treated badly," Noah continues. "Don't waste your time on people who make you cry. You're not going to get what you want from them and you're going to miss out on the fun in the meantime. That's what I'm talking about."

If I weren't so drunk, I'd ask Noah how long he's known, how did it feel watching me walk into the lion's den so many times and not saying anything, but my tongue feels thick and my eyes won't stay open. The spins are settling in behind my eyelids. When I don't respond, Noah tells me he's going to bed. Some murky amount of time elapses before he yells out in the dark to the living room, "Are you going home or what?"

"Yes," I mumble. I know better than to think he might have snacks in his cabinets. My stomach is grumbling. So much tequila, so little food. I crawl over to his bedroom to say good night, and he pulls me toward him in an uncharacteristic hug.

I laugh. "Um, hell no, you had your chance in Vietnam."

Noah pulls away, opens his mouth to say something and doesn't.

"What?" I ask.

"Nothing."

"Say it," I slur, like the belligerent drunk girl I am.

"I didn't want to make out in front of Teddy and Jason," he confesses. Oddly, we're still hugging. "And besides . . . I propped my door open for you."

What!?

The tequila speaks through my mouth and says, "Well, then, kiss me now."

So he does.

And then we start really kissing, and I stop to say, "How weird is this? Aren't you surprised? I thought I'd totally throw up because you're you but you're actually a really good kisser and—"

He starts kissing me again just to shut me up.

After a few minutes, Noah pulls back. "I can't do this. I love you. We can't get weird. Are you going to get weird?"

I crack up. "Don't you know me?"

Noah sighs. "Yes, I know you."

"So, yes, I will totally get weird."

"Right. Okay, let's skip it," Noah says, turning around so his back is to me.

I tap him on the shoulder.

"What?" he asks, annoyed, as if he'd already passed out.

"I love you, too, buddy," I tell him. "Also, wow, killer kisser, watch out!"

"I hate you," Noah says, covering his head with a pillow and telling me to stay on my side.

I wake up and find Noah sleeping on the couch. My head pounding out of my skull, I call a cab and punch him in the arm on the way out, laughing the whole thing off. We were both really drunk and really stupid.

In the cab, all the tequila threatens to come up. The driver is blasting Stevie Wonder's "Isn't She Lovely?" but I've never felt less lovely. I have eyeliner down to my chin, I'm definitely going to throw up, and it's so goddamn hot out. My phone lights up because Noah has texted: "Welcome to 30."

When we pull up to my apartment, the driver asks if I'm all right, and I nod because my jaw is locked and now, one foot out of the cab, I am doubled over, the unapologetic sun beating down as I puke my tequila brains out, and the driver is yelling, asking over and over if I'm okay, but I'm not okay, but he keeps yelling, trying to be heard over that song that's still blasting, gloating, mocking me as I wretch. *Isn't she looovelyyy.*

PULSE

June

SUNDAY MORNING AFTER MY BIRTHDAY STARTS WITH NONSTOP BUZZ-ing. News alert after news alert. A massacre at the Pulse nightclub in Orlando. I sit up, suddenly wide awake, and read through what happened. A lone wolf, a three-hour shootout with police; 49 dead, 58 wounded, a terrorist attack aimed at the LGBTQ community. The deadliest mass shooting in the United States to date.

I reach for my work phone and see there will be a POTUS statement in the briefing room. The itinerary for the upcoming week will be rescheduled so he can go to Orlando and meet with the survivors and family of the victims as soon as possible. The shooter had an assault rifle and a handgun. Most of the victims were so, so young. We are rattled and jaded at the same time.

Just like San Bernardino, Killeen, Fort Hood, Binghamton, the Washington Navy Yard, Newtown, Samson, Aurora, Roseburg,

Charleston, Seal Beach, Manchester, Appomattox, Carthage, and Lafayette, the Pulse nightclub shooting happens on Obama's watch. As he has done in the aftermath of every mass shooting, the president argues for gun reform. And as they have done in the aftermath of every mass shooting, Congress sits on their hands.

Vice President Biden joins POTUS when we fly to Orlando that Thursday. The press pool hold in a windowless room several hallways down from where the president and vice president are meeting with the bereaved. I head outside and stand next to Teddy in the shade while he smokes. "It's so sad in there," he says, looking at the ground. His sunglasses are on and I wonder if he's been crying. "I don't know how POTUS does it," he says. "It's a room full of broken hearts."

THE WEEK AFTER PULSE, I'M IN MY APARTMENT UNPACKING THE BOX of stuff Noah has dropped off from my birthday. I hold up the journal they'd given me, and I weigh the president's heavy pen in my hand before realizing I shouldn't touch it so I can keep his left-handed fingerprints intact.

And then I see the vibrator staring at me from the bottom of the box. Cole, in an effort to make me laugh, had taken it out of its package and stuck the tip in Noah's ear. I dig around for the original packaging, and the charging stand—maybe I can return it and get the $300. I find part of the packaging but not the stand, so I text Noah to ask him if it's still at his apartment. "Oh, so you've come around to it?" he teases. I know he's only joking, but I start shaking as I text back, "I'm just one big joke to you guys."

"Huh?" Noah writes.

"I'm a joke, I don't matter, I'm cheap entertainment."

"Beck, what are you talking about?"

I go into my room and start to hyperventilate. I gave up Sam to be Jason's joke. I've lied to my friends and to myself, I've hated myself for so long, I've spent how many hours crying over this guy who never considered me more than an easy sidepiece. I'm not first-edition-worthy. I'm a disposable piece of plastic, a replaceable cog on the road. I don't know how much time passes before I hear my phone in the other room and look at it just as the ringing stops. Noah has called me seventeen times. Now he's calling again, for the eighteenth time.

"Jesus, Beck, what the hell is going on?"

"I'm a joke. I want to disappear."

"Look, buddy, you're not a joke, and you're not going to disappear."

"But I want to disappear," I say, sobbing.

"Too bad," Noah says. "Now, look, are you okay or not?"

"I'm fine."

"If you're not fine, I will drive over."

"I'm fine."

"What's the matter?"

"He thinks I'm a joke. He gave me a fucking *vibrator*."

I can hear Noah suck in his breath. I've never confided in him this directly about Jason. It's a Rubicon moment. After all, they're friends and colleagues. I'm putting Noah in a shitty position. I'd care, if I weren't having a bit of a breakdown.

"You need to move on, Beck."

Sometimes I love Noah's coolness, but right now I resent it.

"Okay, thanks, I'm hanging up," I tell him.

"I know I'm giving you tough love, but it's the truth. You're not going to get what you want from him—not now, not ever."

"I'm aware. See you later."

"You can hang up on me once you promise you're not going to hurt yourself."

"I'm not going to hurt myself," I tell him. But in my head, I say, *I'm not going to hurt myself too badly*.

"I can come up there if you want."

"No, I'm fine."

"Okay. I'll check in with you tomorrow, then."

We hang up and I start digging around in drawers. I've never been physically self-destructive, but Noah, in his attempt to protect me from myself, has inspired me. *What would help me disappear?* I ask myself as I run my finger over the knives. I realize this is why people cut—to distract themselves from the deeper pain. I hold up a dull vegetable peeler with a lime-green plastic handle and envision pulling back a thick strip of flesh, from wrist to the crook of my elbow. Maybe this will make me feel better. But what if it doesn't?

I put down the peeler and pick up Bodhi, my big, sweet cat, who doesn't give a fuck about Jason or Air Force One or how many months are left in the Obama administration. Bodhi meows at me as Mary Jane weaves figure eights between my legs.

Maybe I should call someone. I reach for my phone, but when I pick it up, Noah is already calling me.

"What?" I answer.

"I'm downstairs with Cole. Come say hi."

I walk down the five flights, and through the glass of the front door I see them leaning against Noah's car. My eyes well as I open the door. Friends. Real friends. They may be dicks half the time, but they show up.

"Jesus, Becky," Cole says. "You get stung by bees in both eyeballs?" Cole is more affectionate than Noah and brings me in for a hug. "I brought you a red Gatorade. That's your favorite, right?"

"Mine and POTUS's," I remind him.

"Oh, right, yeah, he wanted to come, too, but we told him maybe another time."

"Come here, Becky," Noah says, grinning.

"I told you I was fine," I say.

"Yeah, but we just thought, eh, what the hell, it's a nice night, let's go see our friend Beck."

These are men in their thirties whom I'm not dating, who won't even wait for me at a concert when I go to the bathroom. Of course, I start crying—blubbering. Because even though we're not going to talk about Jason, these guys are here because of him. If there is a bro code, they're also on my team. They care.

I ask them if Teddy knows.

"Of course not." Noah laughs.

"That would require him looking up from Clash of Clans," Cole adds.

I look at the ground as I wipe away my tears, embarrassed by all of it, but also so deeply touched that they've shown up, I don't know what to do with myself. I can't believe they're here.

"You're going to be fine, Beck," Cole says seriously.

"You really are," Noah agrees, looking me in the eye before reaching over and mussing up my hair. "Now go get some sleep, would ya?"

I wave as the boys drive away. They're right. I'm going to be fine.

TURN AND FACE THE STRANGE

July

EVERYTHING IS BECOMING A LAST. IT'S SECOND SEMESTER OF SENIOR year, and we're trying to gorge ourselves and prepare ourselves, practicing distance from the people we've learned to love the most, even though they can be annoying as hell. We've grown up together.

We fly to the DNC Convention in Philly for POTUS to support Hillary Clinton as she officially becomes the Democratic candidate for president. The vibe in Washington and, arguably, across the country, is that Hillary will win. I don't tell anyone, but I'm really sad. Before POTUS goes onstage, I go out back to the loading docks where the boys are smoking. I need air. I need to be outside the HRC bubble, because they're acting as though she's already the forty-fifth president and I haven't prepared myself for the peaceful transfer of power.

Granted, nobody is cooler than Obama, but some of Clinton's

closest aides make me worried about Trump. I've played in too many soccer/basketball/lacrosse games where we knew we were better than the other team, and then we got a sluggish start, played down to their level, and were still tied at the half, actually down by one with six minutes to go, and then whoops, there's the buzzer and we lost because nobody deserves anything until they've earned it.

After flashing my hard pin at a Secret Service agent who'd grabbed my arm a little too hard—he's been traveling with HRC and doesn't know me—I walk into the arena and post up on the side of the stage. There are so many people here, everyone cheering and chanting and holding signs.

When the spotlight finds POTUS as he walks onstage, I clap and cheer as if I'm at a concert, begging for an encore. *One more song, POTUS, one more song.* I feel someone's eyes on me and it's David Plouffe, standing with a huddle of other alum senior strategists. We smile and wave to each other. I look across the arena, at all the blue Obama signs: It's a sea of believers, a congregation of hope. It's only when POTUS takes one of his famous pauses that I hear myself praying. I am asking, pleading, begging, moving my lips through the mantra, *Please don't go, please don't go, please don't go.*

But change is coming—quickly.

COLE'S GOING-AWAY PARTY DRAWS A DIVERSE GROUP OF FORMER AND current White House staffers, wealthy donors, Secret Service agents, even a few celebrities. After eight years of working for Barack Obama, Cole has made a lot of friends, both in high places and in the stenographers' office. Jason and I have barely spoken to each other since my birthday party, but here we are, at a rooftop bar, celebrating our friend.

"Let's take a picture," I suggest while standing around with Teddy, Cole, Noah, and Ingrid. After all, when will we all be together again? The boys are obedient and don't fight me on squishing together for a photo—but then Cole calls over to Jason to get in. As Jason puts one arm around me and one arm around Ingrid, I smell his mint gum and ignore that familiar light-headed feeling.

Around midnight, we grab a cab to go to another bar, where more of Cole's friends are meeting us. An hour later, we go to another bar, where we close the place down. As the group separates, everyone hailing cabs and heading to their beds, I tell myself to leave. But I don't.

"Can I walk you home?" Jason asks.

"It's a long walk," I tell him.

"Let's do it."

We walk block after block, hand in hand, talking and not talking. This time next year, neither of us will be here. In six months, POTUS won't be POTUS. Will I love Jason less then, when I don't see the Wagoneer parked on West Exec every day? I squeeze his hand tighter. I don't want to let go. I may be miserable, but I don't want anything to change. As Jason follows me into Megan's building, I justify to myself, *Tonight is for old times' sake, one last time.* We're barely in the elevator when he bends down to kiss me, and I realize I'm drowning—not in the Pacific Ocean, but in lasts.

Only after the first gray slant of morning peeks through my blinds do I realize Jason is still lying next to me. We must have passed out. I reach for a glass of water on my bedside table and see Jason's phone lit up and vibrating next to the glass. It's Brooke. The phone stops vibrating and shows she's called several times. I had assumed she was in L.A. this weekend.

"What will you tell her?"

"That's the difference between you two," Jason says, leaning down to kiss the top of my head. "She doesn't ask."

SLAM-DUNK
THE OUTSIDE
SHOT

August

THE PRESIDENT LOVES HIS BIRTHDAY. EVERY AUGUST 4, I THINK ABOUT
adding to the pile of cards and well-wishes that stack up on Ferial's
desk in the president's personal mail cubby, and every year, I chicken
out. I don't want to make him feel awkward. I work for him; we're
not actually friends.

Last year, I went so far as to order an old photograph off eBay of
the 1985 NBA slam dunk contestants. I searched all over for this
photo, because it's one of the few that includes both Dr. J—the president's all-time favorite player—and Michael Jordan, who led the
Bulls to victory while POTUS was working as a community orga-
nizer in Chicago and thus holds a special place in his heart.

But it takes another year, this year, the president's last year in office, for me to screw up the courage to do something with the eBay
photograph. Noah not only encourages me to give the president a

card, but also promises to hand deliver it to POTUS. "Just bring it to me in the outer Oval," he texts me.

But when I arrive in the outer Oval, Noah is nowhere to be found. Only Ferial is in the office, and I almost turn back. But Ferial, whose intimidating beauty is offset by her warmth, smiles at me from behind her monitor. I hand her my manila folder and confess that I've been too self-conscious to do it in years past. She grins and tells me he'll love it, that he appreciates every card because—and here we share an insider smile—he really loves his birthday.

It's my last chance to take a buzzer shot, I tell myself. *I'm just trying to make my boss feel special on his birthday, even if my boss happens to know the nuclear launch codes.* When I get back to my desk, Lisa yells at me for disappearing. "You always just, like, leave without saying anything!" she says. As I take the heat, I see a new email arrive in my inbox. It's from Ferial, and she's asking me if I can come back to the outer Oval. Lisa rolls her eyes when I ask her permission to go to the bathroom.

Walking across West Exec, I take a deep breath and prepare myself to graciously take back my note and act like it's not a big deal that I'm too much of a creep. Instead, Ferial smiles broadly as I enter the outer Oval.

"He *loved* it!" she says. "He asked me to make sure you got this, right before he motorcaded over to the Pentagon."

Ferial hands me a small envelope with my name printed on it. My heart stops. I know that handwriting. It's the president's.

QUIT
THIS
SHIT

September

EVERYONE ELSE IS TALKING ABOUT THEIR PLANS AFTER HRC WINS. NOT only do I not have a plan, but pretty soon I won't have a place to live. When Megan returns to D.C. as a lauded speechwriter for the first female president of the United States, she'll want her apartment back.

"Just think, Beck," my brother says on the phone, "this time next year, you'll be a homeless cat lady standing on a street corner in Philly and yelling at passing cars, 'I used to be somebody! I could have been a contender!'"

I know Zach is joking, but the image seems a little too real. What if this was as good as it gets? What if I peaked at the White House but was too heartbroken most of the time to enjoy it?

The next day, as I jog up the airstairs onto Air Force One, I feel I'm sinking faster than a stone in Ophelia's pocket. We're about to fly to New York City for three days to attend a Hillary Clinton fundraiser, our last United Nations General Assembly, and Hope's cowabUNGA birthday. Anxiety is starting to encroach on the excitement.

When AF1 lands at JFK, I walk to Nighthawk 4, pop in my earbuds, and close my eyes for the deafening fifteen-minute helicopter ride to Manhattan, just as I have done dozens of times. When we motorcade to the Gramercy Park home of the restaurateur Danny Meyer for the HRC fundraiser, I don't look up from my phone. I don't take notes about what I see. I don't marvel at the Secret Service staying abeam of us on motorboats in the East River, or the Brooklyn Bridge lit up as another day melts into dusk. It doesn't matter. I've seen it all before.

But then, in the billiard room of Danny Meyer's house, where I'm setting up my laptop and typing in the wifi code, I see Avril Haines across the room. Noah is sitting next to me, typing away on his work phone, and I tell him how much I admire her. I'd heard Avril lead a heated press call on resettling refugees with such eloquence and poise that I'd stopped typing to look her up. She is the first female to be Deputy National Security Advisor. Before this, Avril was the first woman to be deputy director of the CIA. And before that, she and her husband opened a bookstore in Baltimore in honor of her mother, who passed away when Avril was still in her teens.

"This is her first time traveling with us," Noah says, not looking up from his phone.

"No way," I reply.

"Yes way," Noah says, getting up from the couch to check on the president's dinner.

Avril is standing by herself on the other side of a Ping-Pong table, typing on her phone. Admiration carries me to her side before I can stop myself.

"Avril?"

"Hi!" she says, as if she knows me, which I know she doesn't.

I extend my hand and introduce myself, explain my job. "I just wanted to say how great you were on that press call."

"Oh, yes, that was something!" Avril says, her eyes wide but her mouth turned up in a smile, recalling the conservative reporters who saw the resettlement program as a threat to national security. "But that was why we had the call, so I could address those concerns."

Avril is so senior that I realize I should leave her alone, and yet I get the sense she truly does not mind that I've approached her. I wonder if she has a teaching background. She's clearly not a proponent of Vagiantism.

"But you know," Avril adds, "for every staunch opponent, there's a staunch supporter. So you have conservative governors who refuse to work with us on this resettlement program, but then—well, just this week, a farmer out in Idaho called me to say he had several acres and to send as many refugees as we wanted out to him—he'd teach them how to till the land."

"Wow."

"Right?" Avril says, grabbing my hand, smiling in a moment of solidarity.

Josh Earnest walks over to ask Avril a question, so I excuse myself and weave my way through the dining room of big Democratic donors to set up my recorder for the president's remarks. A few minutes into his speech, POTUS says Hillary Clinton will be the next president of the United States. I can't help but wonder, shouldn't we knock on wood or something? Don't we not want to jinx this? But everyone claps, and I scold myself for letting my mom's superstitious nature get the best of me.

As POTUS continues speaking to the room of high-powered New Yorkers, he says, "There's a reason why we haven't had a woman president: that we as a society still grapple with what it means to see powerful women, and it still troubles us in a lot of ways, unfairly, and that expresses itself in all sorts of ways." I scan the room looking for Avril and see her in the hallway, standing next to the Rattler. They're both typing frantically on their work phones. I doubt they heard what the president said, but it doesn't matter—they've lived his words.

THE NEXT NIGHT, AFTER A FULL DAY AT UNGA, I RUN INTO NOAH OUT-side the hotel and insist on going with him wherever he's going. I'm desperate to get out of Midtown, away from the bubble.

We hop in a cab and head downtown to a bar where some former colleagues are waiting for Noah. What starts as fun Hawaiian cock-tails at a tiki bar spirals into an extravagant evening, and the restau-rant fills with the who's who of politics, money, and influence—even a top Clinton aide is there, eyeing my shirt with disdain as I stare at her bedazzled clutch that spells out, in blinding, victorious gem-stones, HILLARY 2016.

I look around and see career stepping-stones all around me, sip-ping Manhattans, passing tuna tartare; any D.C. creature would love to be in this room, crowded with power players. All I have to do is reach out, grab a rung, and pull. These are the connections, these are the inroads. I see the map crystallize in front of me, like a con-stellation coming into focus. My head is spinning with a dangerous cocktail of mai tais, ego, and insecurity, and yet I've never seen life more clearly. Just like those who wear the black-tie disguise of the White House Correspondents' Dinner, these people don't seem par-ticularly happy. Powerful, yes; hungry to prove something, abso-lutely. Excited about life? Not really.

When we get back to the hotel, I follow Noah to the four-story penthouse suite he is sharing with Teddy for UNGA. Because the suite includes half the roof of the Lotte Hotel with 360-degree views of the city, the Secret Service had determined it was not secure for POTUS. The White House would need to pay for it anyway, however, because it was on a secure floor, right next to the president's room, where he's not even allowed to use his balcony and all of his win-dows are blacked out with dark, heavy curtains.

We hear Teddy puttering around at the bar in the suite, the sound of ice hitting the bottom of a glass. "Oh, hey, guys," he says.

"I can hear you smiling, Teddy," I say as I take off my coat and collapse on one of the long, comfy couches. There's a hockey game on the 70-inch plasma flatscreen.

"Kiddo," Teddy yells from the bar, "how badly do you want a White Russian right now?"

"So badly. Can you make me one?"

"Yeah, definitely. I've got all the ingredients right here except for the milk and Kahlua."

"Teddy," Noah yells over before flopping on the couch across from me, "grab me a beer, would ya?"

As I kick off my shoes, I replay the last few hours in my head. "That was kind of intense," I tell Noah. "But fun!"

Noah sits up to receive his beer as Teddy crosses the living room's thick carpet, three green bottles pressed against his chest.

"I can't believe you guys got this suite," I marvel, looking through the floor-to-ceiling glass windows, the skyline lit up a little too perfectly, like the set of a high school play.

"Why?" Teddy asks, sipping his beer. "I mean, we're the most responsible staffers. It makes sense the advance team would trust us with the leisure living suite."

"You're right," I say, leaning over to clink each of their beer bottles with mine. "You guys are totally responsible adults, who always make responsible adult decisions."

Noah puts his beer down on the glass coffee table and looks at me. "Speaking of adult decisions," he says slowly, pointedly, "when are you going to quit this shit job and start writing?"

Talking about my nonexistent writing feels intimate, as if Noah just opened my top dresser drawer.

"Yeah, kiddo," Teddy follows, like a hype man. "When are you going to start—*Goal!*" Teddy jumps up, knocking over Noah's beer as he puts up his arms like goalposts to celebrate the now-tied hockey game.

Noah and I look at each other and laugh, but he doesn't take his eyes off me. He's waiting for an answer. He's holding me accountable for my pipe dream. In a town that's not exactly known for its creative spirit, Noah has always supported my desire to write—the only thing I care about too much to say out loud. My ultimate secret.

"Guys," Teddy says, "I know we're talking about Beck's future and all, but I think we should talk about our collective future for a sec."

"I don't want to," I tell him.

"Me neither," Noah agrees.

It's hard to imagine us not traveling together, not seeing each other most days. Just the thought makes me homesick—or, I guess more accurately, roadsick, hotelsick, planesick, motorcadesick, and, most of all, Obamasick.

"Jesus, you two are so serious," Teddy says, exasperated. "I was just going to ask if you'd be down for ordering room service. I could go for some snacks, you know?"

Twenty minutes later, we dip French fries into pools of ketchup on the roof of the Lotte Palace. I can't help but think how much happier I am here than I was in that fancy restaurant filled with all those power players. Fuck the ladder. Noah is right: I should quit this shit and try to take my writing seriously.

"Love you guys," Teddy says as he licks his fingers and lies back in his chaise longue. I can hear Noah's steady breathing from his lounge chair, already passed out. I curl up into a ball and try to close my eyes but I know I won't sleep. This is my favorite time of day. Awake on the roof of the Lotte Hotel, I watch the sunrise over Manhattan, a triangle of light growing bigger and brighter.

THE SUN WILL COME OUT

November

AS WE SHOULD HAVE LEARNED FROM THE *TITANIC*, THERE ARE NO UN-sinkable ships, or presidential candidates. Despite Hillary's three-million-popular-vote advantage, the ship goes down. It's easy to point fingers—the Russians, Comey, misogyny, the tone-deaf DNC, the electoral college, the fearmongering right-wing media.

But placing blame doesn't make reality hurt less.

This cannot be.

I'd gone home to vote with my family, and we watch the returns in the living room. My dad tucks me in for the first time in fifteen years, tears cutting paths through his stubble. It's the second time in my life I've seen him cry.

The next morning, I take the train back to D.C. I sit in the café car and feel alienated, like I'm surrounded by Death Eaters. How did we let this happen? As we pull into Union Station, my stomach drops as

I recall what FLOTUS said at the convention last summer: "Being president doesn't change who you are—it *reveals* who you are."

I make it to the White House in time to go out to the Rose Garden and watch the president deliver remarks about the election results. Somehow, he smiles. Somehow, he is able to look up from the teleprompter and into the rising sun staring back at him and to remind us—the reporters, the camera crews, the throngs of staffers lining the Colonnade—"The sun is up."

Reporters, usually bloodthirsty for sound bites, are uncharacteristically quiet. Those who traveled on the campaign trail with Trump had endured his harassment firsthand. He kept them in a pen, pointing at them and calling them "sick" and "dishonest" while his supporters booed, jeered, and threw things at them.

How are we going from a man of hope and intellect to one who denies climate change but does not condemn David Duke; who boasts he could shoot a man in the street and get away with it but who won't disclose his taxes; who was caught on tape bragging about sexually assaulting women. That guy, this founder of birtherism and puppet of Putin, will now represent America's interests from the Oval Office.

President Obama's leadership compels him to find the bright side, but I can't look up. I watch Amelia, eight months pregnant, hold her belly as she crouches with her Nikon. Her baby deserves better than Donald Trump. The Death Eaters are on the rise; fear and fight hover in the atmosphere. I look down at my feet, tears dropping onto my black flats. Today I dressed for a funeral. Everyone looks the way I feel—devastated, disappointed, outraged. I focus on the president's voice more than his words, because I'm not ready for the mature message he's delivering about rooting for Trump's success. I know it's in our best interest to wish him well, but we know who Trump is, and he is not what America needs.

When Trump visits President Obama in the Oval Office, I stay home from work. It's a Thursday, my reporting day, but I can't stomach reality, not yet. Peggy says she understands, and Lisa happily goes in my stead. This paragraph just took such a wrong turn.

Later that same day, Noah calls.

"Beck," he says, "you've got to stay."

"Why?"

"You've got to stay after we all leave. Having them here today, it was just—They have no idea what they're doing."

"I can't stay," I tell him. I'd rather be unemployed than work for Trump.

"You're a writer," Noah says, his tone serious. "Of course you can stay. You have to, and then you can write about what you see, because it's going to be insane."

That night, I see I have missed a called from Jason. But Jason never calls. Just then, he texts me: "We need to talk—can I call you?"

And now my phone is ringing again. Jason.

"I'm married," he says over the phone. "Went to City Hall yesterday—it's done." We talk for over an hour, but I don't remember anything else he says. It almost makes sense that Trump's winning and Jason's marrying Brooke would happen in the same week. The world is officially upside down—or had we all just been blind to the evolving reality, the true state of the union, for the past several years?

The next morning, Jason shows up outside my door to help fix the damage he's done to me and the damage I've done to my apartment. We'd had long-standing plans to spackle and paint before Megan moved back in.

I had been holding my breath for Megan's return, quietly expecting her to come back to town as a local celebrity. Layla even believed Megan could be the first female director of speechwriting at the White House. Instead, my brilliant friend is returning to town without a job.

"HELLO?"

Jason lets himself into my apartment because I haven't gotten out of bed since our phone call last night.

"Hey there," Jason says softly as he enters my bedroom, and bends down to give me a gentle hug, as if he knows all my bones feel shattered. He's brought several bags of painting supplies that he starts to unpack. I'm unable to move, defeated.

Jason gets to work spackling.

"Are you happier now that you're married?" I ask.

"I am," he says. "You know, I've been living a shitty life for a long time, Beck." He's filling in all the nail holes I've made. "All this sneaking around and lying makes me nervous." He looks at me. "It's been a shitty life, but I have the chance to make it better."

Jason looks at me, sandpaper in hand. "That's the other thing I wanted to talk to you about," he says slowly. "At some point, Brooke wants to start a family, and so do I."

I don't say anything. I don't move. I don't breathe. I think that maybe if I stay very still it won't hurt as much. It's as if my blue down comforter has become a bed of nails. My head has become a stretch rack. There's nowhere safe in my own mind anymore. Don't move. Don't think.

Jason comes over and rolls me onto my side to spoon me, pressing the backs of my knees with the fronts of his. I am here on my bed, the day before we embark on our last overseas trip, with the man I've loved for years. The man who has married his girlfriend—a woman he wants to be the mother of his children. The man who is holding me tight while my body convulses, the morning sun shining through the window.

"You will be a great dad," I tell him.

"Maybe," he says. It's always maybe with him. My maybe man.

"Please don't lump me in with your shitty previous life," I cry. It's hard to speak. My voice cracks while tears flow in rivulets down my cheeks. My sleeves are soaked.

"I won't," he says. He reaches over and unfurls my clenched fists, tells me I have nice fingers.

"Thanks," I whimper. "Your kids could have had these fingers," I say in a voice cracked from sobbing, and we both laugh.

We watch the gray paint dry. There's a black puppy across the street, trotting on big paws he hasn't grown into yet. Runners are running. Parents are holding hands with their kids as they cross the street and head toward the playground.

Jason puts the lids back on the cans of paint, sits down next to me, tells me he needs to go, he is late for a meeting with POTUS. Jason pulls me across his lap, holds me like a baby, pulls my arms around him so they're draped over his shoulders. This is, by far, the best position to encourage full-belly sobs. I snot up his fleece, wipe it clean, and snot it up again. He squeezes me, brushes back my hair, rubs my back, rests his cheek on my forehead.

But he needs to go. "We'll talk later," he says. I nod even though I know we won't. "I love you, Beck," he whispers in my ear. It feels like a kiss. I watch from far away as he closes the door behind him.

The day disappears. At some point I drag my body into a hot shower. I try to eat leftover Chinese food but end up dumping the whole container in the trash. The sun is up but I crawl into bed, close the blinds, and turn out the light.

IT'S
ABOUT
THE WORK

Later in November

NEWS OF JASON'S MARRIAGE PRECEDES OUR ARRIVAL WHEREVER WE GO, chasing us on our last overseas trip to Greece, Germany, and Peru. And too often I'm next to him when someone approaches to congratulate him on the best decision of his life: "Just heard the great news, Jason! Well done! She's a lucky girl!"

One night in Berlin, I get dinner with Noah and Teddy. We don't talk about Jason's marriage or Trump's inauguration. Instead, we talk about my graduate school applications: I've applied to MFA writing programs. "Let us know if we can help," Teddy says, patting my hand.

I'm staying in the press hotel, so the boys walk me back to make sure I get in safely. We stroll past the Christmas market that will be targeted in a terrorist attack in one month's time. But tonight, like every night before, we are lucky. Tonight is all white lights and closed streets and the sound of our footsteps echoing behind us.

As I push my way through the revolving door at the hotel, I hear someone shout my name. I see a young woman in a booth at the hotel bar, and I realize it's Jessie with Terry the speechwriter and Chuck the photographer. Jessie works in Hope's office, and though she's traveled only a few times, she's fun and funny and usually quite buoyant, but as I sit down next to her, I can tell Jessie has been crying.

She tells me that she and Hope had meant to meet up with my dinner group, but wires had been crossed and they'd inadvertently ended up at the Rattler's private dinner with senior staff. And even though everyone insisted that they sit down, it was terribly awkward, and it was obvious the Rattler didn't want them there.

"I don't get why she hates me when she doesn't even know me," Jessie says, looking at me like a kicked puppy.

I grab Jessie by the shoulders. "Do you like them?" I ask her. "Do they seem fun to you? Do you think they'd make good friends?" She shakes her head violently and wipes away her tears. "Then they don't matter," I tell her.

Jessie tells me how much she admires me, that I'm friends with everyone, that she hopes to be like me one day. It's out of the blue, and it's such a big compliment that my heart swells.

I give her a smile. "Don't let them get to you," I tell her. "They're unhappy people. They're jealous that you're happy, that this isn't your whole life, that your career is just beginning." I realize I'm saying this as much to myself as to Jessie. Maybe I have learned something after all.

"Do you like what you do?" I ask Jessie. "In digital strategy?"

She sits up straight and looks at me. "I fucking love it."

"Then that, my friend, is what fucking matters."

Jessie nods and I put my arm around her, the way I used to when I had crying freshman girls rush into my office when I was a teacher on dorm duty. Jessie is good at digital strategy, and I'm good at helping her remember what she's good at. It's what POTUS always says—to White House interns, to Jerry Seinfeld, to young leaders in Vietnam: "It's about the work." How did I lose sight of that? We're in Germany, for chrissake—just a few hours ago I'd transcribed a press conference with POTUS and a woman who, like him, knows it's all about the work: Angela Merkel. You know who else knows it's about the work? Pathahad. And Avril Haines. And Megan Rooney. And Susan Rice. The writers I love, the athletes I admire, the musicians I worship. And Ruth. Just try to tell me someone who knows it's all about the fucking work more than the Notorious RBG.

WHEN WE GET BACK TO D.C., I SAY FAREWELL TO MEGAN'S CONDO, AND Noah clears a space for my air mattress in his guest room until I figure things out. "Just don't get too comfortable, Becky," he says, handing me his house key.

Before the president spends forty minutes doing regional press interviews in the Diplomatic Reception Room in the East Wing, I set up my recorders and go over to say hi to one of my favorite agents, Willem. "What's up, Gator?" he asks, nodding at my gold alligator necklace. "You sticking around?"

"I really hate Trump," I tell him. You're not supposed to discuss politics with agents because they have to be apolitical—same with the military aides—but at this point, who cares?

Willem looks at me and smiles. His blue eyes twinkle. And then, his hands still gripping his lapels in standard agent stance, he stares ahead. We hear the president's voice down the hall.

Without affect, Willem recites, "Whether 'tis nobler in the mind to suffer the slings and arrows of outrageous fortune, or to take arms against a sea of troubles."

I stare at him.

"That's Shakespeare," Willem says, grinning. "*Hamlet*—ever heard of it?"

"I've never heard an agent quote Shakespeare before," I finally muster.

"I've never heard a stenographer say they hate the incoming president," he says. "Don't buy into the stereotypes. Be who you want to be. You can do anything if you're honest with yourself."

"What's going on, people?" the president asks, striding across the carpet, joking with the camera guys as they set up his microphone.

I walk over to hit Record, but not before Willem whispers, "To thine own self be true."

A FEW DAYS LATER I AGREE TO GET COFFEE WITH SAM, WHO IS BACK IN D.C. after losing the race in St. Louis. It's good to see him. We're so comfortable with each other. I tease him about how short his hair is, and he still calls me Cookie. He tells me he's moving back to D.C. because "this is where the jobs are." He says he and his new girl-friend are looking to buy a house that's big enough to accommodate their two dogs.

"That's all I ever wanted," I tell Sam. "I just wanted you and me in a house with a bunch of dogs and cats."

He hugs me and whispers in my ear, "No, that's not all you wanted. You need more than that. You're so much bigger than that."

We say goodbye and I tell him that I'm happy for him. Because I am. I want him to be in a loving, joyful relationship. Ours was too broken. Sometimes the best love stories don't work out.

I think back on the last five years, on what I've ever really, truly needed. A sick playlist. A good book. A pumped-up basketball and half-decent vodka. Friends who want only friendship in return. Run-ning shoes. I think of all the rules I've needed to live by, and all the rules I've needed to break. I'm done with tiptoeing; I'd rather dance around in my pink shoes. I don't need to breathe quietly; I'd rather shout for an encore. I don't need the Vagiants to approve of me when, frankly, I don't approve of them. I'd rather set a new standard for all the Jessies who come after me; I'd rather help them look up, and be respected for the right reasons, not just because they were in the right place at the right time. The future is female because there's a storm of kick-ass women on the rise who will remember to reach back with both hands to help others climb up with them.

POTUS, as usual, is right. It's about the work, and I have so much work to do. I tell Sam I love him but I can't talk to him for a while. I delete Jason's phone number for the last time. I know that that sassy little minx called love will find me when I'm ready, but right now, it's time to write.

MAHALO

December

WHEN WE GO TO HAWAII FOR THE SWAN SONG, I BRING MY YOUNGER sister, Caroline. POTUS makes a big deal over her at Hanauma Bay and asks her if she's as fast as I am. I tell him no way—she's not as fast as I am—she's way, way faster. Caroline looks at me, surprised because we're so competitive. I've had my time with POTUS; let her have a magic moment, too.

I take walks by myself, and I drive to the North Shore alone, windows down, being right here, right where I want to be. I write on the beach, I breathe air that smells and tastes different than in any other place I've been—sweeter, gentler. I say hi to strangers and wave the shaka when locals in rusted beaters stop to let me cross the street. I offer to take photos for families in front of the Banyan Tree. Every breath in Hawaii is a gift. Every moment is a mahalo.

And I run. The morning sun is my church. I lace up my sneakers, inflated with excitement for whatever comes next. As I press Play for my workout soundtrack and set off for Diamond Head, I feel myself returning, swiftly, surely, one step at a time. "Heart It Races" comes on the playlist, and I almost fast-forward. But I decide to listen, as if the song might turn out differently now that Sam and Jason are gone. Now that it's just me. And the funny thing is that it is different, yet familiar, like an old friend all grown up. As I get to the foot of Diamond Head Mountain, Dr. Dog gets to the bridge. I pump my arms and lift my legs in sync with the building beat: *I race alone, I race alone, I race alone, I race alone.*

WHEN WE RETURN TO D.C. IN JANUARY, MY FAMILY COMES WITH ME FOR departure photos with the president. I accidentally step on POTUS's foot as he tells my family I'm his workout buddy, that he could count on only Susan Rice and me in the gym. "And she's a good writer, too," POTUS tells my mom before putting his arm around us for the photo. I'd given Noah a story to give POTUS back in December, a scene I'd written down about him with his daughters from a few years back. I had wanted to say thank you to him the best way I knew how.

"Zach, fix your hair," I scold my older brother before the photo.

"Yeah, Zach, fix your hair," POTUS teases.

I've been in the corner of the Oval a thousand times, but with my family there, it's just too much, and I feel as if I've spent the better part of the morning sticking my finger into different electric sockets.

"It's just a job," Von the butler had told me when we first met. Now, in the Oval, I get it. This is just a room. The White House is just a building. The Constitution is just a piece of parchment. It's what we invest in it that matters. It's the humanity behind it. The magic we breathe into it. I thought that Von was saying that his work was nothing special when he said it's "just a job." Of course it's special. But the moment you start believing the job makes *you* special, that you're an irreplaceable cog, that's when you've become a D.C. creature. That's when you're in peril. We are made of guts and heart and stories, not titles and W-2s. We are lucky but we are nothing special. It's a privilege and an honor and a job. Don't trust anyone who tells you otherwise.

"What's the rug say?" my mom asks after we're escorted out to the Colonnade.

She means the circular rug in the Oval. The rug I've read a million times. The rug beneath the circle of stars on the ceiling that few of us have had the pleasure to look up and notice.

"It says the arc of the moral universe is long, but it bends toward justice."

YOU CAN'T
KEEP THE
END FROM
ENDING

January 2017

PRESIDENT BARACK OBAMA GIVES HIS FINAL SPEECH IN CHICAGO ON January 10, 2017.

Shilpa and hundreds of other White House alums have flown in from everywhere and are standing on the riser and in VIP seats when we arrive from the plane. It feels like the end of *Big Fish* as I see everyone I've met in the past five years: Noah, Teddy, Cole, Ferial, Terry, Lawrence, Chuck, Pete, Rachael, Skye, Kendall, Jessie, Chad, Kelly, Marvin, Marie, Ingrid, Eliza, Lisa, Susan, Avril, Jen, Tess, Hope, Amelia, Layla, the Rattler, and, of course, Jason. He looks over at me, but I see past him. We are both finally moving forward. I am ready to be a better version of myself—I hope he is, too.

Backstage at the farewell address feels somewhere between a frenetic wedding and a funeral, a celebration of life and a memorial service for what could have been.

Weaving through the thicket of people backstage, I find WHCA and set up my recorders next to the speakers.

Here we go.

The president walks onstage to "City of Blinding Lights" one last time, and I find Shilpa in the alumni riser. We hold hands and cry as the U2 chorus hits us like a bag of bricks, like hearing "the song" in the middle of a breakup.

It turns out a farewell address isn't too different from a final-tour concert—POTUS plays the hits—*Yes we can*—along with some new stuff. "Yes, we did," he says. "Yes, we did." I cry my face off because he brought together people from all over, people who don't look the same but who hold the same values of equality and justice in their oversized, open hearts; people he inspired to advance a greater good through scrappy grit as much as brilliance or relentless hard work. I look around and find myself in a room with seventeen thousand friends who fought fiercely to get this paragraph right.

"Thank you. God bless you. And may God continue to bless the United States of America," POTUS says slowly, taking in the crowd, the moment. He steps away from the lectern to deafening applause, and Bruce Springsteen's "Land of Hope and Dreams" plays as the First Lady, Malia, and Joe and Jill Biden join the president onstage.

"I need to set up for an interview," I say to no one in particular. I get myself backstage but my feet are suddenly cemented as the familiar post-speech chaos buzzes around me. *Time needs to stop. Please stop. Please make everything stop.* Someone taps me on the shoulder. It's Jackie, the president's makeup artist. She gives me a side hug as she slides a package of tissues into my blazer pocket. *This can't be real life.*

I find the sound crew, switch on my microphone, do a quick mic check like I've done a million times before. POTUS shows up and does a double take at my wet cheeks. As I hold my microphone and stare into the fluorescent lights to stop the tears, all I can think of is that there must be a way to slow things down, to go back, to change the future. This is all a bad dream. I'm not ready. No one is ready.

But he's here. He's found us. Tick Tock Croc. I guess he was here all along, waiting.

My instinct is to run. In my head, a ticker tape repeats: *This is it. This is it. This is it.* But I can't listen to my brain because my heart is beating faster than it has during any race, as though it's going to pound itself into cardiac arrest or pop out of my chest. It is thumping, thumping, thumping, beating, beating, beating, *go faster, go faster, go faster.*

But that's the thing: You can't outrun time any more than you can outrun yourself.

ON THE FLIGHT HOME, CHRISTINE, ONE OF MY FAVORITE FLIGHT ATTEN-dants, delivers a Cape Codder that Krissy, my Air Force One mom, has made especially for me—too strong, just her style. And then I choke up because this AF1 crew, they've become my family. I know so much and so little about them, but I love them. Tess and Hope flank me in my seat and we raise a toast to Krissy, who has taken care of us en route to more than sixty countries, across hundreds of thousands of miles.

POTUS comes into the staff cabin and walks over to us. Hope jumps up to thank him.

"No, thank *you*, Hope," he says, wrapping his arm around her.

I want to tell POTUS that his speech reminded me of the best fireworks I'd ever seen—that every time I thought this *must* be the finale, he kept going, each line the best line. But I don't. He looks exhausted. I just smile and hope that he knows.

I remember the first time I heard the click and groan of the gate. I remember the first time I saw POTUS crouch to hug a little boy so they were the same height. I remember the first time I watched him make a whole room—an entire arena!—erupt in laughter, and the first time he trash-talked me on the treadmill. I remember him entering the Roosevelt Room for a background briefing with reporters and thinking he moves like an athlete, and then, ten seconds into the briefing, realizing he thinks like a scholar. I remember what he taught me as I sat there listening to him speak in the Oval Office, at the Newtown vigil, in Laos and Oklahoma, in Argentina and Anacostia through his patience, compassion, thoughtfulness, and openness. He taught me hustle isn't something you outgrow unless you want to get outworked. He taught me to assume responsibility for mistakes, to listen, to stay scrappy, to believe in hope, and to fight for optimism.

When POTUS walks away from us in the staff cabin, I whisper, "Bye, sir, I love you," just loud enough so that only Hope and Tess hear me. They burst out laughing, and Hope raises her glass for a toast. Tess tilts her head, beaming.

"There are so many things to cheers to," Tess says, smiling.

"To that wonderful man, our forty-fourth president," Hope says.

I see tears well up in their eyes through my own clouded vision.

"To Pathahad," Tess says.

"To Amelia," Hope says, because our missing fourth is at home with our brand-new fifth—her baby girl.

We clink glasses, and then I hold mine up again for another toast.

I'm crying openly now and take a deep breath, but my voice still cracks when I finally say it: "Dream big dreams."

I cry harder, but Tess and Hope start laughing at me.

"That's actually kind of cheesy," Tess teases.

"Which is totally perfect," Hope says.

We toast, we clink, we drink. We fly at altitude until we hear the whoosh of the wings, feel the drag of the landing gear. You can't keep the end from ending.

EPILOGUE

Send in the Clowns

Do I believe the total perversion that I am witnessing?
—JOHN KENNEDY TOOLE, *A CONFEDERACY OF DUNCES*

JANUARY 20, 2017, INAUGURATES A WAKING NIGHTMARE. I'M NOW A stenographer in the Trump administration. Remember that pit of snakes in *Indiana Jones*? I work in that pit now. At a pool spray in the East Room, I feel a cold draft behind me and turn to see Steve Bannon lurking in the corner. The West Exec parking lot is no longer filled with Priuses and Chevys but with Porsches and Maseratis. The black frames that line the West Wing no longer display photographs of POTUS shaking hands with world leaders, little kids, and wounded warriors; instead, it's a pathetic display of inauguration day crowds with the aerial shots cropped tight in the attempt to establish yet another "alternative fact."

The deputy communications director tells us they don't need stenographers or transcripts of interviews because "there's video." They don't realize that print and radio interviews will not have video. They don't realize a lot of things. After a few weeks they decide they do want us, "But, like, only some of the time."

I watch the Napoleonic clowns swagger through the West Wing in bad suits. I watch the female contortionists, who believe bending over in a miniskirt and stilettos is a good idea but a woman's right to choose isn't. I watch Hope Hicks summon Bill O'Reilly to the Oval Office for an hour-long meeting before his taped interview with Trump, and marvel over how well this administration wastes the sitting president's time with television personalities. I watch Stephen Miller smirk like a demonic Pee-wee Herman as he cracks jokes about gender equality in a van full of women who are active-duty members of the military. I watch all of it. I force myself to look up so that I can write it all down.

"Where are your pink shoes?" Leo the Secret Service agent asks as I enter the West Wing.

"I'm in mourning," I tell him.

He winks and smiles as if to say *Right on.*

I wear my pink hat through the gate every day, intentionally give new employees wrong directions in the EEOB, and nuzzle "the liberal media" in front of the Trump press office team. I'm basically begging to get fired.

"Back in Afghanistan," a nurse tells me, "I had to administer medicine to Taliban prisoners—so I'm basically approaching these people the same way."

In the Oval Office during the first pool spray I attend with Trump, I notice that the table behind the Resolute Desk, once crowded with Obama family photographs, is now empty except for one framed picture of Trump's father. There isn't a single photo of Barron, or Melania, or even Ivanka. *If only Fred had told his son he loved him, that he was proud of him—maybe none of this would have happened.*

When I fly to Mar-a-Lago with the Insane Clown Posse, I hear Fox News blasting from every cabin so loudly I can't hear the whoosh. After takeoff, Trump gets lost while giving Melania a tour of the plane. I don't know how he gets lost, but he does. Air Force One is a beautiful bird, but it's no different from any other commercial 747 in that there's one narrow hallway that takes you from the front to the back. Nevertheless, Trump ends up standing over my seat, which is more or less a cul-de-sac—no need to come over here unless you want to talk to me. I stand up because he is, after all, the president. Even if he is totally lost.

"Hello," he says.

"Hi, sir," I say, taking a step back, just as I've learned to do with President Obama. Give the most powerful man in the world room to breathe. But when I take a step back, Trump takes a step forward, into my personal space.

"Hello," he says again, with a smile he must consider charming pasted on his face. It looks like he's spent the last decade staring directly into the light of a tanning bed. I look to Melania behind him, but she stares at the ground. On the television screen is footage of Michael Flynn and the new allegations against him. In front of the television screen is Michael Flynn himself, talking with Trump's body guy as he retrieves documents from his briefcase.

Trump is still in my face when a staffer touches his arm, distracting him.

"Right this way, sir," she says, directing him back toward the aisle.

THE LAST TIME I WALK THROUGH THE WHITE HOUSE I DON'T KNOW IT'S my last time. As I cross the Colonnade, I hug myself to fight the cold March air and drag my feet from the East Wing back to the West Wing, dreading the rest of the day, and tomorrow, and the day after that.

Microphone in hand, my eyes on the Oval, I wonder what POTUS would say if he saw me moping in his absence. As a breeze skirts through the Rose Garden and along the Colonnade, every blade of grass seems to take a knee. *What would POTUS tell me if he were here?* Light kisses each petal and stem. The sun is up. Time exists elsewhere. I look through the glass doors and see President Obama sitting in the Oval, taking a sip of tea at the Resolute Desk. He's between meetings, and he picks up a pen and scrawls out a note in his left-handed script.

I watch myself walk into the Oval and turn on my recorder, test my microphone. The forty-fourth president looks up from his desk and flashes that serious yet gentle smile he used to give me before pool sprays. His brown eyes dance with calm amusement. I double-check the recorder and give him a nod. I'm ready. *Well*—he pauses, because he always pauses. And then, in a voice strong and steady, he asks me, just as he would ask you: *What are we going to do about it?*

THANK YOU

Out of all those kinds of people,
You got a face with a view

—TALKING HEADS, *THIS MUST BE THE PLACE (NAÏVE MELODY)*

A TOAST TO **MY PARENTS,** WHO HAVE NEVER MET A DANCE FLOOR THEY didn't like or a problem we couldn't solve. Thank you, **Ninny,** for being an infinite fount of creativity, beauty, support, fun, barbed humor, and compassion. Thank you, **Dad,** for being the best listener, thinker, dancer, fire-builder, and calmer-downer. You guys are the original Dream Team.

Thank you, **Zach,** for teaching me what it means to "pick it up" when I thought I already had, training me for *American Gladiator,* being the family do-gooder, and telling me that David Bowie/Luther Vandross story when I most needed to hear it.

Thank you, **Caroline,** for making playlists full of smooth transitions and harsh judgments that hurt but aren't wrong about my clothes and life decisions. Thank you for being so supportive and insightful this past year when I needed you most.

Becky Sweren, this book is because of you. My darling girl, thank you for your humor, poise, patience, eloquence, and grounded brilliance—your very Beckyness. Calling you my agent is like Wilbur calling Charlotte some spider he used to know. I'm forever grateful to have you in my corner, and this project benefited immensely from your genius.

Thank you to the devastatingly cool **Julie Grau.** Your ability to cut to the truth makes you a top-notch editor; your patience to guide me there makes you a soul Sherpa and honorary member of Pathahad. I wish I were Sugar or Sheba so we could walk together every day. Thank you for helping me go toward the good and for holding my hand all the way here.

Thank you to the entire Spiegel & Grau team, especially **Mengfei Chen, Ted Allen, Emily DeHuff, Annie Chagnot, Denise Cronin, Maria Braeckel, Barbara Fillon, Anna Belle Hindenlang, Mary Moates, Isabella Biedenharn, Leigh Marchant, Jessica Bonet, Andrea DeWerd, Theresa Zoro, Debbie Glasserman, Tom Perry, Greg Mollica**, and **Cindy Spiegel.** Thank you, **Gina Centrello**, for making my dreams come true/nonfiction at Penguin Random House.

Thank you, **Vanessa Haughton**, the first to read this stuff and see a book. I can't wait to revel in the wild success (and fun!) that awaits you, my lovely lady.

Thank you, **David Remnick** and **Emily Greenhouse**, for reading the early essays and suggesting that I insert my own story, which changed exactly everything.

Thank you, **Dylan Loewe**, for empowering a cog in the initial stage of this project.

Thank you, **David Litt**, for your guidance and generosity about book stuff.

Thank you, **Dr. Janice Hillman**, my #1, for being so delightfully funny, cool, and wise.

Thank you, **Dr. Ron Shectman**, for always bringing it back to the writing.

Thank you, **Dr. Mel Singer**, for your sage advice, killer coffee, and easy laugh.

Thank you to my teachers: **Mr. Michael Segal** and **Ms. Jill Knight** at Lower Merion, and **Professor Gertrude Hughes, Professor Gayle**

Pemberton, and my thesis advisor/saving grace, **Professor Stephanie Kuduk Weiner** at Wesleyan.

Thank you, **Siobhan Troy-Carranza** at Tranquil Space, for laughing with me through the discomfort that is pigeon pose/life. How's this for a heart opener?

Thank you, **Matthew Martin**, **Matt Levy**, and **Neil Rosini**, for your kindness, humor, eagle eyes, and *Jaws*-like legal chops.

Thank you, **Peggy Suntum** and **Regina Wagner**, for the opportunity of a lifetime.

Thank you to my **extended family** for being such a fun and smart group of goons.

Thank you, **Bird Bones** and **Wide Wale Corduroy**, for your enthusiasm, support, and willingness to overlook my crude language and poor choices.

Thank you, **Mommom**, **Tamara Stein**, for being such an animal-loving, key-tickling trailblazer, a forceful but ever-polite political hell-raiser. I hope this was delicious.

Thank you to the **Larkin-Gilmores**, the best BTBs a girl could ask for. To the hunt!

Thank you to the **Evergreen Club** for a childhood of beach walks, fire talks, and family feelings.

Thank you, **Minta**, **Mattie**, and the **Sayres/Watson family**, for being so fun and lovely.

Thank you, **Chris Arnone**, for toasting with me despite my cocktail preferences.

Thank you, **Jeremy Doernburger**, for the support and enduring my endless chirps.

Thank you, **David Turner**, for your confidence in me and for our chapter. I am proud of you and hope that all your candidates win and favorite bands stay together.

Thank you, **Jim Loftus**, for illuminating the peril of writing, the importance of Dorothy Parker, and that truth about poetic ideas and barroom floors.

Thank you, **Caitria Mahoney**, for teaching me about turtle shells and making me laugh about wine corks. Cheers to the big nights, early mornings, and Luke's boat.

Thank you, **Bobby Schmuck**, for the thoughtful conversation on so many rides to Andrews. Thank you for enduring my post-Kesha session and always delivering fun surprises, funny digressions, spot-on impressions, sharp jokes, and sharper insights.

Thank you, **Luke Rosa**, for reminding me that life is just one big buffet if you remember to appreciate the spread. Here's to a lotta ins, outs, wakey-wakeys, and Caucasians. Before there was Bodhi, there was you, my sweet, leisure-living Big Cat.

Thank you, **Joe Paulsen**, for the tough love, good times, and crinkly eyes. Thank you for including me in the best nights, seeing me through the worst, and for always encouraging me to write. May you purify yourself in the waters of Lake Minnetonka and receive total consciousness, Joe Cool.

Thank you, **Sam Tubman**, for the friendship, style recs, and protocol consultations.

Thank you, **Tomas Pagan Motta**, for showing me how to get "Up and Away."

Thank you, **Caitlin Owens** and **Kelly Nash**, for investing your time in my happiness.

Thank you, **Laurel Waterhouse** and **Rachel Steinberg**, for being so much wiser.

Thank you, **Sandy Tattersall**, for being a good man, worthy of missing every day.

Thank you, **Nick Hiebert** and **Ellie Doig**, for the circle of friendship and paper trail of letters, stories, and poems I cherish more than you know, and for not going illegally.

Thank you, **Kerry Rose** and **Chris Dorbian, Isaac Katz**, and **Erin McCarthy**, for being golden friends as well as my golden couples.

Thank you, **Jill Bronson**, for a lifetime of love before the life-changing legal guidance.

Thank you to my childhood pals who have become my adult Narby Neighbor lifelines: **Jen and Ryan Denholm, Lish Berenson**, and **Austin Hoggan**. You guys have taught me so much and fed me so well. Love you sweetly.

Thank you, **Charlotte Hastings** and **Emma, the OG Swanns**, for helping me through nine head staples, unemployment, and "one" pitcher of margaritas from Lauriol Plaza.

Thank you, **Sarada Peri**, for dignifying this dream by saying it aloud, and for telling me to devote everything to it in your delightful matter-of-fact way.

Thank you, **Kat Narvaez**, my sister in sports and three-legged Peruvian dog bites, for a lifetime of adventures, broken bones, magic, and mischief.

Thank you, **Bernadette Doykos**, for the book recs, fresh beats, and brilliant insights. Thank you for being the earliest reader and my entrusted confidant for this book.

Thank you, **Megan Rooney**, for sharing your home, dry humor, quick wit, and compassion. You're the most generous of writers, and forever the geek to my freak.

Thank you, **Joani Walsh**, for the hikes, shenanigans, wine, and wisdom you shared with me everywhere we went. I love your big-sister bossiness, atrocious sense of direction, unruly cackle, and protective bulldog instincts. You are my ravioli.

Thank you, **Amanda Lucidon**, for teaching me some of the most important life lessons. Thank you for always chasing light and helping me find my good side. I love you for your kindness, goofiness, wide-lens view of the world, and, of course, your killer dance moves.

Thank you, **Shilpa Hegde**, for being my twin, my Kesha companion, kindred animal spirit, and the only one who loves Bodhi and MJ as much as I do. There's no one I'd rather dance on a chair with as we worried no one was going to show up. We've worn a lot of glitter, but none of it sparkles like you, Shilp.

Thank you, **Jamie Nash**, for your Pollyanna smile, strength, and truth-speaking self. You are the unsung hero of this book, the anchor through the best and worst and funniest. You are my Pop-Tart and sweatpants on a Sunday night, my "one more episode" pal, the whisk to my hammer. Now stop being a genius-in-waiting and go get wild with pots, pans, and plans. Do the damn thing you were born to do.

Thank you, **Hope Hall**, hippie warrior of love, for showing me what the universe can do when you go toward the good. Thank you for your endless—if sometimes embarrassing—faith in this book, when it was still just a twinkle in my eye. This is because of Hope. You are your father's daughter, and I am your biggest fan.

Thank you to the men and women who serve without flash or fanfare, but with dedication, pride, and sacrifice. You made my time at the White House full of joy, surprise, humor, and kindness. To the **Military Aides, Medical Unit, Air Force One Crew, Technology Team, Secret Service, Valets, Ushers, Butlers, WHCA, WHTV, Grounds Crew, Janitorial Staff, Ike's Staff, Post Office Staff, Navy Mess,** and **Eggnog Makers**—I am forever in awe and eternally indebted to you for millions of reasons and moments. Thank you for looking out for me and laughing with me.

Thank you, **White House Press Corps**, for sharing your audio, laughs, and snacks.

Thank you, **Philadelphia Eagles**, for proving hungry dogs really do run faster.

Thank you, **Vice President Biden** and **Dr. Biden**, for your endless optimism and contagious compassion. You make every house a home, and every stranger a friend. I can't tell you how often I quote you. Thank you for being the truest of teachers.

Thank you, **President Obama** and **Mrs. Obama**, for the tireless work you did and continue to do. You demonstrate what grace and leadership look like, especially when the cameras are off and the crowds are elsewhere. You're simply the best, and the funniest, and the coolest. It was the honor and privilege of a lifetime. Thank you.

And thank **YOU**, dear reader. It was my greatest hope and biggest dream to land here, in your hands, but that doesn't make printing such personal stuff any less terrifying. Thank you for coming along for the ride. I hope you heard the *whoosh*.

ABOUT THE AUTHOR

A graduate of Wesleyan University in Connecticut, BECK DOREY-STEIN worked as a White House stenographer from 2012 to 2017. Previously she worked as a high school English teacher in New Jersey, Washington DC and Seoul, South Korea. This is her first book.